Cities on Rails

Cities on Rails

The redevelopment of railway station areas

Luca Bertolini and Tejo Spit

Utrecht University, The Netherlands

E & FN SPON
An imprint of Routledge
London and New York

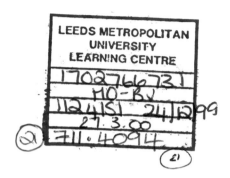
This edition published 1998
by E & FN Spon, an imprint of Routledge
11 New Fetter Lane, London EC4P 4EE

Simultaneously published in the USA and Canada
by Routledge
29 West 35th Street, New York, NY 10001

© 1998 Luca Bertolini and Tejo Spit

Typeset in 10/12 Times by Keystroke, Jacaranda Lodge, Wolverhampton
Printed and bound in Great Britain by the Bath Press

British Library Cataloguing in Publication Data
A catalogue record for this book is available
from the British Library.

Library of Congress Cataloging in Publication Data
A catalogue record for this book has been requested.

ISBN 0 419 22760 1

Contents

Preface

'Fundamentally the importance of the King's Cross story is the struggle over whose definition of reality is to prevail', as Michael Edwards, planner and economist, concludes (Edwards, 1992, p.14). To those involved in any of the ambitious station area redevelopment plans sprouting across Europe, the word 'chaos' must have often come to mind. Euralille's master planner Rem Koolhaas defends his choices there by arguing that 'We are not deliberately introducing chaos; it is the contemporary system that is doing so, with its contradictory assemblage of architectural wills, populist sensibilities, financial policies, triumphant dreams, and so on' (*l'Architecture d'Ajourd'hui*, 1992, p. 168). In the face of this 'chaotic' accumulation of demands, the planner and designer must be 'dedicated to resisting it'.

What makes the redevelopment of railway station areas such a daunting task? Is it the challenge of making order out of chaos? Or is it the challenge of sifting through the diverse perceptions of the problem and prescriptions for its solution? If the forces of chaos can be resisted, how are planners to arm themselves for the struggle? Perhaps the answer lies in recomposing divergent perceptions. With these questions in mind, we embarked on the theoretical and empirical journey that has resulted in this book. During the trip, the authors met, to compare notes and to absorb the ideas of others.

The whole project was triggered by Franco Corsico at the Politecnico di Torino. In 1992 he suggested that Bertolini should consider the theme of station area redevelopment for his PhD dissertation. At first he hesitated, but then accepted, trusting Corsico's renowned intuition. The choice could not have been more timely. Since then, waves of enthusiasm for and disillusionment with station area development have produced a groundswell of interest in the research. At an early stage, the advice given by Luigi Falco and Giuseppe Dematteis, also at the Politecnico di Torino, was essential. In particular, Dematteis' analysis of the complex relation between a *geography of networks* and a *geography of areas* helped to structure the approach to the theme. In fact, his insights are still bearing fruit. The work of fellow researchers such as Paola Pucci of the Politecnico di Milano was also a source of inspiration during that period. At the outset, the project was intended as an international comparative study. In France, the United Kingdom, and the Netherlands, the response of those involved in the projects under scrutiny (and of colleagues at local universities) has been outstanding. Their cooperation has been perhaps the single most important condition for the achievement that followed. Space does not permit us to mention all of them here, but at least Michael Edwards at the Bartlett School and Michael Parkes, both in London, together with Anton Kreukels at the Universiteit Utrecht in the Netherlands deserve explicit recognition. Their enthusiasm and suggestions were essential to both the initial results and the later development of the study.

For various reasons – including a fascination with the qualities of Dutch urban civilization – Bertolini looked for ways to pursue his career in the Netherlands after completing his PhD. At that point he met Tejo Spit, thanks to the mediation of Frans Dieleman (director of the research school NETHUR). Together, Bertolini and Spit wrote three research proposals to work out the findings reported in the dissertation. Two of the proposals were successful. First came a research grant from NS-Vastgoed, the newly founded property subsidiary of the Dutch railways. The firm's managers showed an unusual willingness to reflect on and learn from experiences in other countries. This project allowed the researchers to update and expand the empirical basis of the study. Again, the readiness to collaborate shown by those involved in the initiatives studied was critical to the project's success. In some cases, their cooperation went far beyond expectations. This was true of Martin Skillbäck in Stockholm and Andreas Fischer in Basel. Colleagues Stefan de Corte in Brussels and Richard Wolff in Zürich provided a fantastic blend of generous hospitality and challenging debate, a combination that helped to focus the analysis. The second research proposal that received funding was a three-year project supported jointly by NWO (the Dutch Organization for Scientific Research) and the RPD (the Dutch National Planning Agency). This project, which is still running, led to the appointment of Bertolini as a post-doctorate researcher at the Faculty of Geographical Sciences, Universiteit Utrecht, thereby creating the material conditions to develop both the empirical and the theoretical aspects. In Utrecht, he has found a stimulating academic environment at the Utrecht Centre for Urban Research (URU). Utrecht has also been the venue for particularly fruitful exchanges between the two authors and Anton Kreukels.

This book distils the findings of five years of research on the subject, and sets the goals for future endeavours. It combines the expertise on the theme built up by Bertolini with the long-standing research focus of Spit on complex planning challenges. The book remains the product of collective, interactive effort. Yet the specialities of the two authors can be traced in the division of tasks. Bertolini has done most of the writing for Chapters 2 and 3, as well as for the case studies. Spit has written most of Chapter 4 and has outlined the national planning systems. The introduction and the conclusions were a fully concerted effort of both authors, both regarding the case studies and at the general level.

While putting together the material for this book, the authors derived much benefit from the input of various individuals. The assistance of Leonie Jansen, Marinka Van Vliet and Sarah Schendeler was important. Several illustrations, including the national maps that appear at the beginning of each case study, were prepared at the Kartografisch Laboratorium of the Universiteit Utrecht. The quality of the text was greatly improved by Nancy Smyth van Weesep, who had to untangle the first draft within very tight deadlines. At E & FN Spon, Caroline Mallinder proved to be a very professional but gentle editor, effectively combining firmness and encouragement. Last but not least, the comments of the anonymous reviewers of the first proposal and the response by the anonymous reader of the first version of the manuscript are greatly appreciated. The authors have learned much along the way, from start to finish, and hope the reader will too.

Luca Bertolini
Tejo Spit
Utrecht, December 1997

Part One
Conceptual framework

1
Railway station area redevelopment in the spotlight

1.1 Cities on rails: an introduction

Railway stations and their surroundings are the focus of ambitious redevelopment plans throughout urban Europe. A complex set of factors – as diverse as the promotion of sustainable transport and land use, the stimulation of local economies, technological and institutional change, the business cycle and the spatial impact of globalization – drives these initiatives. Both differences and similarities are found among the national and local approaches, and there is certainly much to be learned from looking across borders.

As Europe changes, patterns of urban development are also changing, falling into step with the ongoing process of internationalization. The redevelopment of railway station areas throughout Europe is often an important part of urban restructuring. To many, these processes appear fragmented. Moreover, the information they provide is partial; it rarely sheds light on any relevant developments taking place elsewhere in Europe.

Yet it is surprising how much information about this subject is available on individual projects. It is also surprising how widely this knowledge is spread among the parties involved, so that no one party has the whole picture. Another problem is the rapid obsolescence of the information. The planning and development of railway station areas takes a long time, and so knowledge gets out of date, changes, or simply disappears in the course of the project. It is for the same reason that the actors involved in one redevelopment process learn relatively little from others participating in the same process. As redevelopment plans are continuously changed and adjusted, it does not pay to make the effort to learn. However true this may be for most railway station redevelopment plans, the full scope of the problem is even more apparent when we compare different railway station sites in Europe. Although there is already a wealth of experience in the continent that could be applied, participants in any one project know very little about railway station area redevelopment elsewhere. The benefits of sharing

3

this knowledge are obvious. An open exchange of information helps the parties to put their own experiences in perspective. Furthermore, it can help to solve problems, by showing how similar situations have been addressed.

In a Europe without borders, capital flows can migrate from one metropolitan area to another. It is often concluded that those cities that are the most competitive will gain the greatest advantage. In order to remain competitive, cities and metropolitan areas will have to mobilize their potential to retain and improve their market position for footloose capital. When we assess the competitiveness of metropolitan areas in the European context, we should keep in mind that their strength will depend upon their performance in key sectors. Railway station areas constitute one of these sectors. In a European development market, redevelopment strategies for railway station areas could prove increasingly important in attracting or repelling economic activities.

In those central cities where the redevelopment of railway station areas is impeded by conservation and heritage policies, extra constraints burden the development prospects. While the direct costs of redevelopment are likely to remain at the lowest spatial level – consisting of the railway station area and its immediate surroundings – its benefits tend to spread over a wider area. The metropolitan region is the first to benefit. Because the redevelopment process comprises various issues, as the spatial scale decreases so the need for a more integrated approach increases. Total integration, however, is a fiction. Therefore at this level the aims of economic development and transport and mobility improvement must go hand in hand with the aims of environmental protection and social integration. The constraints mentioned earlier refer to these complex relations. Although the constraints may seem enormous, the actors numerous, and the processes complex, a successful redevelopment of such areas can prove vital for the attractiveness of the city and the region.

The main objective of this study is to provide information about railway station redevelopment throughout Europe, and to analyse it, highlighting the similarities and differences. At the same time, this study places the redevelopment processes within their national contexts in order to understand their peculiarities, to identify which constraints generate specific problems, and to point out opportunities for specific solutions.

The complexity of the redevelopment of railway station areas can be traced back to its different components. The task involves different stages of development, different kinds of location, different actors, and different functions. In studying this complexity, one is free to choose one of these components as a perspective for analysis. The *actor-centred approach* is often used (e.g. Teisman, 1992). Despite the new insights that may be gained through such analysis, the results may be rather one-sided. A more comprehensive analysis – in which the major components are related to one another – seems to be a more promising way to tackle the complexity, because it is just these relationships that are responsible for the internal dynamics (or lack of dynamics) of the redevelopment process. Because the redevelopment of railway station areas can be viewed as a multifocus problem, it should be viewed from several perspectives at the same time; and that requires a more holistic approach.

The analytical framework for this study is derived from the *planning triangle* (Figure 1.1), which provides a general frame of reference. In the planning triangle,

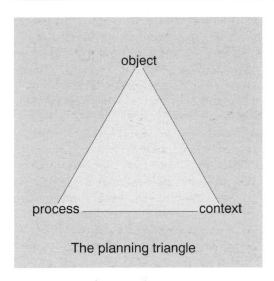

Fig. 1.1 The planning triangle.

object variables (such as site and locational characteristics) interact with *process variables* (such as actors, interests, and intervening developments) and *context variables* (such as national planning systems, the social and cultural trends of each country, major economic developments, and internationalization processes).

The way in which the planning triangle is used as a frame of reference will be elaborated in subsequent sections of this chapter. First, the factors behind the present wave of railway station area redevelopment in Europe will be discussed.

1.2 Driving forces behind railway station area redevelopment

The redevelopment of railway station areas represents a major effort for most European cities in one way or another. Pressure is mounting on these cities to take up the challenge. Most metropolitan areas in Europe have responded to it. Stimulated by the decline in spending by national governments (Spit, 1993), those cities have become more entrepreneurial (Kreukels and Spit, 1990; Parkinson *et al.*, 1991). Throughout Europe, cities have embarked upon urban regeneration projects as a means to market themselves on an international scale. These efforts not only include the redevelopment of railway station areas but also apply to waterfront areas, inner-city housing projects and so forth. This shift towards municipalities' profiling themselves by undertaking the physical restructuring of inner-city areas is visible in most of Europe.

A combination of factors may explain the emphasis on railway station redevelopment initiatives in Europe. The combination includes both structural evolution and policy discourse. With reference to the cases described later in this book, the most important factors fall under five headings. These are elaborated below.

1.2.1 Two distinct types of public policy

Both policies result in the promotion of urban redevelopment at stations. On the one hand there are policies to promote environmentally sustainable transportation and land-use patterns. Among the examples studied here, the most clearly formulated policies are those adopted by the national government in the Netherlands, and also by regional and local governments in Switzerland. On the other hand there are policies to regenerate local economies by restructuring the urban fabric. Such measures are also initiated or favoured by national governments (as in the Netherlands and the United Kingdom) but most explicitly by local governments (as in France and the Netherlands). All the countries and cities mentioned here are confronted by largely similar pressures and trends. These include constraints on public expenditure, deregulation, a shift from social to economic and environmental objectives, the rise (and fall) of public–private partnerships, and an emerging centrality of infrastructure investments in public policies. Particular national and local planning systems, institutional contexts and local political cultures have resulted in responses to these challenges that are sometimes different and sometimes similar.

1.2.2 Positive and negative technological change

Both types of change create urban redevelopment opportunities at stations. Positive changes – that is, ones that make station locations more easily accessible – include the expansion of high-speed train (HST) systems, and also of advanced regional, S-Bahn and RER/TER-type networks. The most notable negative changes – those that make space available for development – are the transfer of freight and heavy industrial activities away from stations and towards other locations. Among the cases analysed, the role of positive technological change is most evident in France (with the TGV), in Switzerland (with the S-Bahn systems), and in the Netherlands and again Switzerland (with massive national rail investment packages). Negative changes are of a more structural nature. While not explicitly mentioned in the national outlines that follow, they are ubiquitous at the local level.

1.2.3 Institutional change

While there is an evolution in the roles of all public and private actors, the most striking and relevant changes are those occurring to the railway companies, as captured by the term *privatization*. The railways are of course key actors in station area redevelopment. Their privatization (however that term is interpreted) has far-reaching implications for the nature of the initiative. In some cases, this might be the one factor that actually triggers a plan. Privatization, however, is an open-ended process rather than a definite state, and it means different things in different countries. Among the cases analysed, it is most advanced and carries the most weight in the United Kingdom and Sweden. There, however, two very different approaches are being pursued, as we shall see. Commercialization plays an increasingly critical role in Switzerland, where its implications are nevertheless still ambiguous. But it also plays a pivotal role in the Netherlands, where it helps to distinguish a first generation of plans from an incipient second generation of station plans. Privatization is the least advanced in France.

1.2.4 The property cycle

Property booms are partly autonomous and partly related to an explosion in office demand at certain locations and times. Their incidence is also a factor in station area redevelopment. Real estate market cycles have had a compelling influence rather than just a contextual relevance in most London station projects. When the boom turned to bust, the market was a decisive factor in the failure of initiatives such as that taken by the London Regeneration Consortium for King's Cross. In Sweden the collapse of the property market first led to a stand-still. Then it prompted a different approach to station area redevelopment, one that is demand driven rather than supply driven. A similar move in Switzerland distinguishes initiatives such as Zentrum Zürich Nord or Basel EuroVille from the 'outdated' Zürich HauptBahnhof Süd West. Anticipating this reorientation, the market in France and the Netherlands appears to have had a deflating rather than an inflating effect on station projects. There, developers and investors alike have been urging caution and raising doubts about the expectations of 'entrepreneurial' municipalities.

1.2.5 Internationalization and metropolitanization

The internationalization of the economy is imposing the need for far-reaching restructuring in the urban fabric of western Europe. Urban economies are under-going a process of spatial expansion, functional 'sorting-out' and division of tasks on a regional scale (Louter, 1996). A *space of flows*, where specialized and integrated clusters of activities are interconnected both within and outside urban regions, is being superimposed on a historical, weakening *space of places* (Castells, 1989). Station areas are potential nodes in emerging transport and information networks (Bertolini, 1996a, 1996b). An awareness of this possibility and of its implications is beginning to surface in the approach to station area redevelopment across Europe. The initiatives of several cities in France, and most notably of Lille, point in this direction. However, too many unverified assumptions still underpin most strategies there. The debate on the potential roles of station areas as transport and information gateways within multicentred urban regions in a global context is gaining momentum elsewhere too, particularly in the Netherlands and Switzerland. Although the direction is somewhat ambiguous in the other countries, the potential role as a gateway could indeed become the main criterion by which to appraise station area redevelopment initiatives in the future.

The station area redevelopment plans peculiar to each country reflect distinct combinations of the factors described above. However, common trends are also arising and, most interestingly, might become stronger in the future. European integration is of course a very important factor in this regard. From the point of view of transformation at stations, the leading role of the European Commission in the privatization of national railways is particularly important. Its standpoint is formulated in Directive 91/440. Also important is the Union's support for rail transport in general and for the development of a European HST network in particular. For instance, of the 14 links envisaged within the framework of the

Trans-European Networks (TEN) programme, nine are rail links. On the other hand, all the evidence presented in the case studies suggests that local and national institutional and policy contexts will continue to be very important in determining how European and 'global' factors will translate in specific cases. Especially interesting is the diversity of responses to the largely similar challenges raised by station area redevelopment, as discussed further on in the book.

1.3 Organization of the book

The underlying structure of the book is quite simple. It consists of two main parts. Part One can be described as the theoretical part. In Part Two, the emphasis is on empirical evidence: a description of seven case studies in five countries.

Part One presents a number of ideas and concepts that are used to analyse the redevelopment of railway station areas in a systematic way. It posits that the issue at stake in this study is part of a larger European approach to urban planning. In the near future, Europe will have no more internal borders, and capital flows will be increasingly footloose. Accordingly, metropolitan areas will do their utmost to promote themselves. The redevelopment of certain inner-city areas is an important element in this campaign. Along with waterfronts, railway station areas can be considered one of the most important assets in this endeavour. The complexity of the subject may be reduced by splitting it into three parts. That division is reflected in the organization of this book. The first part of the book is structured along the lines of its leading (planning) concept. The *process* (who does what and when) and the *object* (the railway station area) are placed against the background of a regional, national and international *context*.

In Chapters 2 and 3, the essential characteristics of a railway station area (the object) are explained. Then in Chapter 3 relevant participants and their respective interests are described. That overview also presents the consequences for the area's development potential (the process). The contextual elements are the main subject of Chapter 4 (the context). Although the structure is segmented, it will be clear that object, process and context are interrelated. Therefore each chapter builds upon elements from the preceding chapters. Consequently, the once simple structure becomes increasingly complex. But in this case a complex structure is the best way to elucidate these complex processes.

Part Two consists of five chapters. Each describes and analyses railway station redevelopment processes in a particular country: France, the Netherlands, Sweden, Switzerland, and the United Kingdom. In each of these five chapters, context, process and object variables are systematically discussed. Each chapter in Part Two includes a brief description of the national planning system, as that forms part of the development context.

In Part Three, the final chapter of the book takes a wider perspective. It seeks to combine the common elements of the case studies with the concepts from Part One. The discussion covers national as well as European perspectives on railway station area redevelopment. This chapter illustrates the liveliness of the debate, its topicality in Europe, the increasing importance of means of transport, with railway stations in a prominent place, and last but not least its emerging relevance for cities and regions.

2

The railway station as node and place

2.1 Nodes and places

As a geographical entity, a railway station has two basic, though partly contradictory, identities. It is a *node*: a point of access to trains and, increasingly, to other transportation networks (Figure 2.1). At the same time, it is a *place*: a specific section of the city with a concentration of infrastructure but also with a diversified collection of buildings and open spaces (Figure 2.2). Both the practice and the theory of railway station redevelopment demonstrate inadequate understanding of the ambivalent nature of the location, as well as of the interactions between its two connotations. As a consequence, its specific opportunities and problems tend to be overlooked. In order to shed light on the unique challenges associated with the redevelopment of stations, we must first design a framework for their conceptualization *both* as nodes of networks *and* as places in the city.

Taking a dual node–place perspective, we see that both positive and negative interrelations may exist between the two domains. For instance, on the one hand, a high level of accessibility may provide the critical mass of demand for the development of particular activities. In turn, a high density of activities may induce the necessary support for the development of transportation networks. On the other hand, dense patterns of use can make a location's transport infrastructure difficult to expand and adapt. In the same vein, optimization of a station's accessibility by all modes may negatively affect its liveability, and thus its attractiveness. These complex node–place interactions form the core issues of railway station redevelopment.

Is there a way to interpret the node and place dimensions of a railway station location, and analyse their reciprocal interactions? In this chapter we first define what we mean by *node of networks* and *place in the city*. Then we introduce some themes connected with the interaction between the two dimensions. Finally, in order to make the argument more concrete, we identify the specific characteristics of railway stations as compared with those of two other classes of node–place: seaports and airports.

9

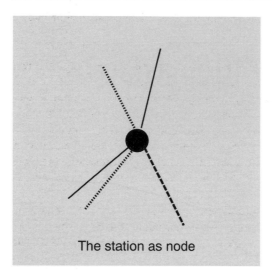

The station as node

Fig. 2.1 The station as node.

2.2 Nodes of networks

In order to understand the specific meaning of networks it is necessary to clarify some definitions. Only when the underlying assumptions are made explicit can the concept be elaborated further. Assuming railway stations are nodes of networks, what do the terms 'node' and 'network' refer to exactly? In common parlance, a *network* is:

- a fabric or structure of cords and wires that cross at regular intervals and are knotted or secured at the crossings;
- a system of lines or channels resembling a network;
- an interconnected or interrelated chain, group, or system [as in a network of hotels].

(*Webster's Ninth New Collegiate Dictionary*, 1986)

A *node* is a point at which subsidiary parts originate or centre (*ibid.*). Together with 'lines' or 'channels' (or 'arches' or 'links'), nodes (sometimes called 'points' or 'vertexes') are the basic components of a network – the points where the lines are 'knotted', 'secured', 'interconnected' or 'interrelated'.

A crucial observation is that 'network' has both a concrete meaning (a fabric or structure of cords and wires) and a more abstract meaning (an interconnected or interrelated chain, group or system). This ambivalence can also be found in the use of the term in urban studies. Here the word has two basic connotations:

The first one comes from common sense and concerns infrastructure systems (highway and railway networks, drainage networks, etc.), the second one regards, *lato sensu*, the spatial interaction among urban places, economic activities and people. If the first one has a 'weak' meaning, describing rather than interpreting . . . , the second one offers, on the contrary, interesting metaphorical implications, but for this reason it seems difficult to use and to submit to an empirical validation. (Camagni and Salone, 1993, p. 1054).

In actual usage, the distinction made by Camagni and Salone is often not clear at all. Attributes of one connotation (that is, of infrastructure networks) tend, quite uncritically, to be attributed to the other domain (to socio-economic networks), or vice versa. Some positive impacts of the performance of, most notably, transportation networks on that of socio-economic networks seem apparent. Activities tend, for instance, to concentrate around transportation nodes such as airports, motorway outlets, or public transport interchanges. However, there are also activities that appear to be repelled by the same nodes, and nodes that do not seem to exert any attraction at all.

This confusion becomes particularly dangerous when we are studying railway station redevelopment. As major nodes of transportation networks, stations are often automatically equated with nodes of socio-economic activities. The Euralille venture, for instance,

is founded on the hypothesis that 'the experience' of Europe is going to change radically under the double impact of the Channel Tunnel and the extension of the TGV network. If this hypothesis is verified, the city of Lille, centre of gravity of the London–Brussels–Paris triangle (30 million inhabitants), will acquire an immediate theoretical importance. It will become the seat of a number of typically modern activities. (Koolhaas, in Simon, 1993, p. 110).

While contentions such as this may contain an element of truth, they cannot be taken as anything more than a possibility. In any case, it must be established for which socio-economic networks a specific station is or may become a node, and under what conditions. In dealing with the problem, we shall use the terms 'network' and 'node' in their first connotation (the railway station as a node of transportation networks). Furthermore, we shall consider relationships, positive or negative, with their second connotation (the railway station as a node of socio-economic networks) as hypotheses to be verified, case by case.

2.3 Places in the city: defining and delimitating the station as place

What do we mean when we call the railway station a *place in the city*? Essentially, a place is a physical environment and a synonym of 'space', or the physical surroundings and a synonymous of 'atmosphere' (*Webster's Ninth New Collegiate Dictionary*, 1986). It is interesting to note that material, quantifiable qualities (as evoked by the term *space*) coexist with immaterial, qualitative attributes (as evoked by the term *atmosphere*). From the perspective of station redevelopment, the focus here is on the *piece of city* incorporating the station – on what is sometimes called the *station neighbourhood* or the *station district*.

This description, however, is still too vague for research purposes. In trying to improve on it, we discover that the railway station as a place has uncertain boundaries. Where does the border lie between the station district and the rest of the city? What makes the former 'different' from the latter? The fact is that there are several overlapping systems ('the city is not a tree', as poignantly contended by Christopher Alexander (1965) many years ago). The influence of a railway station may go far beyond its immediate surroundings. Conversely, entities right next to a railway station may not show any apparent relationship to it. Almost inevitably, any delimitation of the station as place is destined to be somewhat arbitrary. In practice, four approaches to this problem can be identified. These might be characterized as the *walkable radius*, *functional–historical*, *topographic*, and *development perimeter* approaches. Each has its particular advantages and limitations, as outlined below.

- *The walkable radius*. Following this approach, the railway station area is identified as the circular area radiating from the railway station that is considered 'walkable' distance. This is, for instance, the solution chosen by Munck Mortier (1996), who adopts a walkable radius of 500 m. Others use a time criterion: for instance, a 'ten-minute walk'. One advantage of this approach is that it embraces the average user's perspective, which is the least partial of all. But this approach also has some drawbacks. It does not generally coincide with the functional unit of a 'station district' or the area that is the object of a redevelopment initiative. Also, the walkable radius often does not coincide with the actual walkable distances. That discrepancy is due to the existence of asymmetrical physical or psychological barriers, and of different sorts of user.
- *Functional–historical elements*. The railway station area is here considered equal to the sum of the functional elements (for instance, a commercial axis connecting station and city centre, or industrial and distribution facilities with a direct connection to the station), having (or having had) a strong evident locational link with the rail transport centre. Bakker (1994), for example, takes this approach. The advantage of the functional perspective is that it allows relatively rigorous and meaningful criteria. One disadvantage is that it focuses on current or past uses rather than on the potential evolution. Another weak point is that negative 'dysfunctional' relationships tend to be overlooked.
- *Topographic*. From this point of view the railway station area is the surface included within an arbitrary (mostly rectangular) section of a map. The location and extension of this window are determined by a commonsense evaluation of which elements to include in the analysis. However, its arbitrary shape is justified by the need to consider 'all that is there', avoiding a priori assumptions. This is, for example, what Pucci (1996) has done. The advantage of this perspective is that it combines both user and functional criteria. Its main limitation is that the criteria are vaguely defined, and thus are difficult to verify or replicate.
- *A development perimeter*. A fourth possibility is to consider the area included within the perimeter of a specific redevelopment initiative, as done by Bertolini (1996b). This approach has two advantages. First, it adopts the perspective of a specific development plan, and is thus the most concrete. Second, it generally has a better coincidence with administrative boundaries and an acceptable coincidence with functional boundaries. It also has some disadvantages. Areas under the railway station's influence, but excluded from a plan, are neglected. The developer perspective is also the most partial. And if there is no comprehensive plan, this approach is not applicable.

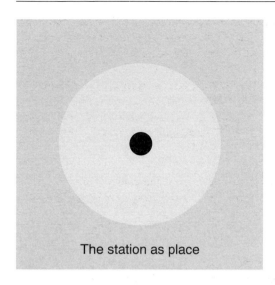

The station as place

Fig. 2.2 The station as place.

In addition to their individual drawbacks, a problem common to all these approaches is that they do not allow for a flexible delimitation of the railway station area. These approaches should be evolving in accordance with progress in understanding of the issues at stake, and/or (with the partial exception of the fourth approach) with changed planning circumstances. A way to overcome part of the delimitation problem could then be by distinguishing between a delimitation prior to analysis and one, possibly different, resulting after closer examination of a case. For this reason, a combination of the approaches described above is proposed. An arbitrary yet use-based definition (walkable radius) was initially chosen. It was then amended according to the specific characteristics of each situation (functional–historical) and the redevelopment process (development perimeter). The meaning of 'place' as discussed earlier is implicit in such a choice. That meaning is made explicit in the following definition of the station as a 'place in the city':

> All the built and open spaces, together with the activities they host, contained within the perimeter designed by a 'walkable radius' centred on the railway station building, as amended to take account of case-specific physical–psychological, functional–historical and development features.

The station as a place in the city is shown in Figure 2.2.

2.4 On the interaction of node and place: railway stations, airports and seaports

2.4.1 Introduction

Railway station areas are nodes and places. Fundamental to the analysis of their redevelopment is a view of the bigger picture. The individual features of the node and place components of a location must be understood in their reciprocal interactions. This is shown in graphic form in Figure 2.3.

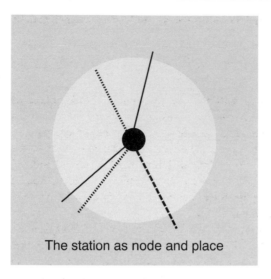

The station as node and place

Fig. 2.3 The station as node and place.

What, more specifically, does being a node–place entail? And how do railway stations distinguish themselves from other sorts of node–place? To answer these questions, in the following pages we shall compare railway stations with two other great families of node–place: airports and seaports. The comparison will be a qualitative and largely intuitive one. It will also deal in the first instance with 'ideal typical' examples of each of the three categories, and refer – quite statically – to the situation now. Yet we believe it helps us to focus on the kinds of variable referred to by terms such as 'node' and 'place'. The comparison will also help to outline some of the key issues raised by nodes–places as development objects, and by railway station locations in particular.

What do seaports, airports and railway stations ('railports') have in common? What are some of the more obvious and less obvious differences? And what implications do these differences have for their development? To make the above definitions and statements more concrete, and to introduce the analysis, these points are dealt with in the following sections, with reference to the European context. By comparing railway stations with seaports and airports, we can shed some light on their differences and similarities. In that way we can better appreciate their specific development potentials.

Not only seaports, but also railway stations and airports were initially built as nodes in a specific transportation network: waterways, railways and flight routes respectively. Increasingly, they are also becoming nodes in complementary transportation networks: the nodes are turning into multimodal interchanges of passengers and/or goods flows. But in addition to their nodal function, they are also places: they all occupy a particular space. This aspect is evoked, for instance, by terms such as *harbour district*, *airport city*, or *station neighbourhood*. And all three names reflect a particular kind of interaction with the area, the direct surroundings and the urban region in which these modes are located. Thus, in addition to a node dimension, they all have a place dimension. From a transport and urban development perspective, relationships between these two dimensions are particularly important. In this light, the opening questions could thus be rephrased: What are – ideally-typically – the similarities and the differences between seaports, airports and railway stations as nodes, as places, and as interacting nodes and places?

2.4.2 Nodes

One basic difference is that railway stations tend to connect a wider range of transport systems than ports and airports do. This wider variety of networks interconnecting at stations is reflected in a more fragmented style of management. No sharp separation exists (yet, in most cases) between the management of transport infrastructure and that of services. And different market and subsidized transport regimes coexist. The opposite, at least in principle, tends to be true of seaports and airports. There, port authorities that commercially exploit the node infrastructure have a longer-standing tradition.

A second basic difference lies in the spatial reach. The reach of the system is more limited in stations (where the regional scale dominates) than in seaports and airports (where the international scale dominates). A third difference is in the adaptability of network configurations: lower for railway networks, higher for air routes and waterway networks. Most importantly, seaports, railway stations and airports offer very different degrees of *space–time compression* and thereby quite divergent transport growth dynamics in their volume of activity. In Europe, the contrast between intense development in air transport and relative stagnation in the other two modes is striking. For stations this pattern is reinforced by the higher spatial constraints on transport growth. As these patterns evolve, the above differences are reflected in the passenger and freight markets served by airports, stations and seaports. Airports accommodate global business and leisure travellers, and transfer higher-added-value freight. Railroad stations cater for daily commuters and city users, and seaports transfer lower-added-value freight.

2.4.3 Places

From a place point of view, a crucial difference between the three modes of transport is the location of their terminals. Most railway stations still tend to be where they were originally built. By now, however, they are immersed in a dense, functionally mixed and historically stratified urban fabric. In contrast, seaports have moved out of their original locations – in or adjacent to the city – and have become the focus of vast mono- or oligo-functional districts. Airports were mostly 'exurban' from the beginning. Yet the picture is all but static. New high-speed train stations are also being developed in peripheral locations (for instance, in the Paris metropolitan area). Airport areas may show the highest urbanization rates of an entire region, and seaports are evolving further into multifunctional complexes. Nevertheless, an important implication of these differences, which are still significant, is that the non-transport world (the 'city close by') tends to have a much stronger presence in railway stations than in seaports and airports. Not only are there more sorts of use and user; there are also more non-transport-related activities and a more fragmented administrative context in the railway station areas. There, node jurisdiction (for example, by transport companies) and place jurisdiction (for example, by the municipality) overlap in particularly complex ways. Add to this the relative scarcity of land and the relatively limited endogenous transportation growth dynamics, and the framework is set for a very different sort of property development around stations. This is dominated by the negotiated renewal of the existing fabric, as opposed to greenfield airport and seaport developments under control of the port authority.

2.4.4 Nodes and places

All the features discussed above converge in determining distinct patterns of node–place interaction. In general, for railway stations the local dynamics and weak impacts prevail, while for airports and seaports regional dynamics and stronger impacts are more prevalent. An important distinction between airports and seaports should be made, however. The accent is on growth in the former, while the latter emphasizes more defensive, 'conservative' developments. Paradoxically, the less intense transformation dynamics of station areas are generally associated with a broader array of actors. Of course, here too some change is taking place. For instance, there is growing resistance to airport expansion among local residents and environmental organizations. The focus of policy and research reflects these contrasts in transport and spatial dynamics. With the possible exception of high-speed train (HST) stops, in the case of railway stations, the policy gives relatively more attention to positive environmental effects (limiting automobility, improving the urban environment) than to economic development (stimulation of the urban economy, diversification of activities and privatization of the railway company). For airports, politics and research are dominated by the issue of growth and its management. Managing growth is an exercise in the distribution of benefits and the mitigation of the adverse environmental effects. Also, for ports, economic development appears to be the core concern, albeit within the context of more limited growth dynamics. Thus the policy emphasis there seems to be on holding a competitive position rather than on accommodating growth.

2.4.5 Towards a conclusion

Node and place concepts are also useful in analysing the development potential of airports and seaports. A comparison – admittedly, more extensive than has been done here – with railway stations can contribute significantly to a further understanding of all three types of terminal separately, and perhaps even in combination. To provide a systematic overview of the similarities and differences Table 2.1 presents a summary of the characteristic features of each type of terminal.

The comparison shown, while stimulating, necessarily overlooks significant exceptions. At least four should be mentioned:

- Within each category there are important differences. Major 'railports' such as Utrecht CS in the Netherlands, Lille Flandres/Euralille in France or Hannover in Germany refer to a totally different order of issues than, say, sub-metropolitan commuter stations such as Didcot Parkway in the United Kingdom. The same could be said of airports (London Heathrow as opposed to Nice) and ports (Rotterdam as opposed to Trieste).

- Especially at the top end of the node hierarchy, there is an increasing blurring of differences. Though perhaps less obviously than for the previous point, complex intermodal interchanges are emerging through increasing inter-connection of formerly separated transportation systems (a top priority of EU transport policy). Under these evolving conditions one transportation mode may dominate, but many others are represented. For instance, there are plans for high-speed rail/air combinations at Schiphol in the Netherlands and Frankfurt in Germany, while interconnection is already a fact at Paris-Roissy and Lyon-Satolas in France. This perspective makes definitions based on a conventional world of distinct mono-network nodes increasingly inadequate.
- Local situations may differ profoundly. For example, consider the different role in the urban–regional context, and the different hinterlands of ports such as Rotterdam and Genoa, of airports such as Frankfurt and Manchester, and of stations such as Utrecht and Lyon. In the case of stations, relative position in the city region may have fundamental implications, as in the distinction between metro–central interchanges (such as the Gare de Lyon-Austerlitz in Paris) and metro–peripheral interchanges (such as Massy in Paris).
- The picture is constantly evolving. For instance, ports were originally next to or close to urban centres. Since then, as we have seen, they have been moved further out, giving rise to distinct geographical entities. Urbanization of previously largely unbuilt airport areas is rapidly gaining momentum. Finally, while most railway stations still are in predominantly urban locations, there is a tendency, most notably in the Parisian region, for high-speed interchanges to be built in a peripheral, if not rural, location.

Some caution is thus required when generalizing about a node–place frame-work. Nonetheless, we still think it can generate fertile insights into the problems at hand. In considering railway stations, airports and seaports, planners are confronted with tasks that are both similar and different. In all three, a node and a place dynamic must be recognized, and node–place interactions must be dealt with. However, different transportation development trends, different types of location, different scales of impact, and different constellations of actors involved have profound implications, as we shall see, on the sort of planning approach adopted.

Attributes of railway station areas cited in the previous pages will be reconsidered and detailed further throughout the analysis of the case studies. Basically, the unique challenge of the development of node–places is the need to deal, *at the same time*, with *both* transport *and* urban development issues. This entails inter alia two distinct and at least partly autonomous and often conflicting sorts of policies, markets, administrative and management structures, and technical domains. We shall see in detail how this fundamental ambiguity translates into a set of characteristic *development dilemmas* of railway station areas, for which analogies can also be drawn for airports and seaports. On the other hand, railway station areas are, at least in most of their present configurations, also different from the other two categories of node–place. Again, schematically, railway station areas are different in that they tend to have a much more articulated place dimension, whereas in airports and seaports the node dimension tends to

Table 2.1 Summary of typical characteristics of railway stations, airports and seaports, following the node and place approach, with reference to the European context

Feature	Stations	Airports	Ports
Node			
Spatial reach from node	Local–(inter)national Dominant scale: regional	National–intercontinental Dominant scale: (inter)national	National–intercontinental Dominant scale: (inter)continental
'Space–time compression' from node	From moderate to high	Very high	Low
Transport pattern	Polycentric distribution Rigid network configuration	Concentration and diffusion (hub) Adaptable network configuration	Concentration and diffusion (hub) Adaptable network configuration
Modal choice at node	High Dominant modes: train and local public transport Main complementary modes: car, bicycle, foot	Limited Dominant mode: aeroplane Main complementary modes: car, train	Very limited Dominant mode: ship Main complementary modes: truck, train, barge
Accent on	Passengers	Passengers and freight	Freight
Main accessory services at node	Passenger care	Passenger care, and goods transfer and storage	Goods transfer and storage
Transport unit cost	Lower middle	Higher middle	Low
Management of node	No separation between infrastructure and services Monopolistic, subsidized regime (but changing)	Separation between infrastructure and services Quasi-market regime, but presence of dominant operators and (hidden) subsidies	Separation between infrastructure and services Quasi-market regime, but presence of dominant operators and (hidden) subsidies
Target market	Commuters (for work or study), city users (for shopping and/or entertainment), some types of long-distance business or pleasure traveller	(International) business travellers and tourists; higher value per unit goods	Lower value per unit goods
Spatial constraints on transport development at node	High	Moderate, but growing	Moderate, but growing
Transport growth dynamics	Passenger: moderate (high external, low internal competition)	Passenger and freight: intense (high internal, low external competition)	Freight: middle (high internal, low external competition)
Place			
Typical location	Urban	Extra-urban	Extra-urban
Land consumption per unit transported	Moderate	Very high	Very high

Table 2.1 continued

Feature	Stations	Airports	Ports
Land use density	High	Low	Low
Variety of uses	High	Low, but growing	Low
Dominant uses	Non-transport related	Transport related and non-transport related	Transport related
Dominant place-connected activities (thus excluding node operation)	Private and public services, shopping, hotel and restaurants, housing Business services growing	Business services, innovative (high-tech) industry, transport and distribution Hotel and congress growing	Transport and distribution, process industry (petrochemical, steel)
Variety of place users	Very high (anything from 'metropolitan businessmen' to the homeless)	Moderate, selected	Very limited
Access	Public	Restricted	Restricted
Land available for property development	Scarce	Yes	Yes
Property development dynamics	Weak	Intense (under conditions)	Weak
Type of property development	Renewal of existing fabric	Greenfield development	Greenfield development
Node–place			
Node–place relationship	Local interaction, regional dependence	Local dominance, regional interaction	Local dominance, regional interaction
Economic impact of node	Weak, and local	High, and regional–national	High, but contrasted, and regional–national
Environmental impact of node	Moderate, and spatially limited	High, and extensive	High, and extensive
Density of actors	High, and fragmented	Moderate, and concentrated, but conflict is growing	Moderate, and concentrated
Administrative framework	Fragmentation of responsibilities	Autonomy, with restrictions: airport authority	Autonomy, with restriction: port authority
Policy context: 1. thematic focus	1. Environment (positive indirect effects)	1. Economic development (positive direct and indirect effects), environment (negative effects)	1. Economic development (positive and negative direct and indirect effects)
2. specific issues	2. Development of public transport, development of HST network, privatization of railway companies	2. Managing growth	2. Conserving competitive position, employment levels
Dominant research perspective	Transport and urban development	Economic impact; trade-offs between economy and environment	Technological change

dominate. While the picture may be evolving, and there are certainly exceptions, in most cases this implies that for station areas the leading, 'ordering' role of transport development is much less undisputed than in the other categories of node, and that, conversely, autonomous urban development trends have a much greater weight. As the cases in Part Two will document, this may open up unique opportunities for integration between the two orders of development, but can also result in problematic stalemates, as one may impede the other.

3
What makes the development potential of a railway station location?

The development potential of railway station areas is closely connected to their features both as nodes and as places. Chapter 2 anticipated not only that there are development potentials on both sides, but also that they can contribute to each other's potential. Next to opportunities, constraints and possible sources of conflict have also been indicated. In this chapter both dimensions of development will be elaborated, starting with the node. The discussion here is centred on the transport of passengers in Europe. Section 3.2 treats place, a dimension that has been receiving more and more attention as interest rises in the station area as an object of property investment. In section 3.3, starting from a discussion of the Japanese example, an attempt is made to show how node and place developments can contribute to each other's development in practice.

3.1 The transport development perspective: the node

The times when trains carried as much as 80–90% of total passenger-kilometres are a distant memory. After an exponential growth – which took off in the first half of the nineteenth century and peaked in most industrialized countries around 1900 – railway transport has entered a period of absolute stagnation and relative decline. Since the 1930s the railway network has not grown globally, and has contracted locally (Grübler, 1990; Grübler and Nackicenovic, 1991). Especially after the Second World War, the train's lower flexibility than that of the car and lower speed than that of the aeroplane have proved fatal for it. Under-investment and ineffective management have added to these weaknesses, together with a generalized trend towards spatial spreading of homes and jobs. This accumulation of factors has brought rail transport into a spiral of declining market shares and profitability.

More recently, however, there have been signs of a comeback. The dominant automobile-centred transport system may be approaching saturation, possibly opening up windows of opportunity for alternative solutions (Grübler, 1990,

Grübler and Nackicenovic, 1991). Concerns about the negative impacts of other modes on congestion and the environment – together with technical and organizational innovations within the railways – may lead (according to some) to the advent of 'a second railway age' (Banister and Hall, 1993). As will be shown, this is perhaps an exaggerated statement. Nonetheless, an evaluation of the future prospects of rail transport is an indispensable basis for any appreciation of station area redevelopment opportunities.

The discussion in this chapter will concentrate on passenger transport in Europe. This is by far the most relevant sector in the light of the theme of this book. Freight operations are disappearing from the passenger station areas that we have analysed. Continuing concentration and economies of scale in the freight transport and distribution sectors mean that goods are increasingly handled in a decreasing number of separate, decentralized intermodal centres. These are arguably also a type of station, but one that would require a quite different analytical approach. Indeed, it is rather the removal of freight activities from passenger station areas that is often a basic condition of the development plans discussed here.

In the following pages the current position of rail passenger transport in Europe will first be outlined. This situation will then be related to wider contextual factors in order to focus on the strengths, weaknesses and future prospects of rail transport. The section will end with an outline of the implications for station area development.

3.1.1 A railway renaissance?

How is rail transport faring in Europe at the end of the twentieth century? The statistics are not particularly encouraging (Cornet, 1993; Batisse, 1994; *Railway Gazette International*, 1994; ECMT, 1996). Market shares have been declining in all sectors, with the exception of high-speed and commuter services. Whereas in 1970 trains accounted for 10.4% of Europe's passenger-kilometres, by 1993 that figure was down to 6.6%. These figures lie in between those found in Asia and the USA. Japan is the industrialized land where travel by train has the largest market share by far. There, about 150 railways carry 19 billion passengers each year, or half of the world's total. In contrast, passenger transport by rail has virtually disappeared from the USA, with the partial exception of the North East Corridor (NEC). In 1991, while Europeans averaged 760 km of train travel per person per year for a total of 0.381 billion passenger-kilometres, Japanese travelled an impressive 3040 km per person and totalled 0.37 billion passenger-kilometres, and Americans only 80 km for 0.03 billion passenger-kilometres. Within the European context there are significant national variations, however (Figures 3.1 and 3.2; Tables 3.1 and 3.2). Perhaps more importantly, there are areas of relative weakness (such as international and suburb-to-suburb relationships) and relative strength (such as high-speed trains and radial commuting).

What structural factors lie behind such a picture? Without understanding these underlying factors no improvement is possible. In the following sections, we shall touch on the two most important ones. On the demand side, we shall consider the unfavourable mobility and urbanization context (section 3.1.2). On the supply side, we shall examine the instabilities of the rail operators (section 3.1.3).

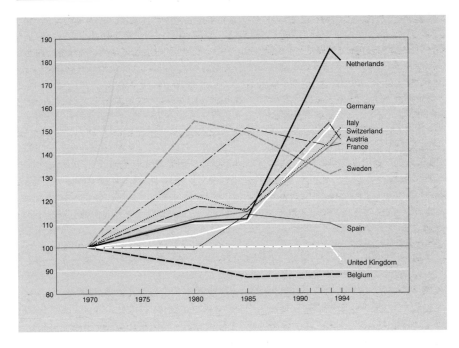

Fig. 3.1 Passenger transport by rail in selected European countries, in passenger-kilometres: 1970 = 100. (Source: own elaboration of ECMT, 1996)

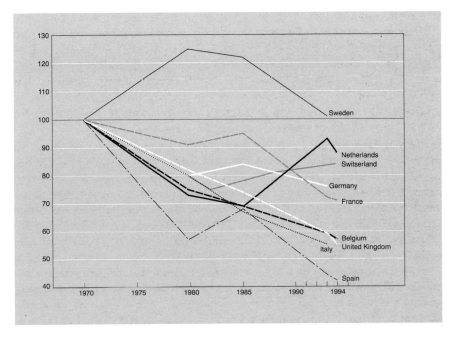

Fig. 3.2 Passenger transport by rail in selected European countries, share of rail in total passenger-kilometres, 1970 = 100. (Source: own elaboration of ECMT, 1996)

Table 3.1 Passenger transport by rail (thousand million passenger-kilometres)

Country	Year				
	1970	1980	1985	1993	1994
Austria (A)	6.28	7.38	7.29	9.61	9.20
Belgium (B)	7.57	6.96	6.57	6.69	6.64
Switzerland (CH)	8.17	9.18	9.38	11.68	12.09
Germany (D)	38.48	40.50	42.71	58.00	61.30
Spain (E)	14.99	14.83	17.07	16.49	16.14
France (F)	40.98	54.66	61.72	58.60	58.90
Italy (I)	32.46	39.59	37.40	47.10	48.90
The Netherlands (NL)	8.01	8.89	9.01	14.79	14.44
Sweden (S)	4.56	7.00	6.80	5.97	6.05
United Kingdom (UK)	30.41	30.26	30.38	30.36	28.66

Source: ECMT

Table 3.2 Passenger transport by rail as a percentage of total passenger transport

Country [a]	Year				
	1970	1980	1985	1993	1994
Belgium (B)	11	9	8	7	7
Switzerland (CH)	15	12	12	13	13
Germany (D)	9	7	7	7	n.a.
Spain (E)	15	9	10	7	6
France (F)	11	10	10	8	8
Italy (I)	12	9	8	6	n.a.
The Netherlands (NL)	9	7	6	9	8
Sweden (S)	6	7	7	6	n.a.
United Kingdom (UK)	8	6	6	5	4

[a] There was no information available for Austria
Source: ECMT

3.1.2 An unfavourable context

Many of the factors that explain the declining trend sketched above are structural in nature and largely exogenous in origin. Without understanding this development, any effort to revitalize the railways (and with them the station areas) would remain wishful thinking. In Europe, contextual forces unfavourable to the development of public transport in general and of the train in particular have been highlighted elsewhere (e.g. Salomon *et al.*, 1993; Orfeuil, 1994; Banister, 1995; Pucher and Lefèvre, 1996). It will be useful to summarize these points here. In general, the continuous growth of personal wealth is paralleled by an ongoing increase in car ownership ratio, while processes of social differentiation and emancipation bring about more complex mobility patterns, for which public transport is often ill equipped. Trends in the job market (such as short-term contracts, part-time work, multiple-income households, and the participation of women) also contribute to an increasingly multidirectional, diffused mobility. Furthermore, the locational preferences of many if not most firms and households seem to be for low-density, car-oriented, suburban and exurban locations. The decentralization of activities and the growth of automobility appear to reinforce one another, following a trajectory that is proving extremely difficult to change.

Reinforcing the problem, and turning to the supply side, administrative fragmentation makes it difficult to manage mobility at its 'natural' regional scale, or to integrate transport and land-use policies. In addition, and paradoxically, while more control of transport and land-use developments is advocated, there is a general trend towards the retreat of the state. As a result, public transport companies, including the railways, are torn between (very material) pressures to become profitable, and (too vague?) pressures to contribute to an environmentally and socially sustainable mobility.

Given the quantitative weight of mobility at the regional scale (see below), particularly important issues among those cited are the emerging diffused distribution of activities within vast conurbations, or *urban fields*, and the connected exponential growth of criss-cross (auto)mobility (as extensively documented by Salomon *et al.*, 1993). In recent decades, population growth and (increasingly) employment growth have been maximal in peripheral, car-oriented locations all across Europe, including cities as diverse as Paris (Orfeuil, 1994), Manchester (Haywood, 1997, unpublished), and Amsterdam (Van der Berg, 1996; Louter, 1996). In the Netherlands, for instance, since 1960 the population trend has been one of increase outside and decline inside the four major municipalities of Amsterdam, Rotterdam, Utrecht, and The Hague (Van der Berg, 1996). At the same time, growth has been highest in municipalities without a railway station (Bakker, 1994). Between 1987 and 1993, employment has grown by only 4% in the four major cities but by as much as 21% in suburban areas (Louter, 1996). In the Amsterdam region, only 75 000 out of a total of 500 000 jobs are still in the central city. Meanwhile, several subsidiary employment centres in the suburbs and beyond have been rapidly growing. The booming airport area already counts 60 000 jobs (Lambooy, 1994). Similar pictures can be found elsewhere in Europe (Salomon *et al.*, 1993).

The implications for mobility patterns are far reaching. Commuting data on the Dutch and French situations, among others, are quite revealing in this respect. Suburban and exurban trips already account for a significant share, as shown in Tables 3.3 and 3.4; and they are also growing the fastest (Jansen, 1993; Orfeuil, 1993). The problem is that trains and public transport tend to be stronger where the flows are declining: that is, on radial, centre-to-suburb trips. In the Netherlands, trips between the central city and the surrounding area accounted in 1987/88 for only 14% of all trips and 45% of all travelled kilometres in the four large metropolitan areas (Korver *et al.*, 1993). In Paris, public transport in 1984 – with a share of about 30% – was a serious competitor to the car only for trips between the central city and the suburbs. But these were merely 11% of all trips within urban areas of more than 20 000 inhabitants (Orfeuil, 1993).

Trends such as those outlined above are neither fixed nor unavoidable. They are constantly evolving, and can be to some extent reinforced or weakened by public intervention. Indeed, policy variables explain to a significant degree the striking differences that still exist between the mobility patterns of Europe, Japan, and the

Table 3.3 Commuter flows in Ile de France, Paris, 1982 (percentage share)

Place of residence	Place of work			
	Central city	Suburban ring	Exurban area	Total
Central city	17	4	1	22
Suburban ring	13	24	2	39
Exurban area	8	7	24	29
Total	38	35	27	100

Source: Jansen (1993), p. 118

Table 3.4 Commuter flows in Amsterdam metropolitan area, 1985 (percentage share)

Place of residence	Place of work			
	Central city	Suburban ring	Exurban area	Total
Central city	36	4	4	44
Suburban ring	10	21	3	33
Exurban area	16	7	excluded	23
Total	62	31	6	100

Source: Jansen (1993), p. 118

USA (Orfeuil and Bovy, 1993; Pucher and Lefèvre, 1996). Also, within Europe 'supply factors' are possibly the single most important explanation for internal variations in the modal split (Bovy *et al.*, 1993). In this respect, on the continent differences are still significant, harmonization pressures from the EU not-withstanding (Salomon *et al.*, 1993; Pucher and Lefèvre, 1996). However, the relevance of unfavourable mobility and urbanization patterns does imply that any reversal of the decline in public and train transport cannot come from within these sectors alone. A different set of contextual conditions is also needed. Further-more, this implies that, if a mobility and urbanization context is given, any change or attempt at developing public transport – including the train – threatens to be marginal if these contextual factors are not taken into account.

3.1.3 An organization in transition

Many consider the poor performance of the train in Europe to be a consequence of two situations. One of course is the unfavourable development of external factors (that is, the context) discussed above. The other is the fact that train services have become the product of the restricted freedom and autonomy of the railway companies. This is often connected to their being operated as public services instead of private businesses. To this (not unquestioned) line of argument one could add a destructive comparison with profitable passenger services in south-east Asia (*The Economist*, 1996). An examination of the performance of western European railways in the period 1977–1990 (*Railway Gazette International*, 1994) shows a varied picture. All railway companies had productivity gains. Train kilometres per staff member rose on average from 2302 to 2926. Internal differences were pronounced, ranging in 1990 from a high of 4484 km per staff member in the Netherlands to a low of 1568 km in Italy. However, in all cases receipts were less than the expenses. Also, the cost recovery ratio worsened: it dropped from an average of 59% in 1977 to 46% in 1990. The sole positive exception was in the UK, where it rose from 71% to 82%. Furthermore, the report saw evidence of a deteriorating financial situation. This was attributed mainly to inadequate public service compensation for social services, and failure of investment to produce adequate returns. Other sources confirm these points. For instance, the supply of social, non-profitable services is currently estimated at about half of the costs of rail operations in the UK, France, and Germany (*The Economist*, 1996). Indebtedness is particularly severe for railways that have taken the path of otherwise much needed massive investment spending (Batisse, 1994).

In the period covered by the *Railway Gazette International* (1994) report, the market share of the train decreased from 7.6% in 1977 to 6.7% in 1990. The exceptions were in the Netherlands, with a rise from 6.4 to 6.9%, and Sweden, with a rise from 5.4 to 6.1%. The biggest market shares in 1990 were those of Austria and Switzerland, with 11.1% and 10.8% respectively. The lowest were in Ireland, with 3.6%, followed by Norway (5.1%) and the UK (5.4% and declining). The UK data are disturbing: they give the impression that any higher cost recovery may be at the expense of market share. Indeed Fitzroy and Smith (1995) reach this very conclusion.

Many initiatives have been taken in an attempt to reverse these trends. In Europe, a quite remarkable (if not always unambiguous) consensus exists on the need to defend and further develop the railways. Emergency measures, reforms, recovery plans, restructuring, investments and cut-backs: all these approaches have been tried, sometimes with noteworthy results. A persistent problem is the extreme compartmentalization of policies and programmes at the national level, with little communication between European railways. While there are some recent signs of change, several parallel, alternative programmes are for example running for the development of high-speed technology. This is a striking example of the absence of the international and open approach that has been fuelling innovation in the air and sea transport sectors (Batisse, 1994). A similar conclusion was reached in our interviews with the property departments being set up by railway companies throughout Europe (Bertolini and Spit, 1996). There was interest in each other's experiences, but actual knowledge appeared to be limited; and there was little evidence of learning any lessons from across the border.

Paradoxically, the range of possible organizational innovation is limited by the European Union's agenda, outlined in Directive 91/440. The Union pursues for its railways (Cornet, 1993) management autonomy, clearance of past debts, separate accounting for infrastructure and operations, fees for the use of this infrastructure, the possibility of creating new railway ventures, infrastructure access rights for these ventures, and special access rights to infrastructure for intermodal transport operators. For its part, the International Union of Railways (UIC) has also agreed on a set of objectives, which entail (Cornet, 1993) complete autonomy in international traffic, special contracts for transport covered by public service

27

obligations, total freedom in the management of human resources, a substantial increase in the level of investment, harmonization of the conditions of competition between all modes, a significant reduction in production costs, improvement of the financial situation, separation of infrastructure and operating accounts, balancing of the budget on a company level and in each business sector, increased market shares in profitable growth sectors, and internalization of external costs for all modes.

While there are significant shifts in emphasis, a common orientation seems thus to be taking shape. But there are several fundamental questions still awaiting an answer. Some particularly important ones are the following:

- Should railways concentrate on areas of strength (high-speed lines or commuting, for example) or on improving the whole network?
- In what measure should railways enter the business of travel-accessory services?
- Which are the most appropriate institutional arrangements in the light of national heritages, which are often strongly conditioning?
- What is the right mix of cooperation/integration and competition/ disintegration between railway companies and services?

In each European country different, tentative answers to these questions are being tried. There is as yet no unequivocal picture emerging. The challenge is daunting: European railways have to find ways of making more efficient use of a transport mode that is gradually losing market share. In this context a particularly important development appears to be the move towards separation of management of operations and infrastructure. However, here also there are in practice many different interpretations, ranging from simple separation of accounts to total disintegration, with France and the UK occupying the two extremes in Europe (Bowers, 1995; Brooks and Button, 1995). And the real point may be yet a very different one. In a study of 16 OECD countries, Oum and Yu (1994) concluded that, besides contextual factors, it is not so much the ownership regime but rather the degree of freedom for managerial decision-making that is the crucial variable in achieving economic efficiency.

The situation is thus still one of continuous change. A balance sheet is hard to draw up. However, it is already apparent that until now no approach has unequivocally solved the central dilemma of how to increase economic efficiency while also satisfying wider political goals such as sustainability, equity and regional development.

3.1.4 Strengths and weaknesses of railway transport

Capitalizing on strengths
In the light of the points raised in the preceding sections, the current phase can be defined as one of intense turbulence, many uncertainties and some opportunities. Despite this complexity, it is essential to try to map out scenarios for the future. This and the following sections constitute an attempt to sketch the future development of the sector by evaluating rail passenger transport's comparative strengths and weaknesses.

Frequently cited strengths of the train are that it is relatively environment-friendly, it is safe, and it is reliable. Its frequently cited weaknesses are its lack of flexibility, its generally unreactive and cumbersome organization, and – with a few exceptions – its poor performance and image. Any revival of the train would have to capitalize on the sector's strengths and find ways of overcoming its weaknesses. The following sections are devoted to each of these points.

On the plus side are especially the train's comparatively lower external costs. Accordingly, any revival appears to be closely connected with a more adequate internalization of transport's social and environmental impacts. The current financial balance in favour of automobile use has a direct effect on the modal split. This has been demonstrated, among others, by Pucher (1988) and Pucher and Lefèvre (1996). From an environmental point of view, the advantages of rail transport seem significant. While the visual and acoustic impacts of road and rail transport are roughly comparable, rail scores much better on land uptake, chemical pollution, energy consumption, and safety. Congestion is another area of externalities where a shift towards the train would be welcome. The costs of road congestion are high and growing. According to an OECD study (*Railway Gazette International*, 1996) the annual cost of road congestion in the EU is 120 billion ECU, or 2% of the Union's GDP. And this sort of evaluation does not include the less quantifiable negative impacts of road transport, such as the loss of public use of streets for other than traffic purposes.

These general findings for the European Union are supported by material from individual countries. Troin (1995) for France and Ellwanger (1990) for Germany report the following figures on the environmental and social impacts of road and rail:

- *Land consumption*. In France, a two-track high-speed line has a net width of 12–13 m, while a 2×2 lane motorway is 34 m wide, though the former has a much higher capacity. One thousand passenger-kilometres consume 15 m^2 on the roads but only 3.2 m^2 on the rails. Similar figures are reported for Germany.
- *Chemical pollution*. In France, the train is responsible for 2.1% of the carbon emissions attributable to passenger transport (while carrying 11% of the traffic); in contrast, private cars account for 94.8% of the emissions. In Germany, road transport pollutes eight times as much as rail transport per unit transported.
- *Energy consumption*. In France, consumption per passenger-kilometre is a factor of 1 for the TGV, 2.7 for the car and 4.2 for the aeroplane. In Germany, road passenger transport consumes 3.5 times more energy per unit transported than rail.
- *Safety*. In France, the yearly average of deaths per billion passenger-kilometres in the period 1977–1992 for train and plane was 0.18; for road it was 18, or 100 times as much. In Germany, accident rates in 1985 (number of victims per million kilometres) were a factor of 1 for train, 0.8 for air transport and 24 for road.
- *Environmental and social costs*. Environmental costs in France were calculated for 1993 to be Fr 87.5 billion for road transport, Fr 4 billion for rail transport, and Fr 16 billion for air transport. In Germany, the internalization of

social costs (accidents, traffic jams, air pollution, and noise) would have amounted in 1989 to 30.4 ECU per 1000 passenger-kilometres for road and 1.65 ECU for rail. The Environment and Forecasting Institute of Heidelberg has calculated in detail the social costs of road transport on the basis of the full life-cycle of an automobile (*The Guardian*, 1993). These would amount to DM 6000 per car per annum – including the external costs of all forms of pollution, accidents and noise after deducting income from all sources of vehicle and fuel taxation. While the numbers may differ, the same general picture is confirmed by other studies (e.g. Renner, 1988; World Resources Institute, 1992; *De Volkskrant*, 29 July 1995).

The implication drawn by Rommerskirchen (in Ellwanger, 1990, p. 11) is that 'liberalization concepts, which are geared solely to market mechanisms, will fail to cope with ecological issues as long as external effects are not internalized.' Also, Pucher and Lefèvre (1996, p. 207) contend that 'the pricing of automobile use at its full economic, social, and environmental costs must be regarded as a long-term objective if any improvement in urban transport is to be achieved.'

Overcoming weaknesses

There are signs that Europe might, albeit partially, move in the direction indicated by Rommerskirchen. However, little will be achieved if the structural weaknesses of rail passenger transport are not also taken into consideration. Some of the lessons that Webber (1986) learned from the evaluation of BART (the mass transit system of the San Francisco area) provide useful material for reflection. Webber concluded that modal choice is made on the basis of money and time costs for the entire door-to-door trip; that time spent waiting is charged at several times the time spent travelling; that large-vehicle systems are most appropriate where there is high density at both the residential and the employment ends of the trip; and that there appears to be a point of no return in the land-use transport nexus, beyond which land-use concentration cannot be simply induced by transport concentration.

Financial and other car-restraint policies (such as traffic buffers, pedestrian zones, bus lanes, parking restrictions, and bicycle lanes) can be successful only if an adequate train and public transport system is developed at the same time. This must also, and most notably, include a lower-cost, low-capital, flexible approach for suburb-to-suburb and 'rural' trips. For instance, there must be (connecting) van services, minibuses or shared-ride taxis. The conclusion of Webber (1986, p. 49), while geared to the West Coast US context, is thought-provoking: 'The design criteria for an alternative future transport system must reflect the (flexibilities) that the modern city form requires.' Ideally, a mass transport system is needed that is 'capable of providing random access, just the way the telephone network connects everywhere to everywhere – directly, and on demand.'

Next to the development of innovative, hybrid forms of public transport, the main issue is the consideration of journeys from the point of origin to the destination point, and thus of chains of trips and combinations of modes. More attention to transfer points, to terminal trips (before and after the train) and to fare integration is thus needed. Rail transport integration is indeed a leading theme in the European Union's transport policy. Two concrete translations of this policy are investment in trans-European networks (TEN: 9 out of the total of 14 planned are rail links), and interoperability (to allow high-speed trains to run non-stop between cities in neighbouring countries). Integration is also the key word in a recent green paper by the EU transport commissioner Neil Kinnock (*Railway Gazette International*, 1996). In this document, which considers ways to make public transport sufficiently attractive to get people out of their cars, integration is the key concept. It calls for physical integration at nodal points, coordination of timing of services to connect operationally, and coordinated fares, ticketing and information. The starting point, we may add, could be the integration in wider transport networks of commuter and high-speed links, which are the railways' most competitive services, as discussed below.

3.1.5 Development prospects 1: commuter trains and intra-metropolitan mobility

From a quantitative point of view, the great majority of rail trips, as of trips in general, are in the short and medium range. For instance, on an average day 2 million suburban travellers pass through Paris's stations, as opposed to 35 000 TGV and 100 000 main-line passengers. In Tokyo, 30 million persons commute daily by train, as opposed to 300 000 long-distance passengers on Shinkansen, which is the world's longest-running high-speed rail system, with 1800 km of railway tracks through Japan's densely populated areas. It is thus at this *regional* scale that the battle for transport share is fought. Suburban travel is a captive market for the train, especially in dense, highly populated metropolitan areas around the world, as there is often little or no alternative. While an increasing percentage of trips are made for reasons other than work (about three-quarters in most European countries), commuting, together with study trips, is an area of relative strength of the train. In the Tokyo region, the train has an astonishingly high share of home-to-work trips (75%). In London, with a share of 45% this is more than significant. In the Netherlands (Van Nierop, 1993), as many as 30% of all train travellers were commuters, 21% were students, while shopping and recreation accounted for only 9% and 8% respectively of all trips by rail. This relative orientation is confirmed by data elsewhere. In London, for example, 65% of all train trips may be ascribed to commuters (Bayliss, 1991).

Against this background, two crucial questions arise:

- Is the train sufficiently equipped to retain its relative strength in commuting and student transport?
- Can the train capture a bigger share of the faster-growing categories of non-work, non-study trips?

In order to answer these questions in the affirmative, the decisive move appears to be improved integration between train and other forms of transport, both public and private, as sketched above. Train travel is seldom, if ever, an isolated experience. For instance, of all the commuters that come to London by train, 40% also use the Underground (Bayliss, 1991). In the Netherlands, 52% of all train passengers arrive at the railway station by bicycle, while only 22% are close enough to walk (Ministerie VROM *et al.*, 1992). As Webber (1986) emphasizes, transport options are perceived – and evaluated – by passengers as part of the door-to-door package of a full intermodal chain, and time spent waiting is weighed particularly heavily. As a result, the quality of connections is especially important. There are some successful examples: the RER system in Paris, fully co-managed by SNCF (the French railways) and RATP (the local transport company); and the S-Bahn systems in German and Swiss cities. Also promising may be the development of car–train complementarity. This has been introduced in numerous French and Swedish railway stations. It is also in place at commuter interchanges on the edges and in the hinterland of metropolises such as London and Milan. Furthermore, there are some unconventional approaches. One is the train–taxi fare and service integration, as in the *treintaxi* system in the Netherlands. Another consists of rent-a-car and rent-a-bike facilities (the former expanding at HST stations, the latter being a standard provision at Dutch railway stations). Last but not least, it is important to have an excellent connection to local pedestrian routes.

3.1.6 Development prospects 2: high-speed trains and inter-metropolitan mobility

At the intra-metropolitan scale, the issue appears to be one of holding onto market shares. At the inter-metropolitan scale, the introduction of high-speed trains (HST) has been perceived by many as a real breakthrough for the train, if not the trigger of a 'new railway age' (Banister and Hall, 1993). There are expectations that, in Europe, HSTs could capture as much as 80–90% of all trips in the distance range between 160 km and 500 km, and about 50% up to 800 km (Hall, 1991). That share of the market is currently held by airlines. HSTs have already had a strong impact on travel patterns in the countries where they have been introduced. In all cases, however, the outstanding performances of the first lines, often linking the two main national centres, were followed by less striking results of subsequent additions to the system. For example, the success of the Paris–Lyon TGV has been beyond expectations. So has the success of the Hanover–Wurzburg and Stuttgart–Mannheim ICE and the Madrid–Seville AVE. But there have also been somewhat poorer performances for subsequent expansions of the network, such as the TGV Atlantique and the TGV Nord in France.

In both France and Germany – the European nations that are moving most rapidly and consistently towards the implementation of a national HST network – the first lines had a 15% return on their investment, but these figures have since been steadily decreasing. The expected return for the TGV Méditerranée, for instance, is 8%, mainly because of environmental impact mitigation measures. Installation costs are rising rapidly. While the TGV South-East cost Fr 26 million per kilometre, the cost of the TGV Atlantique climbed up to Fr 42 million per kilometre (Troin, 1995). Because of these trends the alternative use of high-speed tilting bodies on existing lines – a solution that is both less intrusive and less expensive, though not as fast – is gaining favour. This solution has been successful in Italy (the Pendolino) and Sweden (the X 2000). Following their example, this technology was recently chosen for the upgrading to high speeds of the Boston–Washington North East Corridor (NEC) in the USA.

These trends suggest both an acknowledgement of strong but selective impacts, and wariness of easy generalizations. Is it also possible, on this basis, to sketch the future prospects for HSTs in the context of rail travel as a whole? The experience is still very limited. In 1991, HSTs accounted for just 1% of total train travel in the world. Two-thirds of that share was in Japan alone, and one-fifth in France. Gains in overall market share due to the introduction of HSTs have been relatively modest so far. For example, long-distance travel by train increased in Germany in 1992 following the introduction of the ICE, showing slight growth: it rose to 15.5% afterwards as compared with 15.1% before the introduction of ICE. However, these modest results have to be placed in the context of structural decline, as sketched in the preceding sections. Perhaps most significantly, these results must be viewed from the perspective of future developments, and above all the probability of a continental HST network. It is expected that with the implementation of a European HST network – including crucial links such as the Channel Tunnel, Transalpine and German east–west connections – average speeds on international journeys within Europe could improve from the current 98 km/h to 154 km/h, and that market share would follow. The crucial question is when and in what measure such a continental network will be in place. Assuming that those plans will go ahead, the next question is how inter-metropolitan transport share will be redistributed between airline carriers and high-speed trains.

Most studies assume that there is, and will be, a certain amount of competition between train and air transport on selected routes. Experience in France and Japan suggests that analogous trajectories on the main links of first substitution will be supplemented by a stabilization of the modal split. Four years after the TGV line was opened, 75% more personal and 175% more business trips by rail were recorded between Paris and Lyon. Rail accounted for a 10% increase of personal trips and a 20% increase of business trips in the corridor. Initially, nearly half of the passengers previously travelling by air shifted to the train, but by the beginning of the 1990s both flights and trains were travelling at full capacity. In the period 1980–1985, 30% of the growth of TGV passengers had come from air and 18% from car trips, but as much as 49% was autonomously generated traffic. A similar development unfolded in Japan on the Tokyo–Osaka line. After the opening of the Shinkansen in 1964, Nagoya airport (lying in between the two terminals) lost three-quarters of its passengers. But after seven years Nagoya returned to its initial traffic levels. From 1969 on, the train–air modal split has remained constant (Brotchie *et al.*, 1991).

A report of the Institute for Air Transport in Paris (*Railway Gazette International*, 1992) draws several conclusions. Below 250–350 km, the TGV is faster. The modal split would be in favour of rail up to 600 km. Above 1000 km, the plane would always be better. It should thus be expected, according to the study, that as a result of HST development there will be less road traffic and conventional train traffic but more complementary train–air traffic and autonomously generated HST traffic. Other studies reach similar conclusions (Brotchie *et al.*, 1991). In France, the redistribution of passenger shares between aeroplanes and HST in favour of the former after deregulation of internal air travel is a clear sign of the limits of a purely subsitutional perspective (Zembri, 1997).

Finally, we should mention a political argument in favour of HST–air integration. A diffused improvement of accessibility in Europe would also require integration rather than competition between air and HST (Lutter, 1994). By itself, HST would strengthen inequalities and polarization, as has been demonstrated for the French case (e.g. Boursier-Mougenot and Ollivier-Trigalo, 1993). The current orientation of train and air operators in Europe reinforces these points. An example is the collaboration between Air France and SNCF, which is manifest in the connection of the airports of Paris-Roissy and Lyon-Satolas to the TGV. The idea behind this collaboration is that the TGV will act as (inter)national feeder for (inter)continental flights. Outside France, Amsterdam and Frankfurt airports will also soon be connected to the HST network, and similar collaborations are under study.

If complementarity appears to be the way forward with regard to air travel, integration of HSTs in the regional transport system is also important. The French experience is particularly interesting in this respect. The HST system was initially developed solely according to the commercial logic of SNCF, that of 'the fastest connections between the biggest traffic generators' (Zembri, 1995). For all those places in between, the TGV was like 'a plane in the sky'. When it became apparent that, unlike planes, it would disrupt local activities and natural or historical environments, opposition picked up momentum, as in the case of the TGV Méditerranée (Troin, 1995). It is now clear that to gain the necessary acceptance in France, the TGV has to be more than a plane in the sky. Progressively, and mostly thanks to the pressures of local and regional governments, it is being integrated into the regional transport systems. A good example of this shift is the construction of Euralille – pivot of the North European HST network – next to the existing central station rather than on the peripheral site initially proposed by the French railways. SNCF seems to be learning from the mistake of building TGV stations that are disconnected from regional networks. Now, SNCF speaks explicitly of the TGV 'irrigating a territory'. Passengers are responding well to this strategy: in 1996, 4 900 000 passengers travelled by TGV between Paris and Lyon. In the same year, however, a striking 21 000 000 passengers used the TGV on the same line to get to other destinations (data cited by SCNF chairman L.Gallois at the Eurocities conference in Lyon on 13 June 1997).

The most recent and promising orientations of HST development all point in the direction of enhancing its network impact by improving connections with other modes and the conventional railway system, and by increasing the flexibility of both the infrastructure and the rolling material. Two very clear examples of this emerging approach are the recent radical reconsideration of the French approach to TGV development and the exploitation strategy for the future Channel Tunnel Rail Link (CTRL) between London and the Channel. In the first case, next to the scaling-down of the ambitions of the original *Schéma Directeur*, new directives advocate the introduction of tilting trains and improvement of integration of the TGV network in the conventional railway network (Zembri, 1997). In the second case, it is envisaged that new fast commuter services will also use part of the high-speed link, and that through international services towards the North of England will bypass the main London terminal at St Pancras and continue on conventional rail.

3.1.7 Implications for station area development

What are the implications of all this for station areas? The argument of the preceding sections can be summarized as follows. *If* a series of conditions is realized, including the internalization of the social and environmental costs of travel, adequate investment in rail infrastructure, and appropriate land-use planning, *then* railway traffic might be expected to grow, albeit moderately, and at least retain its share of the market. The impact of even just holding its own in an already saturated railway station infrastructure would still be significant in absolute terms. For example, according to Cornet's (1993) low-growth scenario (without a European high-speed network), the absolute growth of long-distance traffic in the period 1988–2010 would still be by a factor of 148 (1988 = 100). His high-growth scenario would mean almost a *doubling* of the total number of transported passengers. Furthermore, the impact of any growth will in all likelihood be unevenly spread. Most demand would be concentrated at peak times in centrally located terminals with already severe spatial constraints. The pressure that growth of any order of magnitude would place on the existing capacity is thus enormous, just as the required investment would be. In the Netherlands, for instance, in order to achieve the goal of doubling rail traffic between the years 1995 and 2010 an investment plan of 8.7 billion ECU has been deemed necessary. At 3.1 million ECU per kilometre of rail, this is far above what is envisaged in most other European countries (*Rail Business Report*, 1994).

Equally important are the qualitative implications of the contextual factors sketched in the preceding pages. The essential condition for growth of rail transport is intermodal integration. From a qualitative point of view, a railway station's essential feature thus appears to be its function as an intermodal interchange, rather than as a 'place where trains arrive and depart'. The railway station is to be seen, as Amar (1996) suggests, as an *urban exchange complex*. What does this mean in practice? Railway stations have traditionally been important transport connection points. But until now they have also tended to remain a juxtaposition of separate elements (for example, a train station, a metro station, a bus station, a taxi stand, parking, shopping and information facilities) rather than becoming an integrated whole (an interchange). The railway station has to offer full connectivity in both the *hard* sense – the infrastructure – and the *soft* sense – the services. The passenger will evaluate and choose on the basis of the full travel experience – the door-to-door trip – including travelling conveniently, changing from one system to another, and making use of accessory services.

All this places severe demands not just on the physical structures but also on the organization. Integration involves many different actors in a unified terminal management. Experiences in Paris, as at La Défense and Gare du Nord, appear to be leading the way in Europe (Amar, 1996). Outside Europe, the vertical integration of railway and other operations in Japan could provide food for thought. In most cases the required transformation would be a matter of (re)ordering the existing elements, and of dealing with continuous change, rather than of creating something from scratch. In the process, a railway station turns into *a place to be*, not just *a place to pass through*. This outlook leads towards the next section, which treats the property development perspective.

3.2 The property development perspective: the place

Traditionally, railway stations have been described in the first place in terms of their transportation functions, or through a transport development perspective as sketched earlier. More recently, because of factors cited in the introduction to the book (section 1.2), interest has arisen in the development of railway stations in combination with their surroundings. That is, railway station areas are increasingly perceived as urban districts with more than a transport function. This implies that they are seen as objects of property investment as well. In other words, the place dimension of the railway station area is becoming more central. In this section, the prospects for railway station locations are discussed in an urban context. We interpret the term *property development* rather loosely, as comprising any alteration of the physical fabric at and around stations that results from quantifiable investments made by one or more actors. Thus we do not limit ourselves to the conservation or expansion of the transport-related structures of this area.

The property development prospects of a station location at a given point in time will depend on many external factors. These include the economic and property market cycles, the relative attractiveness of investment in real estate, and general and specific demand characteristics. However, location-specific conditions will play a role too. These conditions are of special interest in this paragraph. Location-specific conditions of railway station sites are closely connected to the station's transport development prospects. A crucial feature of the location is its accessibility, but there is more. A firm or household considering a change of location (perhaps within a station area) will take into account not only node but also place features. It is not so much the absolute performance of the location that will be important but rather the performance relative to alternative locations, both in the same city and elsewhere. Evaluation of the node component will include positive factors such as the degree of accessibility offered, and negative factors, such as disturbances caused by the concentration of infrastructure and traffic. Assessment of place characteristics will involve a complex of factors, including the availability and cost of accommodation, expectations of synergy and/or conflict with other activities in the area, the global perception of the location (its identity, security, liveability, liveliness etc.), and contextual factors such as government policies and market trends.

Railway station locations do not tend to score well on several of the criteria mentioned above. Indeed, they more often come close to the profile made by Troin (1995) of a typical station location in France. He describes it as an obsolete fabric with degraded housing and shops, the pejorative connotations of an area of transit, and a predominance and poor integration of transport functions in the pre-existing urban structure. Also, where there has been investment on station *buildings*, typically little or nothing has been done to improve the functionality and the image of the station *neighbourhood* (Troin, 1995, pp. 89–91). Though these might be common features, there are many different kinds of railway station location and diverse ways of looking at them. When assessing property development prospects, these differences have to be accounted for. In several cases, both the image and the function of the area are changing drastically. Besides the varying degrees of accessibility, some other basic distinctions are the sort of city that the railway station is in, and its location in that city. We begin with these latter distinctions. We then move on to a discussion of accessibility and other relevant factors affecting the attractiveness of railway station locations. To conclude, we review the strengths and weaknesses of railway station areas as locations for property investment.

3.2.1 Setting station locations in their urban context

Context II: in which city?

Until the 1960s, Christaller's central place theory and Perroux's growth pole theory could be used in describing the two fundamental types of city to be found in Europe: *regional centres* and *industrial cities* respectively (Zoete, 1997, pp. 31–33). In the ensuing 30 years, the impacts of economic change have undermined the two basic assumptions that both theories have in common. These are the assumptions that (a) proximity is a fundamental variable, and (b) cities are about the valorization and commercialization of local resources. Today, relationships of complementarity and competition between cities have become more important than relationships between a city and its hinterland. Behind this transformation lies a combination of factors that can be summarized in the notion of *globalization* of the economy (Borja and Castells, 1997). Increasingly, world macro-regions participate in a global space of international finance and technological innovation. Within macro-regions (of which Europe is one), cities tend to be either nodes of specialized technological and/or financial networks, or bridgeheads for international capital in a specific regional/world market (Bonneville *et al.*, 1994). In Europe, this evolution appears to have brought about more sectoral specialization. For instance, it has led to the concentration of financial services in Frankfurt, of international insurance companies in Amsterdam, of modern industry in Stuttgart, of retail and distribution in Lyon, and of research and development in Grenoble (Bonneville *et al.*, 1994).

Globalization processes have intervened in Europe on a macro-regional urban structure that, because of its long and rich history, is not expected to experience major changes (Bonneville *et al.*, 1994; Kunzmann, 1996). Yet there are developments that have a potential spatial influence within this framework. They include (Kunzmann, 1996) the completion of the trans-European high-speed rail network, the growth of international airport complexes, the spatial implications of new telecommunication technologies, the removal of inner European borders, and urban and regional competition. Furthermore, a spatial impact could also have more hypothetical processes such as immigration and integration, a paradigm shift of European agricultural policies, and the emergence of regionalism.

The combination of global and local factors with the developments cited above results in a set of emerging urban types in Europe. These include, again following Kunzmann (1996), international finance and service centres, modern R&D spaces (technopoles), traditional industrial complexes, modern production complexes ('just in time' regions), inter-regional distribution centres, urbanized transportation corridors, urban backwater spaces, rural industrial complexes, marginalized rural regions, gentrified rural areas, aerovilles (airport cities), and leisure worlds (Disney worlds). Not all of these urban types are equally relevant to station area development, but each type has specific implications for the station area(s) it contains, and this is the point. For instance, most demand-driven station area projects in Europe are currently to be found in the category of international finance and service centres. By contrast, supply-driven projects are often promoted in evolving traditional industrial complexes, while railway stations may have an important complementary function in both aerovilles and leisure worlds. In the other emerging urban types, passenger station locations tend to play a more marginal role.

Context II: where in the city?
At the intra-urban level, globalization has meant an increase in the functional division of space. Next to an ongoing decentralization of activities towards ever more distant metropolitan 'rings', a selective (re)concentration is being observed in both core and peripheral areas. While production globalizes and segments, abandoning the traditional regional logic, and consumer services follow the sub-urbanization of homes, control and command activities, representative functions, cultural institutions, and specific areas of consumption show a tendency to concentrate within a diminishing number of central locations. Most importantly, both decentralization and concentration have a markedly selective character. These processes tend to gravitate toward locations that offer the best access to (tele)communication networks and new kinds of agglomeration effect.

Such shifts cannot be accounted for by traditional centre–periphery opposition. Simply equating decentralization to suburbanization and (re)concentration to (re)urbanization would not only be misleading; it would also make it difficult to explain their coexistence. Current developments may be better understood within the framework of a network spatial paradigm. According to this interpretation of the metropolitan space (see, among others, Dematteis, 1988; Castells, 1989; Borja and Castells, 1997) systems of specialized integrated nodes are emerging, connected with each other and with nodes in other metropolitan areas by both material (e.g. transport) and immaterial (e.g. information) networks. What has also changed is the scale of the urban phenomenon, which is now increasingly that of '100-mile cities' (Sudjic, 1992), where locations have to be placed in the context of vast multinodal, dynamic, functionally rather than physically determined 'urban fields' (Friedmann and Miller, 1965). Differences are still marked, but they are thus less (at least in tendency) between urban centres and urban peripheries and more between high-value geographical clusters (be they peripheral or central: edge cities or downtowns) and the 'rest' (be it peripheral or central: peripheral estates or inner cities) (Dematteis, 1988; Castells, 1989; Borja and Castells, 1997).

Invariably, the most dynamic station locations from a property perspective are those in the former category. The transformations of station areas in the Amsterdam region are a striking example in this respect, with both central and peripheral stations increasingly anchoring specialized and integrated clusters of activities interconnected on a metropolitan or regional scale (see case study in Chapter 6). Dynamic station areas are among the places where both global connection and local disconnection are expressed in their most radical forms. Both extremes of the social spectrum (as typified by the global businessperson and the local homeless) are to be found here. This may offer a unique chance of 'interaction among differents', but can also only reinforce indifference and even generate destructive conflict (Bertolini, 1996a; Bertolini, 1996c)

The position of a station location within the emerging urban networks is, as the case studies will show, a crucial ingredient of its property development potential. But, besides their urban context as sketched above, is there something specific to station areas? What are some of their striking competitive advantages and disadvantages from a property development perspective? To answer these questions, we turn to the following sections.

3.2.2 Developing station locations

A concept that is both an effect and a factor of globalization is the *time–space compression* (Harvey, 1989) allowed by innovations in transport and communication technologies. In the transport domain, progress has to be mostly ascribed to infrastructure with limited entry points such as motorways, air routes and, most recently, high-speed rail links. This has meant a relative valorization of the most accessible connection points, or nodes, including selected station areas. At the same time, it has meant a relative degradation of the simple cut-across, or inadequately connected spaces (for these impacts of high-speed rail links see Troin, 1995). Accessibility is, however, not the only criterion. The station is also a specific sector of the urban space with unique characteristics. Within the emerging network geography outlined above, many railway stations hold, at least potentially, a favourable position. Typically, the stations were erected in the course of the last century at the limits of the city. Today, those sites may be in the midst of revitalizing metropolitan cores or densifying and diversifying peripheries. Often they include large and unfragmented portions of disused or underused land (most notably because of the relocation of annexed freight yards). All these processes mean that, in several cases, both the characteristics of station areas as nodes (that is, the quality of connections) and as places (that is, the value of adjacent land uses) make them possible anchors for forming or consolidating metropolitan activity concentrations (Bertolini, 1996b).

The position of railway station areas in the property market is further reinforced by planning policies promoting concentration of activities around public transportation nodes, in an effort to reduce dependence on the automobile. While the Dutch ABC location policy (Ministry of Housing etc., 1991b) is perhaps the most explicit example of this effort in Europe, public-transport-oriented development is high on the agenda everywhere. Furthermore, the shift of European railways from the public to the private sector, in whatever form, has meant a ubiquitous rise in interest in the exploitation of the companies' property assets. Land and buildings next to stations that were seen only as instrumental to transport operations are now regarded as potential sources of profit and cross-subsidization of less profitable transportation activities.

As a result of a complex of factors, the transportation node is thus becoming a magnet for more than transport-linked activities. Offices and shops are in all development plans, but sport, recreational and cultural facilities, exhibition and convention centres, hotels, government buildings, housing and – to a lesser extent – light industry may also be present. It has even been suggested that stations could become the centres of an emerging European 24-hour urban economy. However, this emerging multifunctionality often appears to be superficial – a mere spectacle of urban diversity. As will be shown in the case studies, the high cost of development, coupled with limited public subsidies, is in favour of short-term, high-return property approaches, where offices tend to dominate.

The accessibility issue

Crucial to the evaluation of the property development potential of a railway station location is an assessment of the relative role of its accessibility. The Euralille venture, as pointed out earlier, is founded on the hypothesis that under the double impact of the Channel Tunnel and the extension of the TGV network, Lille will acquire a number of typically modern activities (Simon, 1993, p. 110). Similar arguments are voiced elsewhere (see the case studies). The critical point in all these contentions is the idea that an increase or decrease in physical accessibility would have a direct, and proportionate, economic impact. However, accessibility remains a highly problematic notion. As it lacks a clear definition, there is no unequivocal way of measuring it. Most importantly, its relationships with urban development are all but straightforward.

While some progress on definitions and measures has been made (see, for instance, Banister and Edwards, 1995, unpublished; Townroe, 1995), our understanding of the link between transport and urban development remains weak, as concluded in a recent review of the state of the art (Banister, 1995). Empirical evidence shows ambiguous relationships. There are both positive and negative effects of accessibility, while other factors often play a more decisive role. The following examples of the impact of the HST illustrate this point in the case of railway station locations.

In reviewing studies of the station area development effects of high-speed rail in Japan and France, Sands (1993) summarizes their most important conclusions. In Japan, at the regional level, the introduction of the Shinkansen high-speed line appears to have redistributed, rather than generated, growth towards stations. At the station level, major differences emerged. Three new peripheral stations opened with the introduction of the Shinkansen line in 1964. There were no significant development impacts when high-speed trains stopped in existing intercity rail stations. The marginal increase in passengers attributable to the high-speed line was an important explanation. Instead, where a new station was built near the existing city centre, and was provided with a good link to the existing station, development within the city shifted towards the new station. The frequency and level of train services, the quality of connections with the existing city centre, and land speculation pressures as opposed to proactive, long-range planning practices have been the crucial discriminants between successful and less successful examples.

Also, in France, the studies reviewed by Sands (1993) suggest a shifting of spatial focus rather than autonomous economic growth at the regional level. On the TGV South-East line (opened in 1981–1983), significant station area development was observed only at Lyon Part Dieu. The area, a doubling of the spatially constrained traditional CBD of Lyon, was already under development at the time of the opening of the TGV station. However, the TGV had apparently reinforced the dynamics of what has become the city's most sought-after office location. On the TGV Atlantic line (opened in 1989) there were signs that development initiatives had been successful in Le Mans and Nantes. Next to the TGV, other important explanatory factors were the quality of other transport connections, the proximity of the existing city centre, proactive public–private development partnerships, and the state of the local economy. The failure to attract development at TGV stations such as Le Creusot, Vendôme or Macon showed, on the contrary, how the TGV alone is not enough.

These and similar points are restated in other literature reviews (e.g. Troin, 1995). The TGV, just like the Shinkansen, appears to be essentially a *catalyst* of development when other conditions are in place. Those conditions include lively local economies and property markets, availability of land or buildings, excellent connection to local and regional transport networks, and strong public investment and leadership. The important conclusion is that a *combination of factors* should be taken into account when discussing the case studies.

3.2.3 Strengths and weaknesses of station locations: an open issue

The preceding sections have considered both the potentials for and some prerequisites of railway station area development from a property perspective. Let us now try to narrow the discussion by focusing on the location's balance of strengths and weaknesses. This will not lead to definitive conclusions. Whatever their potential, the market feasibility of station development plans remains a controversial point. We provide a sense of this debate by summarizing the issues at stake in the Netherlands (Provincie Zuid Holland, 1991; MBO, 1993; Bongenaar, 1994; Cüsters, 1994; Rutten and Cüsters, 1994; NSC, 1994; NIROV/ Sectie SEIROV, 1995). Some of the problems brought up in this discussion are peculiar to the Dutch context, but most are typical of station location development elsewhere in Europe (for instance, several similar points are raised for the Swiss case in CEAT, 1993), and may therefore be instructive. Striking national peculiarities, when applicable, will be highlighted.

According to most developers, investors, and independent property consultants operating in the Netherlands, railway station areas have some strengths and many weaknesses. These areas can be developed only if various conditions are met. The main strengths are their excellent accessibility by public transport, the associated high flows of people, the proximity of the historic city centre (in most cases), and public policy in support of development.

More extensive is the list of recurring shortcomings. A crucial one is the typically high development costs and comparatively low revenues, which mean that a financial deficit is structural (as in other European countries, with the possible exception of very central locations under favourable market conditions, as for instance in central London and Paris during the 1980s property boom). Generally, initial ambitions (such as multifunctionality and open spaces) are not checked against financial–economic feasibility, nor are they translated into hard programme demands/requisites. The inevitable result is downsizing in the course of the process (there are a few exceptions in Europe, for instance Euralille and Zentrum Zürich Nord). A solid foundation of the programme in market surveys is often absent (again, Euralille and Zentrum Zürich Nord are more positive examples). Partly as a consequence there is a strong orientation towards office development, and inadequate differentiation in developments around different stations (with a few exceptions elsewhere). Insufficiencies in urban design quality, access and car parking as well as environmental constraints pose great limits to (re)development. As a result of all this, the price–quality relationship of the location is not competitive, particularly with respect to locations on the urban periphery (more true in the Dutch polycentric urban system than in other contexts). In trying to reverse this situation, there is too little harmonization with developments elsewhere in the region, and no clear political priorities (in contrast with, for instance, several French cases). Finally, there are a whole series of destructive difficulties (ranging from insufficient coordination to uncertainties about intentions of some parties and fragmented landownership) connected to the multiplicity of actors that characterizes station development in the Netherlands, as in other countries.

The list of conditions considered necessary to realize the development potential of station locations in the Netherlands is equally long. Most importantly, enough car parking and good accessibility by car are also to be guaranteed, while public transport must drastically improve its standards. A broader functional mix is required, including offices, but also shops, public services, and housing. This mix must be complementary rather than concurrent to that of the city centre and of peripheral locations. The functional programme must be grounded in feasibility studies and market surveys, reflecting the acknowledgement that each location is different, and that not every station area is a development area. Furthermore, the implementation strategy must entail an answer to the question of how the mix of profitable and non-profitable elements is achieved, and how the latter are financed. In any case, substantial public investment seems unavoidable, while land for development must be made available at the right time, and constraints have to be imposed on development in competing locations. Finally, from an urban design point of view, better integration between buildings, public spaces and transport infrastructure is needed. The attractiveness and security of the open spaces must increase. And a good, short and 'natural' link to the city – or other adjoining – centre is desirable.

The remarkable conclusion of analysts in the Netherlands is that

> Station areas are from a financial, property and investment perspective in first instance unattractive development locations. Their redevelopment into successful, potentially attractive investment locations is only possible through an enormous effort of municipalities, a restrictive investment and location policy and financial support from the national government. (Wolting, 1995, p. 2).

That conclusion should be put in perspective, and not only because of the peculiarities of the highly regulated, risk-averse Dutch property markets (on this subject see Needham *et al.*, 1993). According to a more recent, leading review of the now recovering Dutch property market (Kloosterman and Venema, 1997), railway station areas were actually the most sought-after office locations! The problem, here as elsewhere, is that appraisals have to be more specific, both in space and in time, and that a complex of factors has to be accounted for, including but going beyond accessibility and touching on development processes and evolving institutional contexts. Before considering these points, we shall combine the various lines of argument pursued so far in an integrated transport–property development perspective.

3.3 Towards an integrated transport–property perspective

3.3.1 Defining the matter

The two preceding sections have shown how railway stations are imbued with the dynamics of both the transport and the land-use domains, and how this results in distinct but interrelated transport and property development perspectives. Both positive and negative interrelations may exist. For instance, a high level of accessibility may provide the critical mass required for the development of particular activities. In turn, a high density of activities may translate into demand for transport. However, dense patterns of land use may also make a location difficult to reach, and optimization of its accessibility by all transport modes may also negatively affect its liveability and thus its attractiveness. As anticipated in Chapter 2, such a field of complex node–place interactions belongs to the core issues of railway station redevelopment. The unique challenge of station area (re)development seems to be, on the one hand, to exploit synergies and, on the other, to manage conflicts between node-based and place-based activities – between people *moving* and people *staying*. This complexity is well represented by the dilemmas facing railway companies. The railroad operator is an actor who has to forge a difficult synthesis between multiple – often contrasting – goals. For instance, should property development get priority and all land be put to its maximum use? Or should the accent lie on transport development, whereby space is reserved for future infrastructure needs? And what should be the share of offices in the programme? From a property perspective, offices are perhaps a financial need. But from a transport perspective, they generate only peak traffic, which is the most expensive and least profitable to deal with. The aggregate additional demand for rail travel that a concentration of offices would generate, even assuming very favourable modal splits, would be relatively marginal for most stations. Furthermore, the dominance of offices may create security problems at off-hours, thus discouraging potential passengers and users (Portheine, 1994).

In moving towards a combined transport–property perspective, we should first consider what, at least at first sight, could be seen as an ideal-typical case. We can then outline the contours of an integrated typology of possibilities of station areas in Europe. However, a more refined conceptual framework will emerge only after the presentation and evaluation of the case studies further on in the book.

3.3.2 The Japanese example: an ideal-typical case?

From an integrated transport and property perspective, Japan can be seen as an ideal-typical case of railway station development; but there are important limits to replicating the example in Europe because of great differences in context.

In Japan's major metropolitan areas, interchange stations (where passengers can transfer between commuter trains and local transport) have been the focus of intense property development, mostly promoted by private railway companies. Tokyo stations such as Shinjuku, Ikebukuro, and Shibuya, where the commuter

43

and national radials intersect the circular Yamanote line, provide some striking examples. The same can be said of similar radial/circular interchanges in Osaka, namely Umeda-Hankyu and Umeda-JNR stations. Even through the recent crisis of the Japanese property market, such sites have remained popular with investors (Bongenaar, 1996). The following description of the Shibuya district in Tokyo may express some of the flavour of these highly complex nodes–places:

> The Ginza line enters the station at the third floor level, just under the level of the Shuto motorway which passes above it. Other lines arrive under ground level, and together with the Toyoko, Inokashira and Yamanote lines that arrive there passing above street level, they make of Shibuya station a tridimensional intersection. Around the station a surprising bundle of alleys and small streets is animated by a multitude of small shops, restaurants, boutiques, cinemas, hotels and [most importantly] various department stores . . . The square in front of the station . . . is a popular meeting place for the inhabitants of Tokyo. On the edge of the district are areas traditionally devoted to night life, as the *sakaribas* of Marumayacho and Dogenzakacho, . . . and luxurious residential neighbourhoods as Shoto and Daikanyama. (Kurata, 1994, p. 105).

In Osaka (Edgington, 1990; Roty, 1996), development gravitates around the Umeda North terminals area and the Abeno South terminals area. These are connected with each other and the underground by a circular loop line. Around both clusters of terminals is a concentration of shopping and entertainment facilities. Between them lies the central business district, where more than a million people work daily. The local authorities are promoting an integrated strategy for station areas in the central city (Edgington, 1990). The loop is the support of the Naniwa Necklace Project, a string of complementary, multi-functional urban redevelopment projects on former railway yards and factory sites. A media city, a fashion town, museums and other cultural facilities, commercial and entertainment concentrations, housing and office complexes are being developed on 10 station sites totalling 259.4 ha. Furthermore, both in Tokyo and in Osaka, railway stations are also the focus of suburban development, as the example of new towns around Tokyo poignantly shows. Den'en Toshi – promoted by the Tokyu Railway Company since 1953 – is in this sense prototypical (Jonker, 1996).

Developments on such a scale are made possible in Japan by a set of unique features. First and foremost of these is the much more central role of the train in mobility patterns and especially in commuting in the Tokyo and Osaka areas. The train has 35% of the passenger transport market share in Japan as a whole, and 90% in central Tokyo (as compared with 5.6% in the UK and 75.5% in central London, and 8.7% in France and 59% in central Paris; Bongenaar, 1996). In the Tokyo metropolitan region in 1988, 25% of the 74.1 million daily trips were made by train, 25% by bus, 26.8% by foot, 17.6% by bicycle, and 27.5% by car. In contrast, in the Ile de France region in the same year, 30% of the 19.3 million daily trips were by public transport, 10% by soft modes, and as much as 60% by car (Suzuki, 1996). On average 2.5 million passengers *a day* pass through Shinjuku, the busiest station in Japan (and in the world). At Osaka, a combination of six rail and metro stations provides the Umeda districts with a daily flow of 2.3 million people, with peaks of 640 000 for Osaka national railway station and 630 000 for Hankyu-Umeda private commuter station (Roty, 1996). For the sake of comparison, the busiest station in Europe is Paris Nord, with 300 000 passengers a day, while Waterloo, the busiest in London, has 180 000. Because of this dominant role of rail transport, the distance from a station in Japan largely determines the value of land; and that in turn creates the conditions for the integration of the financing and management of rail infrastructure and urban development.

Second, the large share of railway travel in passenger transport in Japan is possible only because of the much higher net population density. There are about 1550 inhabitants per square kilometre of habitable area in Japan. By contrast there are only 350 in the Netherlands, 260 in England, 160 in France, and 50 in the USA. Tokyo is not only densely populated; perhaps more importantly, the densely inhabited area has a wider scale than in European examples. The population density in the core is about half that of Paris (13 300/km^2 against 20 500/km^2) but in the periphery it is double (7700/km^2 against 3300/km^2). This makes the Tokyo region a multicentred agglomeration, with relatively continuous high densities, a feature reinforced by current planning policies (Jonker, 1996). Within this context, station areas provide the region's 27.6 million inhabitants with the most important opportunities for public contacts, entertainment and shopping. At Shinjuku station, for instance, there are 33 commercial streets and 3275 shops; at Shibuya, there are 31 commercial streets and 3421 shops (Suzuki, 1996).

Third, institutional differences are important. Most notable among these is the division of roles between an (until recently) more conventional national public railway company and the private railway conglomerates. Besides operating regional commuter networks in the bigger metropolitan areas of Tokyo, Osaka, and Nagoya, these conglomerates are also active in the retail sector, hotels, real estate, construction, travel, advertising, resorts, media, entertainment, museums, universities, garden cities, and more. They are highly diversified companies with a strong territorial base, historically grown around the concept of the *total living industry*. The typical business formula combines three elements in a single operation: an urban pole including the railway terminal and a department store/ shopping centre; a development of the garden city or campus type along the line; and, at the other end of the line, a leisure and entertainment complex (Roty, 1996). An employee of one of these companies is likely to live in an apartment built by the group's real estate subsidiary, to travel between home and work on trains or buses run by the company, to shop in its supermarkets, to spend the weekend in its museums, amusement parks and golf courses . . . and, of course, to be a supporter of the group's baseball team (Kurata, 1994).

3.3.2 Towards a typology of possibilities

The set of conditions identified in the closing part of the preceding section allows Japan to have a degree of integration of rail transport and urban development and of cross-subsidization within railway company operations that is unthinkable in the present European context. While the Japanese example certainly gives us something to reflect on, any strategy for Europe's station areas would thus have to be based on an understanding of Europe's own characteristics. Recalling what has been said on the specificity of mobility and urbanization patterns in Europe, the best starting point might be what is already happening here. The case studies presented in this book provide some critical inspiration. In this final section, a preliminary sketch will be made of the requirements of an integrated transport–property typology of possibilities of railway station areas, on the basis of various studies. The objective of such a typology should not be to constrain the variety of individual options; it should rather be to make a contribution to a much needed differentiation of the notion of railway station location. *The* railway station area as such does not exist. Rather, there is a wide range of types. These must be identified on the basis of criteria including the relative position of the location within urban areas and within transportation networks.

While there are still several open questions, some useful efforts towards the construction of an integrated typology of station areas in a European context have already been made. However, a central problem is that approaches tend to be based on *either* a node *or* a place perspective, and rarely account for process and institutional variables. An example of a strongly place-based approach is that of Lambooy (1994). Lambooy has proposed the following typology of Dutch station locations:

1. Centre major city with underground

   (a) with strong central position (work, retail, entertainment) respective to own and other urban regions
   (b) without strong central position

2. Centre medium-sized city, with strong regional functions

   (a) without a specific supra-regional function
   (b) with a specific supra-regional function

3. Extra-urban location

   (a) with one dominant function
   (b) with different dominant functions

4. Edge-city location

   (a) with 'just' one limited function
   (b) with a relatively complete set of functions

5. Centre small city

6. Stations in big commuter municipalities

7. Other

A major drawback of such a classification is that it considers primarily, if not exclusively, place variables. The urban context, or 'what is next', is the determining factor. Node variables, 'what is accessible', or the position in the transportation network, while implicit, fail to gain an autonomous relevance. At the other extreme, Zembri (1995) and Troin (1995) rely heavily on node variables.

Zembri (1995) categorizes the connection of cities to the TGV network in France as:

1. *gares de désenclavement* or 'access stations', built in the urban periphery and unrelated to the conventional railway network;
2. *gares bis* or 'secondary stations', also external to the city but with a connection to the existing railway line;
3. bypassing an HST line with a connection to the conventional line but without a new station;
4. superimposition of new and traditional lines when crossing an agglomeration;
5. interruption of the new line when crossing an agglomeration.

Troin (1995) typifies the link of a station to the TGV and its impacts as:

1. simple improvements of passenger accommodation, with weak development effects;
2. remodelled or rehabilitated stations, with the modest implantation of tertiary activities in the station neighbourhood;
3. stations reinserted in the urban fabric, with the animation of a tertiary district;
4. newly built central stations, with the concerted development of a high-level business district;
5. 'green' or 'bis' stations built in the open fields, with effects that are hoped for but not get apparent;
6. connection stations built in the periphery, intermodal exchange poles, serving a major facility.

In another part of his book, Troin proposes a classification, adapted from Varlet (1992), on the basis of transport infrastructure criteria alone:

1. *complete*: entailing a classic train station, an existing, planned or possible TGV station, with a direct connection to an airport, a motorway, and a regional rail system of the S-Bahn/RER type (Paris-Roissy; stations in Amsterdam, Frankfurt, Geneva, Zurich);
2. *to be completed*: entailing an existing, planned or possible TGV station, with a direct connection to an airport and a motorway, and a connection to a regional rail system of the S-Bahn/RER type to be improved/developed (Lyon-Satolas; stations in Brussels, Cologne, Orly, Basel, Marseille);
3. *incomplete*: entailing a classic urban train station, with a direct connection to a motorway and a regional rail system of the S-Bahn/RER type (stations in London, Manchester, Dusseldorf, Rome);
4. *limited*: entailing a classic train station, an existing, planned or possible TGV station, with a direct connection to a motorway (Paris Massy, Lille, Bordeaux, Strasbourg, Toulouse).

In all these three typologies place variables may be implicit but are not independently accounted for. Furthermore, the development implications of Troin's first typology, while intriguing, tend to postulate a fixed relationship between a station type and development effects, which fails to take account of process and contextual factors. The obvious shortcoming of these node-only approaches is that very different kinds of station location are thrown into the same category. A more satisfactory typology should distinguish between place and node variables and then combine them to obtain specific categories. Furthermore, the complexity documented earlier in this chapter in sections 3.1 and 3.2 should be fully acknowledged. In the emerging urban geography, the weight of proximity and accessibility factors cannot be merely assumed; they have to be verified each time. Most importantly, more research is needed on the potential roles of railway stations in emerging node-and-network metropolises. A further and final point can be made clear by referring to the analysis of CEAT (1993). In trying deal with the complex of variables relevant to each station development case CEAT adopts the following criteria:

I. Objective context:

    1. type of station;
    2. location;
    3. availability of space for property development in the agglomeration;
    4. availability of space for property development around the station;
    5. socio-economic context (more/less dynamic);
    6. railway context 1: innovation;
    7. railway context 2: need;
    8. potential demand (as synthesis of 1–7).

II. Actual realization of the potential:

    9. actors;
    10. supply features (interests of actors);
    11. demand features (considered or not?);
    12. project management.

While distinctions between criteria are not entirely clear also in CEAT's approach, both node criteria (1, 6, 7) and place criteria (2–4) are present. Also, items that could be defined as process criteria (9–12) and context criteria (5) have been included. Evaluations of railway station area redevelopment cases strongly underline the importance of such process and context variables, be they defined as 'political will' (Fancello, 1993), 'conditions and modalities of implementation and operation' (CEAT, 1993), or 'interrelation of strategies' (Bertolini, 1996b).

In conclusion, an integrated framework of analysis would have to comprise *both* node *and* place variables, but also process *and* context factors. In order to complete such a framework, the latter two factors must be understood. They are discussed in the following chapter.

4

How to realize the potential?

4.1 Introduction

Railway station area redevelopment is becoming increasingly important through-out Europe. The borders of nation states are decreasingly important where economic mobility is concerned. Within the European Union, an open market is taking shape in which the freedom to transport goods, investment capital and business is more or less guaranteed. As a result, the meaning of distance between major railway station areas in Europe is becoming relative. In turn, this development implies an increase in competition between railway station areas within each nation state. But in the near future there will also be competition between station areas in Europe. When it comes to planning the redevelopment of railway station areas, factors of accessibility (by road, rail or water) no longer suffice. Other factors, such as social, cultural and environmental qualities must also be considered (Porter, 1990). Railway station area development as a planning problem is becoming increasingly complex as the number of relevant factors increases, the patterns of activities in the same area increase, and the existing physical surroundings have to be redeveloped. This is the reality for many railway station areas throughout Europe.

The actual picture is even more complex. It should be recognized that the decision-making process in combination with the actual implementation of redevelopment takes a long period. A time frame of 10 years or longer is common. As dependence on the willingness of actors to participate grows, the redevelopment process becomes more intricate. Another complicating factor is the fact that an increase of activities within a relatively small area generates inconvenience and impediments. Moreover, it poses a threat to the immediate environment. As both the population and the legislative bodies become more aware of these problems, new rules and regulations regarding the environment also tend to complicate the process of planning railway station areas. All this exacerbates the controversial nature of railway station area redevelopment as a planning problem.

With reference to the planning triangle sketched in the first chapter, in addition to the process of development and the ambivalence of the station area itself, its institutional setting is of utmost importance to an understanding of the ongoing development. By including the institutional context in the analysis, we see that each development process has common elements (*convergence*) as well as elements that are very specific to the railway station in question (*divergence*). More specifically, some of the latter elements can be explained by referring to the structural and cultural characteristics of the country and municipality involved. The political climate at the local level as well as at the national level is particularly important when trying to understand and explain the redevelopment processes of railway station areas.

There are at least three ways in which one can study the interrelationship between the context of development and the development itself (Hoogerwerf, 1995, pp. 253–256). The first perspective is an organizational point of view; the second perspective is derived from actors acting in networks; the third and last one is the institutional point of view.

- In *organizational sciences*, one tries to analyse development processes by studying the behaviour of the participating organizations. Organizations react to each other, but they also develop internal characteristics. The latter can be dominated by cultural or social elements. Against the background of these characteristics, the interaction of organizations is studied as part of the development process. The analysis carried out from this perspective takes place at an aggregated level (the organization). In contrast, in the next perspective, the level of analysis shifts to a lower level: the individual within the organization.
- Within the *networks perspective*, the analysis focuses on actors interacting with one another in more or less permanent patterns. The patterns themselves are determined by a mix of variables: these include the interests of the organization, plus social and cultural factors, but also a personal interpretation of the actors' position. From this perspective, the key words in the analysis are *power*, *flows of information*, *goals and objectives*, and *relation patterns*.
- Third is the *institutional perspective*. Although this is rooted in a long tradition of legal–historical research, it received renewed attention during the 1990s, sometimes referred to as *neo-institutionalism*. This perspective tries to explain spatial developments by referring to institutions within the context of each particular spatial project. Institutions are defined as common denominators for structural relations or developments of interactions among the actors involved. Essentially, this perspective is based on the same frame of reference as economic choice theory. The common denominators are not only to be found in rules and legislation. They are also – and especially – found in un-written codes of behaviour, tradition, and cultural aspects within or between organizations. Therefore neo-institutionalism can be viewed as an extension of economic choice theory. All the relevant advantages and disadvantages of this theory also apply to an institutional approach.

An adequate analysis of complex planning problems such as the redevelopment of railway station areas would have to take aspects of all three perspectives into account. With reference to the planning triangle mentioned earlier (section 1.1), *context* variables (institutional arrangements and developments) ought to be combined with *process* variables (actors and organizations) and *object* variables (the node and place dimensions of station areas). Although each of the perspectives mentioned can provide relevant insights, it is important to construct a balanced model for analysis in which all three aspects of the planning triangle are given due credit. The actual analysis of railway station area redevelopment has to take place in three steps. The first step is to formulate a frame of reference in terms of the institutional arrangements (context) and their history, the relevant actors (process), and the actual situation (object). A static picture is thus obtained. In the second step, the picture is set in motion, and ongoing developments are described. Finally, in the third step the whole process is analysed. It may be expected that the differences between case studies are huge in each step (divergence). In order to overcome these differences a more or less general frame of reference has to be developed. This will take shape in the three steps mentioned above. Therefore, in the next sections the three steps will be elaborated in a general sense (convergence).

4.2 The institutional conditions

Convergence and divergence are processes that can take place alongside one another, but also at the same time. Furthermore, these processes can take different shapes and represent different standpoints. They can have varying degrees of importance at different times during the development process. The institutional conditions under which railway station redevelopment takes place can be extremely important. National planning systems, political and cultural conditions respond in different ways to similar planning problems such as those that occur in railway station redevelopment. In this section we first consider the national planning systems (section 4.2.1). Then we look into more or less similar pressures originating from the institutional conditions that influence the redevelopment of railway station areas throughout Europe (section 4.2.2).

4.2.1 The national planning systems

The redevelopment of railway station areas is subject to opportunities and constraints caused by the national planning system in each country. Yet, as public authorities at all levels of government have often a stake (in one way or another), a certain 'leniency' can be expected towards these projects. This accounts for both opportunities and constraints. Consequently, although the influence of the national planning system on these projects cannot be denied, it touches them less than it would other projects. It is for this reason that in this study we limit ourselves to a concise characterization of the planning systems in general, presented in this section, and an equally short introduction to each planning system at the beginning of the case studies.

According to Healey and Williams (1993, pp. 701–720), planning systems can be characterized by variations in national legal and constitutional structures on the one hand, and by administrative and professional cultures on the other. Inspired by this distinction, Newman and Thornley (1996, pp. 27–75) try to identify

Legal families **Administrative families**

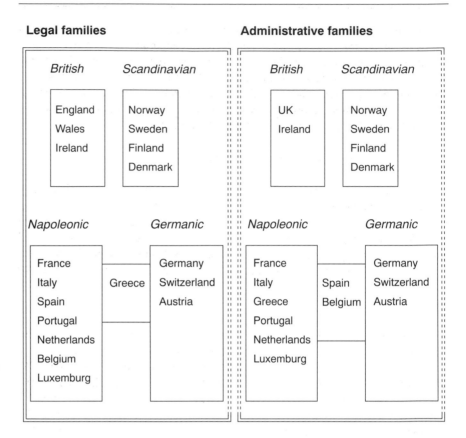

Fig. 4.1 Legal and administrative 'families' in Europe. (Source: Newman and Thornley, 1996, p. 29)

families of legal styles and families of administrative structures. Their legal and administrative typology is based on the criterion of how these structures affect planning at the local level. Within each type or family one can expect similar approaches in tackling complex planning problems such as the redevelopment of railway station areas. Newman and Thornley (1996, pp. 28–30) use the concept of *legal style*, which denotes the distinctive elements that give the system its particular form. Factors that contribute to this style are its historical development, its legal mode of thought, and its ideology. They identify four different European legal styles or families (Figure 4.1).

The grouping of these national planning systems shows a close relationship with a north–south division. This distinction not only makes sense (e.g. Page and Goldsmith, 1987), but can also be traced back to the balance between central and local government. The locus of power may be presumed to have a significant effect on the autonomy and strength of urban planning. In the literature, according to Newman and Thornley (1996, p. 30), there is general agreement on the four categories presented in Figure 4.1, although the labels may differ. It can be regarded as a good starting point for analysis in an international comparative framework.

In conclusion, although the redevelopment of railway station areas may entail such large projects that it falls outside the sphere of influence of national planning systems, at the same time it is part of the national planning system. Thus a rather schizophrenic and sometimes tense relation can exist whereby redevelopment projects may be obstructed by elements of the national planning system (building permits), but sometimes may be assisted or supported by it (compulsory purchase). Consequently, in trying to understand and assess each case study, it is important to keep in mind the institutional setting under which the redevelopment of railway station areas in different countries takes place, including the pressures derived from it. Those pressures will be dealt with in the next section.

4.2.2 Pressures from institutional conditions

Next to differences between national planning systems, there are also many similarities. The institutional conditions in Europe suffer under more or less similar pressures. In Europe the most important common pressures on the institutional conditions are deregulation, constraints on public expenditure, a shift from social objectives towards primarily economic and secondarily environmental objectives, the rise (and fall) of public–private partnerships, and the emerging centrality of infrastructure investment.

Deregulation
In most countries in Europe deregulation is an important political topic. However, if we consult empirical studies on this subject, we are likely to conclude that its practical importance is negligible. In the Netherlands, for example, only 7% of municipalities have taken up some kind of deregulation activity (Spit, 1993, pp. 139 140). Deregulation can be directed at the regulations themselves, or at the implementation and monitoring of those regulations. Although a relation with the ideological dimension of a 'withdrawing' government is sometimes apparent in the background, deregulation seems to be a pragmatic process. Both in the official world and on the political agenda, it appears to have little meaning. At least in the Netherlands, municipalities are likely to think that few rules are superfluous, and that deregulation would contribute very little in financial terms.

The British experience with deregulation presents a characteristically mixed picture, which also sheds light on development elsewhere. During the Thatcher years, planning was certainly under attack as a bureaucratic restriction on the operation of the free market. Practice, however, has shown that even former anti-planners (such as Michael Heseltine) have called for more regulation, for example in areas with rapidly escalating problems of congestion (Bell and Cloke, 1990, pp. 3–28). Railway station areas are known to be vulnerable in this respect. This mixed picture can be found throughout Europe, but is at its most extreme in the UK. On the one hand there are situations in which the private sector demands more regulation (and planning), while on the other hand there are areas where the tendency is for planning and control to be almost completely abolished. It will be clear that, against the background of their vulnerability, in railway station areas there will be always a certain amount of planning and regulation, dependent upon their existing use and further plans for redevelopment.

Constraints on public expenditure
The desire to decrease the budget deficit, which is persistent at the level of central government, is ubiquitous. This is expressed in a wide range of policy measures

towards municipalities, some of them more coercive than others. Jointly, they create fiscal stress of some kind, which constitutes the strongest effect on municipalities. The institutional arrangements are the key to implementing measures to mitigate fiscal stress. The static design and the dynamic process of inter-governmental relations are important elements in the analysis. But the specific circumstances (historical or spatial) also have to be taken into account.

The persistent budgetary problems of local government in the 1980s plagued not only European municipalities but also those in the USA (Clark and Ferguson, 1983; Clarke, 1989). In order to tackle the problems caused by decreasing budgets, municipalities forged particular strategies. The strategies developed in one country are often similar to those devised in other countries.

As far as the redevelopment of railway station areas is concerned it is important to notice that retrenchment policies at all levels of public government have opened new opportunities for private initiatives as the strong emphasis on socially oriented public policy has gradually shifted towards a more economically oriented policy. This tendency will be elaborated in the following subsections.

A shift from social objectives towards primarily economic and secondarily environmental objectives

The general tendency in Europe to cut back public expenditure has also had its effects on public policy objectives. Throughout Europe the once common emphasis on social policy has shifted towards more economically oriented policies. In its slipstream, however, it can generate environmental damage or, otherwise formulated, can increase the volume of existing damage. Therefore, next to economic policy objectives, environmental rules and regulations are developed to counteract expected environmental damage from economic development. In planning literature on this subject, it is sometimes referred to as *growth management* (Stein, 1993; Cullingworth, 1997). The combination of emphasis on environmental policies and economic development can cause problems in the development process, as they represent each other's 'natural' counterparts. This shift has also opened opportunities for public–private partnerships, especially in those countries that lagged behind in this respect. This development will be illustrated in the next subsection.

The rise (and fall) of public–private partnerships

The rise and fall of the importance of public–private partnerships is closely related to the transition from a socially oriented public policy towards a more economically oriented policy. The role and meaning of public–private partnerships tended to change after the transition. This tendency was visible throughout Europe, albeit with different national accents.

If we look at public–private cooperation in Europe from a historical perspective, in general three periods can be distinguished since the Second World War, though each period may differ somewhat from one country to another:

1. The period of recovery and reconstruction of city centres, especially in those countries that suffered damage in the war. In this period a technical approach was considered. This period runs from about 1945 to 1970.
2. The period of socially oriented urban renewal, which runs from about 1970 to the early 1980s.

3. The period of urban innovation with an entrepreneurial approach, from the early 1980s up to the present (Kreukels and Spit, 1990).

Not only the actual developments but also the cultural and socio-psychological climate distinguish these periods from each other. In the first period, which runs from shortly after the war to the late 1960s, public–private partnerships arose as a common form of cooperation. Public–private partnerships are therefore by no means a new phenomenon. Especially during the period of reconstruction after the Second World War, when big projects were realized in order to make up for lost time in the years 1940–1945 with regard to spatial planning, this was often done in some form of public–private cooperation. Forced by the – for both parties – pressing objective that the projects be realized as soon as possible, and pushed on by a growing economy and a substantial rise in real estate prices, large-scale projects were initiated in this period, particularly in the field of infrastructure development and housing. In this period cooperation between the authorities and trade and industry came into being, which could be characterized as simple, yet pragmatic, and seldom caused problems against the background of those days (Lemstra, 1987).

From the late 1960s onwards the social and economic circumstances began to change. In this period, pressure groups and interest groups succeeded increasingly in convincing the authorities to focus more attention on predominantly social objectives in government policy. The contribution of trade and industry was often out of step with this policy. This explains why cooperation with trade and industry was exchanged for government projects. The real estate sector was drastically eliminated in the urban renewal of those days, in a pronounced and active approach from the government. The sector in this period lost touch not only with the authorities, but also with the cities. All this had a great influence on policy programmes and the administrative organization. Planning, planning procedures, and methods of financing were directed by government as the central actor.

The antagonism between administration and trade and industry in the 1970s continued with these policy frameworks in the next period, which started with the economic crisis of the late 1970s and early 1980s. Mainly under the pressure of rapidly rising governmental responsibilities (and, related to this, government spending), but particularly the rapid rise in value of real estate, the authorities increasingly realized that you could not exclude the involvement of the real estate sector over a longer period without substantial losses in building and housing. Local authorities began to focus attention on alternative possibilities for project financing, pressed by shrinking budgets. All kinds of modernization process appeared.

At the end of the third period, the once euphoric expectations have come down to more realistic terms. As one could expect, as both parties have become more experienced with these kinds of project, the related problems have gained wider recognition. The problematic aspects of developing complex spatial projects in a public–private cooperation are once more regarded with some distrust. However, this distrust does not focus on the same arguments as before. Nowadays it often has more to do with a kind of reluctance to accept the unavoidable delays and complications that appear to be inherent in public–private partnerships.

As huge interests are at stake for both public and private parties concerning the redevelopment of railway station areas, public–private partnerships constitute a self-evident way of organizing it. Consequently, when the institutional conditions are not favourable, this generates significant effects on the redevelopment possibilities for railway station areas.

The emerging centrality of infrastructure investment
Governments invest continuously in infrastructure. However, it is not easy to present a general overview of investment in infrastructure in Europe. Although infrastructure has the general character of a collective good, investment in it is not solely public. Private enterprises (or semi-private enterprises, such as most railway corporations) also invest in infrastructure. Yet the bulk is public investment. Through the 1970s and 1980s in countries in Europe investment in transport infrastructure has been decreasing, as Table 4.1 shows.

Although Table 4.1 shows figures until 1989 only, it is important to notice that most countries show a decline in investment in infrastructure during this period: a remarkably sharp decline can be seen in the Netherlands, France and the UK. Only Italy and Sweden are capable of creating an increase in investment after a minor setback. Table 4.1 shows that most countries in Europe are in arrears, and are trying to make up for it, as Table 4.2 shows for rail infrastructure.

The figures in Table 4.2 are derived from operational plans in each country. Although this makes the intentions in each country clearly visible, it does not guarantee their execution as planned. Therefore Table 4.1 can be interpreted only in general terms. Relatively speaking, the Netherlands is in a leading position, while the UK has planned to invest only some 9% of the Dutch investment per route-kilometre (Spit and Jansen, 1997, pp. 6–7).

Investment in infrastructure differs not only in time, but also between countries, as is shown in Tables 4.1 and 4.2. As the finance of infrastructure is a matter for national governments, in combination with (sometimes highly subsidized) public transport companies, an increasing tendency towards centralization can be seen. This tendency is completely consistent with the efforts in spatial planning to combat congestion problems in densely populated urban areas, but also with a returning interest in infrastructure investment as a means of stimulating economic development. This tendency towards centralization, however, is not peculiar to infrastructure development; it can be seen in all kinds of policy making throughout Europe. Yet at the same time an opposite movement is shown: decentralization. The two developments represent opposite sides of the same coin. This will be the subject of the next subsection.

Centralizing and decentralizing tendencies in national policy making
Centralizing and decentralizing tendencies refer to changes in policy making in levels of scale, especially between national governments and municipalities (Page and Goldsmith, 1987). The need to change policy making between levels of governments is often felt to be inescapable. The need is most sharply felt at a regional level of government, often referred to as the *regionalization problem*. This is relevant for large infrastructure development; although the immediate costs are spatially limited, its benefits spread out widely.

Table 4.1 Development of investments in transport infrastructure by constant prices 1975–1989 (1975 = 100)

	1976	1977	1978	1980	1981	1982	1983	1984	1985	1986	1987	1988	1989
Austria	98	103	117	122	123	110	100	103	102	–	–	–	–
Belgium	105	106	98	102	110	100	88	70	62	50	50	43	48
Denmark	100	96	104	91	84	68	62	61	56	45	43	40	36
Germany	97	98	101	99	94	85	79	77	74	75	79	79	76
Finland	97	92	89	97	97	96	97	92	93	86	90	94	90
France	101	87	84	77	90	82	73	79	68	65	71	78	85
Greece	103	91	82	88	71	72	79	88	99	79	64	50	56
Ireland	78	105	120	127	134	171	193	202	190	210	215	185	159
Italy	87	75	76	74	81	90	101	117	129	115	145	156	174
Luxemburg	88	100	107	110	107	95	91	99	100	91	98	100	110
Netherlands	94	81	83	83	86	78	–	–	–	71	63	67	66
Norway	101	109	115	107	105	95	91	99	100	91	98	100	110
Portugal	59	95	90	75	97	120	117	105	70	43	53	61	65
Spain	93	91	58	55	54	53	61	75	53	35	50	56	80
Sweden	92	85	92	91	88	75	76	84	84	130	133	136	148
Switzerland	108	96	87	83	76	78	76	78	75	86	87	90	97
United Kingdom	89	70	70	74	72	68	72	73	74	78	78	78	76
Yugoslavia	126	134	165	181	158	128	101	100	99	–	–	–	–

Note: The year 1979 is not represented in this table because of missing data
Source: *derived from*: ECMT (1988) *Investment in Transport Infrastructure in ECMT Countries*; ECMT (1992) *Statistical Trends in Transport 1956–1988*. Both taken from Bruinsma and Rietveld (1995), p. 102.

Table 4.2 A comparison of planned investment in rail infrastructure in Europe, as of 1994

Country	Railway company	Investments (millions)	Investment (million ECU)	Length of route (km)	Million ECU per km	Rank
Netherlands	NS	G 18 718	8 689.1	2 798	3.105	1
Switzerland	SBB	SFr 10 990	6 516.7	2 982	2.185	2
Belgium	SNCB	BFr 264 000	6 470.3	3 466	1.867	3
Germany	DB	DM 119 949	62 463.2	45 706	1.367	4
Denmark	DSB	DKr 10 440	1 372.1	2 344	0.585	5
France	SNCF	Fr 133 333	20 019.4	34 322	0.583	6
Norway	NSB	NKr 16 106	1 933.2	4 027	0.480	7
Spain	RENFE	Pta 916 650	5 940.4	13 060	0.455	8
Portugal	CP	Esc 300 000	1 541.1	3 910	0.394	9
Sweden	BV	SKr 38 100	4 080.5	10 970	0.372	10
United Kingdom	BR	£ 3 307	4 386.5	16 588	0.266	11
Finland	VR	Fmk 4 800	737.1	5 853	0.126	12

Source: *Rail Business Report* (1994)

The regionalization problem arises when that (subregional) level is lacking. Such a gap is caused by a confrontation between sector-specific developments and administrative boundaries. The sectoral and administrative interests conflict, drift apart, or are hardly connected any more. That gap is still widening as a result of societal developments. The spatial consequences of this gap are dynamic, while the administrative structures remain stationary. Here we define regionalization as an administrative process. It originates in attempts to close the gap between administrative structures and the optimal scale for public service. This process is related to networks and coalitions within the various sectors of the economy.

We distinguish two kinds of regionalization process: changes from the bottom up, and changes from the top down. The bottom-up process refers to municipal activities originating at the local level that are eventually carried out at a subregional level. Two more or less autonomous economies of scale explain this phenomenon.

First, there is a technical increase in scale. Municipalities often lack the money and manpower to satisfy all the demands that have been voiced by the public. In order to optimize their level of services, and concomitantly their effectiveness and efficiency, municipalities try to minimize the problems engendered by changes in scale. In many cases they negotiate with other municipalities to create joint facilities. Activities organized in this way include waste disposal, health care, water purification, energy distribution, and environmental control.

Second, there is a general trend towards enlargement of scale. Spatial developments and administrative borders hardly coincide anymore. This is because societal developments with spatial consequences have become increasingly dynamic, whereas administrative structures have remained stationary. Considering both kinds of scale enlargement, it is not surprising that municipalities show a growing need for cooperation. The need is particularly acute in the areas of planning, coordination, and implementation of municipal policy.

The other kind of regionalization, a top-down process, is characterized by delegation of activities and responsibilities from the central government to the subregional administrative level. For the central government, this seems to provide new opportunities for the ongoing decentralization process. Yet there are hardly any administrative structures capable of coping with these newly acquired responsibilities. Therefore, sometimes new ways are developed for dealing with the administrative gap between the national level and the municipality.

From a sectoral point of view, these kinds of regionalization reinforce each other, as the basic impetus for both is virtually the same: a growing realization of the need for more efficient public administration and a revised planning concept. The processes differ, however, on the criteria for the optimal scale of government activities. A distinction can be made between the problems arising from economies of scale and a sectoral need for more adequate planning tools. This distinction reflects an administrative perspective.

Centralizing and decentralizing tendencies are important in railway station area redevelopment, as both kinds of pressure are visible. From the top down there is an urge to improve public transport rapidly in order to alleviate traffic problems and develop the surrounding areas. A similar urge is felt at the local level, but at the same time – as the costs of development are felt most at the local level – countervailing powers are prominently present to slow the development process down. This is not surprising, as there are numerous actors in the redevelopment process, and their interests differ accordingly. This factor will be dealt with in the next section.

4.3 Actors involved in the process

In general, railway companies come first to mind when thinking of possible actors involved in the redevelopment of railway station areas. Research (e.g. Bertolini and Spit, 1996) shows that railway companies do indeed have an important role. However, the interest of railway companies is not one-dimensional. It consists of different kinds of interest. There can be a real estate interest, a general transport interest, or an exploitation interest (regarding transport and the station itself), for example. These interests can converge, and thus can contribute to the redevelopment process, but they can also diverge. For example, in the case of Euralille, SNCF (the French railway) did not at first agree with the development of the HST station in the city centre: not only was it considered too expensive, but a stop in central Lille would imply a loss in time and thus in profitability. Later in the process, other actors (the state, the region Nord-Pas de Calais, and the city of Lille) made a considerable contribution, amounting to some Fr 800 million, which compensated for the objections of SNCF (Bertolini and Spit, 1996, p. 8).

This French example introduces some other important actors, including national, regional and local governments. Although the interests of the national and regional governments coincided, at the local government level there was some difference of interests. The city of Lille was strongly in favour of the project, but opposition came from the municipalities of Lille's hinterland, through whose territory the TGV must pass, and who feared that they would just get the negative effects of it. During the process it took time, guarantees and compensation in order to convince them to cooperate. This example shows how not only within one actor different interests have to be met, but also how within one kind of actor (in this case the municipality) different interests are shown. The 'hindering power' of the latter can be such that considerable efforts have to be made in order to compensate for it. In general, the involvement of governments within each nation state with the redevelopment of railway station areas is considerable. The European Union, through its promotion of the expansion of a European high-speed rail network, also plays a role indirectly.

In Europe the concentration of high-value land uses around railway stations by means of large-scale urban redevelopment projects is strongly supported not only by national and local policies, based on environmental policy (promotion of public transport use) and economic objectives (strengthening of the competitive position of cities), but also by others. Worth mentioning in this perspective are investors, developers, local businesses, and residents. Yet, as with municipalities, their interests can coincide with the redevelopment, but can as easily be against the plans for it. The redevelopment of Stockholm City West was relatively easy. As there were no neighbours, little opposition emerged, although in this case both market actors and the local population were cautious: they were only slowly recovering from the market crash and some unhappy public–private deals in the 1980s (Bertolini and Spit, 1996, p. 26). A more or less similar situation can be found in the case of the redevelopment of Zentrum Zürich Nord. Also, in this case the number and variety of actors were limited. The shared vision of the two main actors, the city (represented in the alderman, Ursula Koch) and the private landowners, can be considered the key to its success. Other cases, such as King's Cross and the Utrecht Centrum Project, showed much more complex and controversial pictures.

The examples mentioned above illustrate that when redevelopment processes become more complex and more actors get involved not only is it increasingly likely that interests might diverge, but also the planning and implementation process is lengthened, which generates a similar effect: a greater chance for a divergence of interests, diminishing the chance of success. The number and kind of actors involved in the process, including their specific interests, are strongly related to the specific circumstances under which the redevelopment process takes place. Therefore the specific circumstances should be taken as a starting point for analysis. The next section goes into this subject, and tries to identify common distinctive features in railway station redevelopment.

4.4 Railway station redevelopment: the starting point for analysis

How can railway station redevelopment be characterized? What are its common denominators? In the introduction we mentioned the complexity of railway station development. In subsequent chapters we shall discuss specific aspects of it. In this section we try to reduce the complexity by examining some recurring characteristics. It is a systematic search for convergence. Elaborating on Bruijn *et al.* (1996, pp. 26–55) we can distinguish at least seven common features, as detailed below.

Scale and complexity

Railway station redevelopment is by definition a large project: not only in terms of capital investment, the number of actors involved, and the organization, but also in terms of its impact on its direct and indirect surroundings. It can generate a positive effect on employment and a vast improvement of transport facilities, next to an upgrading of the existing physical structure.

Uniqueness

Each railway station area is unique: not only because of its spatial qualifications, but also in its requirements for redevelopment. This sets limits on the potential for learning from one another. Also, comparison of planning performance between railway locations is impeded by their uniqueness.

Partiality

The relatively large scale, in combination with the continuity of a relatively long process of decision making and implementation, makes partiality an autonomous characteristic of railway station areas. Such huge projects are often referred to as one, but in reality end up as a sum of many smaller projects. The unity of development often represents the label under which many projects are programmed. Partiality is one of the main impediments to an evaluation of the success or failure of such huge projects.

Interdependence of design

The overall design of the development project is mostly complemented by more specific designs for limited projects within the territory. Each individual design is preceded by a specification of technical, financial and organizational requirements. Each specification deals with different details of the design. Each individual design has to fit into the overall design, but at the same time it has to deal with changes in the conditions under which it is developed, and has to tune in with other designs that are developed at the same time. The interdependence between the overall design and the other designs thus mortgages the success of development. Interdependence of design is therewith closely related to partiality as a feature of railway station redevelopment.

Colliding functional interests

Within a relatively small territory many activities take place, in both the node and the place dimensions. Not only is the number of activities (or functions) important, but so especially is their intensive use of space. Redevelopment implies almost automatically an increase in the use of space. Consequently, the spatial interests of the activities or functions involved are going to collide. As space becomes more scarce, conflicts of interest will intensify, and the plans for redevelopment will get more complex in order to solve the emerging problems. As both planning and implementation take a relatively long period, new technical options can help in finding solutions. Although the latter refers to a positive aspect of the planning and implementation process, it also introduces an element of technological uncertainty in the process. In this respect the concept of *equifinality* is relevant. Perrow (1984) described this concept as a manifestation of uncertainty in the planning process. As there is more than one option for finding a solution, equifinality can turn out to be a new source of conflict between the actors involved.

Public and private involvement

With reference to section 4.3, which dealt with the actors in the process, an autonomous feature in railway station area redevelopment is the dominant presence of both public and private parties. Both kinds of party are committed to one another, in trying to redevelop the area. However, not all parties are actively involved in the realization process. Public involvement in railway station area redevelopment extends itself also to those parties that display activities in this area, such as living, working, shopping, visiting, passing through, and travelling. From a negative point of view, support of indirectly involved parties is necessary, as they have considerable power to block redevelopment. Through either legal or political procedures they can yield power to block or slow down the redevelopment process. More positively formulated, when these groups support redevelopment plans, perhaps their activities within the territory may expand, and in an economic sense the area will profit from this intensified use. Therefore public support is of the utmost importance, either directly or indirectly.

Risk and risk management

In general the redevelopment of a railway station area implies an intensified use of an area that already has heavy demands made on it. In the literature three main views on risk and risk management are displayed (Fischhoff, 1981). The first is a technical point of view, and deals with the chance of accidents. This perspective is often taken by governments, but is generally under heavy attack. A second view is displayed by the concept that in cases such as railway station area redevelopment, technologically complex systems are linked to one another. Risks are displayed at two levels: within each complex system, and in the linkages between the systems. Complex systems are vulnerable by definition, as each part of the system adds to its vulnerability. As dependence grows between complex transport systems, such as bus and train, the linkage gets more vulnerable as well. Hence a new dilemma shows itself: whenever within a railway station area complex systems (such as transport) are optimized in order to reach their full potential, in economic terms development is most promising, but at the same time the risks will also be highest.

A third approach directs itself towards the acceptability of risks. This represents the most pragmatic of the three views. The measure of acceptability is determined by negotiation. Based upon the outcome of negotiation on the most preferred alternative, risks are calculated and authorities are consulted about public acceptability. As in the technical view, laymen are not involved in the discussion. Assessment of acceptability is exclusively in the hands of authorities and experts. Although risk and risk management certainly have a technical element in them, a pure technical variant of risk management is highly contrary to the high public involvement and public interest in risk situations.

This set of issues will run through the analysis of the cases in Part Two of the book, and they will be taken up again in the conclusions. Analysis of the cases will follow a similar format. First, the national planning context will be sketched. Second, railway station area redevelopment in each country will be introduced. Each chapter will then centre on an extensive analysis of one or two cases, touching on both the process and content aspects of the redevelopment, and will be closed by an evaluation. In Part Three the cases will be compared, and in the light of the issues raised in Part One, conclusions and an agenda for practice and research will be drawn up.

Part Two
Cases

5
Euralille

5.1 Preamble: the national planning system

The *Napoleonic family* is the label that best describes the French planning system (Newman and Thornley, 1996, pp. 27–76). The French planning system is largely shaped by a national codified law (*Code de l'Urbanisme et l'Habitat*). Historically, its roots go back to the French Revolution, and it could until recently have been characterized as very centralistic. At present there are four levels of government involved in physical planning: *state*, *region* (22 on the continent and 4 overseas), *département* (100) and *commune* (36 666). The state produces national laws and guidelines. The national ministry responsible for local and regional planning has local offices in the larger metropolitan areas. The local representatives (*préfets*) of the national government exercise a strong influence over local authorities. At the intercommunal level a planning framework may be provided by a cooperative master directive plan (SDAU). The master directive plan defines the general orientation of planning objectives applicable to a defined number of communes, which can be considerable. The SDAU of Lyon, for example, consists of 71 communes (ISOCARP, 1992, pp. 71–80).

Both the state and the region have specific interests in economic and physical planning. The planning objectives are periodically formulated in national plans. Recently, the 22 regions were also allowed to make their own development plans, but until now few have done so. The départements do not have many specific instruments for physical planning. They do have a considerable range of functions, which indirectly influence urban development and planning decisions.

Essentially, the French planning system is a two-tier system based on the *loi d'orientation foncière* of 1967. Decentralization and recentralization administrative developments are also important in France. Recently, for example, administrative powers were shifted to the office of the mayor, which has given these officials a prominent position with respect to special projects such as railway station area redevelopment. Although strategic plans can be initiated by a commune, they must be agreed upon by a majority of communes in the region. Because of the fragmented structure of the communes, strategic plans are more often than not a joint responsibility of the commune and the state, wherein the state representative takes a leading role. The content of plans may vary but must be consistent with the general objectives and infrastructure.

Though the national government has a strong position with regard to infrastructure planning, the local level of government also has considerable instruments. The POS (*plan d'occupation des sols*) is a specific responsibility of the communes. All larger communes (with more than 50 000 inhabitants) have such a POS, which is a strict zoning plan. Additionally the French communes have instruments for the implementation of plans as well. Compulsory purchase is an example of these additional instruments.

Urban development is generally carried out either through comprehensive development (*zones d'aménagement concerté*, the so-called ZACs), or through a land subdivision plan. ZACs are primarily meant to facilitate urban development operations carried out by authorities and private developers. This institution has been a great success since its introduction in 1967. Over 3000 ZACs have been created since then, including most station area initiatives. An important element in such a planning document is that it includes a programme for the construction of public facilities and their capital investment. The local authority as well as a private developer can carry out projects. Sometimes, however, implementation is carried out by a specially created public agency with a commercial status (*établissement public d'aménagement*), or by a limited-liability planning agency of which the communes are a major shareholder, the so-called *société d'économie mixte* (SEM), as typically with railway station area redevelopment. In the former, the government is primarily responsible for development operations as well as for financial risks. In the latter, the local authority controls development but is only partially responsible for the financial result of the plan (Acosta and Renard, 1993).

5.2 Context: railway station area redevelopment in France

The main driving force behind station area redevelopment initiatives in France in the last 15 years has been the gradual expansion of the high-speed TGV network, following the commercial success of the Paris–Lyon link completed in 1981–1983. In 1996, our literature survey turned up no less than 23 major station area projects spread across the TGV network (Figure 5.1).

Local governments have tended to see a connection to the TGV system as a boost to the local economy, and have accordingly lobbied intensively to obtain it. In combination with the high-speed connection, ambitious urban development schemes have been launched next to stations, often in partnership with private actors. Much has been written on the inflated hopes raised among municipalities by the coming of the TGV, on the importance of factors other than the TGV in realizing its development potential, and on the fact that economic growth has typically been redistributed rather than created (see, for instance, studies and experiences reviewed by Sands, 1993, and by Troin, 1995). In the end, the TGV proved to be no more – but also no less – than a catalyst for development when a lively local economy was already in place and a set of conditions was

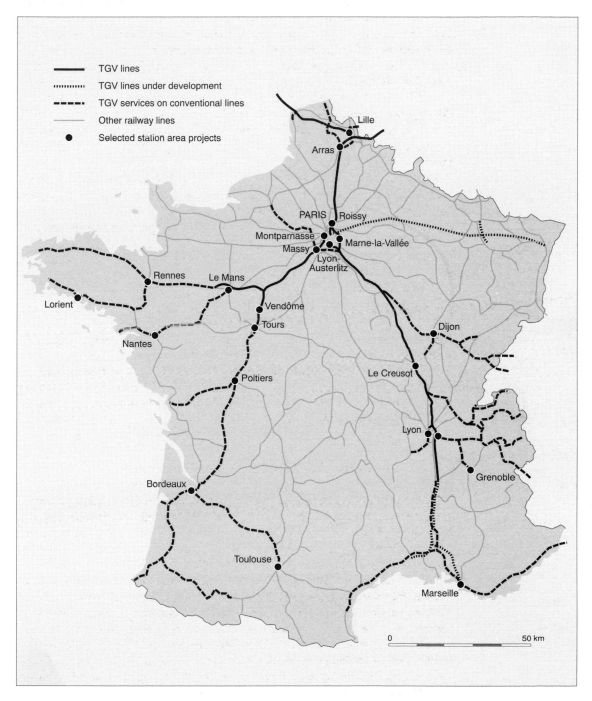

Fig. 5.1 National railway network and main station area projects in France.

met. Furthermore, negative effects have been also underlined, such as increased inequalities in accessibility at the national, regional, and local levels.

Two contrasting developments have determined the actual connection of localities to the TGV network. On one side, the French railways (SNCF), guided by their own commercial imperatives, were aiming at the fastest connections between the biggest traffic generators. In practice, they were set on connecting Paris with the main centres at the other ends of the lines. On the other side were local governments along the TGV network (city, metropolitan and regional authorities), often supported by local market partners (such as chambers of commerce and banks). These coalitions were trying to get the TGV to stop there, and possibly in the heart of the agglomeration. The implemented solutions are largely compromises between these two aims, and reflect the relative strengths of the players in each situation (Troin, 1995; Zembri, 1995). Interestingly, the direct role of the state has been rather weak in this respect. No national strategic guidance was provided, let alone promoted (Zembri, 1995). The same tendency appears to continue into the current effort to expand the TGV network in the southerly and easterly directions (Troin, 1995).

In practice, what have been the impacts of the TGV at the station level? Especially in the larger centres – for instance in Lyon-La Part-Dieu, or in Nantes – dramatically improved accessibility to Paris has given momentum to (often pre-existing) local development dynamics. However, in several cases – as in Mans, and most notably in Lille – the local authorities have had to fight hard to get a TGV station at the heart of the city instead of on the periphery, as was the original intention of SNCF. In many other cases the location of railway stations has not been able to escape the narrow logic of the transport operator. Some medium-sized localities have had no stop at all. Others just got an exurban 'desert station', with nominal TGV frequencies and poor connections to both the local transport networks and economic activity centres. Especially in this last category, urban development effects are still far below expectations, as in Vendôme, Mâcon-Loché, Le Creusot or Haute-Picardie.

Railway stations in Paris constitute a special case. For those in the core, integration with ongoing urban development has been 'natural' but rather haphazard (Gare de Lyon, Montparnasse), while a more coordinated approach seems to be emerging (as at the Gare d'Austerlitz, and in the further development at the Gare de Lyon). Stations in the periphery (Massy, Marne-La Vallée-Chessy, Roissy-Charles de Gaulle) were essentially born out of technical considerations (the possibility of bypassing congested central Paris or interchanging with other transport modes). They have since been launched as anchors of edge city developments, but they have not yet entirely proved their worth in that respect. The airport station at Satolas, outside Lyon, has similar characteristics, though with more uncertain development prospects.

5.3 Euralille as node and place

5.3.1 *The node*

Euralille is a development centred on a complex transport interchange that includes two railway stations: Lille-Flandres (currently with TGV services to

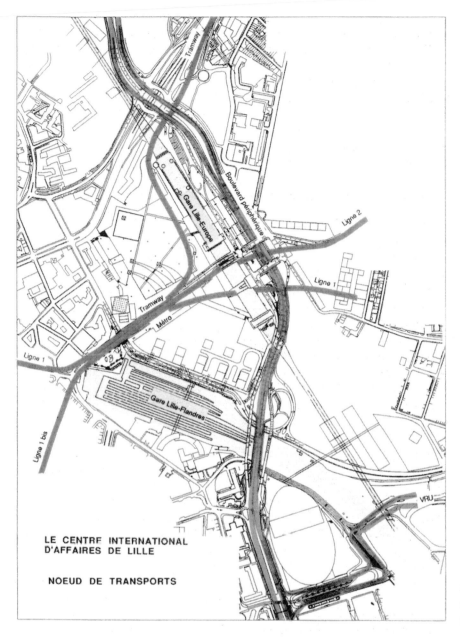

LE CENTRE INTERNATIONAL
D'AFFAIRES DE LILLE

NOEUD DE TRANSPORTS

Fig. 5.2 Euralille, the transportation node. (Source: Euralille)

Paris and regional trains) and Lille-Europe (with international HST services). In the transport node, the following converge: high-speed lines (in the three directions of Brussels, Paris and London), conventional trains, the underground, rapid trams, buses, through roads, and a motorway bypass (Figure 5.2).

Thanks to the TGV, Lille is just 1 hour from Paris (53 minutes from Roissy Airport), and will be 25 minutes from Brussels and 2 hours from London. Before the TGV these times were 2 hours 7 minutes, 1 hour 30 minutes, and 4 hours 45 minutes respectively. In 1995, 70 000 passengers a day passed through Lille-

Flandres and 8000 through Lille-Europe. In the first quarter of 1997, on an average weekday, 45 000 passengers used the TER (Train Express Regional) and 13 500 the TGV.

The transport infrastructure that had to be built (a programme now virtually completed) included the new TGV line and station, a new metro underground line and station, a new rapid-tram stop, the reconstruction of the motorway bypass next to the TGV line, a new road viaduct, and underground parking providing a total of 6100 places.

5.3.2 The place

The development site of Euralille lies in between peripheral, lower-density neighbourhoods and the historical centre of Lille (Figure 5.3). Lille itself is a city of just 168 000 inhabitants, but it is also the core of a truly polycentric metro-politan area, where a total of 1 100 000 people live, not counting the 500 000 inhabitants of the adjoining Belgian municipalities.

The location of Euralille is unusual. Because of military rights, there was a vast amount of unbuilt, underused land next to the existing station of Lille-Flandres. That vacant land lay between the city centre and the bundle of rail and road infrastructure separating it from the surrounding municipalities. When Euralille was conceived, the station neighbourhood was that of a typical obsolescent central station, with a mixture of shops, services, and housing of moderate quality. There was some tertiary development along its margins, but the general property dynamics were low, partly because of the many infrastructure barriers. The areas on the other side of the tracks and the motorway were essentially residential, and had little contact with the social and economic life of the city centre. The construction next to Lille-Flandres of the new TGV station, and especially of the

Fig. 5.3 Euralille, the place. Lille-Flandres is at the bottom right of the picture, Lille-Europe at the top left. The city centre is at the bottom; peripheral residential neighbourhoods are at the top. Between the two stations is the new multifunctional complex of Euralille. Just outside the picture, at the top right, is the new event, congress and exhibition centre. (Source: Euralille. Photo: NAI)

tertiary complex of Euralille, was revolutionary. It had few, if any, antecedents in developments nearby. The scale of reference, here to a more extreme degree than in other station area projects, appears to be that of the far-away places brought closer by new and improved transport networks. The ambition of Euralille is to deal with the fact that

> the space of daily life will be at one time that of the immediate proximity, the territory contained in a radius of 30 km around the centre of Lille, and the triangle London–Paris–Brussels, of which Lille becomes a sort of epicentre. (*Urbanisme*, 1993, p.55)

However, as we shall see, integration of such distant realities raises many difficult issues.

5.3.3 *The process*

The story of Euralille is at one and the same time that of an extraordinary chain of events and that of the determination of the local élites to profit from emerging opportunities. In short, everything about this case is exceptional. Its position is exceptional, thanks to the location; it has become the hinge of the north European high-speed train system. The consequent increase in accessibility is unprecedented on the continent. The FAST study of the European Union (cited in Arenas *et al.*, 1995) concluded that in 2020 Lille will be the most accessible city in Europe, up from eleventh place in 1991. Not just quantitative but also qualitative accessibility is important. Lying between London, Paris, and Brussels, Lille is within reach of some of the world's most densely populated and economically active regions. Exceptional also is the availability of ample reserves of virtually unbuilt land next to the station and the city centre, all in public hands. Exceptional is the personal leadership and political influence provided by Pierre Mauroy. He has been the mayor of Lille for 25 years, president of the Communauté Urbaine (the metropolitan government) since 1989, prime minister when the crucial decisions (Channel Tunnel, North European HST, HST through Lille) were taking shape, and well connected at all times. Exceptional too is the local economic context, and the magnitude both of the past crisis of the regional industrial economic base (textile, coal, metal), and of the present transition to a service and high-tech economy.

As a result of the accumulation of all the above, there is a 'sense of urgency, of inevitability' that in Lille 'generates an incredible dynamic' (*de Volkskrant*, 1994), and which has no equal elsewhere. Referring to the Euralille initiative, Mauroy admits:

> We have been lucky, without a doubt, because if one of these conditions would not have been satisfied at the right moment, the project would probably not have seen the light of day. (Simon, 1993)

All of this has to be kept in mind when evaluating the case of Euralille, and when reviewing the three phases into which its story could be divided.

Phase 1: strategic decisions, 1986–1987

At the beginning of the 1980s, finally breaking centuries-long hesitations, the British and the French governments (Mauroy was then prime minister) decided that the two countries were to be linked by a tunnel under the Channel. The decision was formalized in January 1986. Car shuttles and high-speed trains were the transport means to run through the 'Chunnel'.

In 1987, another important step was taken. The transport ministers of France, Belgium, Germany and the Netherlands signed a treaty for the joint development of the north European high-speed train network. Meanwhile Mauroy, who had gone back full-time to his local responsibilities, took over the leadership of a broad regional coalition of public and private interests to lobby for changes in the HST route. They wanted it to run through the Nord-Pas de Calais region, not the Picardie; and they wanted it to run through the centre of the city of Lille, not on a peripheral course. Initially, SNCF (the French railways) did not agree with the idea. They found it too expensive. Moreover, the stop in Lille would mean a loss in time and thus in profitability. Later, however, a compensation for the increase in costs and the missed profits made SNCF change its mind. The extra Fr 800 million needed was contributed by the state (Fr 400 million, as a result of the mediation of Mauroy), the region Nord-Pas de Calais (Fr 264 million), and the city of Lille (Fr 136 million).

Not all the conflicts were resolved, though. Opposition to the route came also from the municipalities of Lille's hinterland, on whose territory the TGV would have to pass, and who feared they would get just the negative effects. Little by little, guarantees (mitigation of impacts) and compensations (redistribution of the advantages) induced them to change their opinion. Some of the other big projects started in other centres of the metropolitan area should be seen as part of the building of this consensus among municipalities (and, one could say, of the 'foundation' of the Lille metropolis). Examples include the Euroteleport in Roubaix, the multimodal transport platform in Roncq, the expansion of the airport of Lille-Lesquin, the technopole in Villeneuve d'Ascq, the graphic arts and packaging pole in Tourcoing, and the inclusion of a tertiary complex under construction in the bordering municipality of La Madeleine within the perimeter (and the sphere of influence) of Euralille. On a municipal level, an extensive renewal programme of the old city centre is also part of this list of complementary actions.

Phase 2: planning, 1988–1990

The regional mobilization and negotiations were successful: in December 1987, the decision to let the TGV stop in Lille was official. Immediately afterwards, in February 1988, the constitution of Euralille-Métropole was announced. It consisted of a public–private study partnership that was to evaluate the feasibility of urban development on the site of the TGV station. The partnership was presided over by Deflaisseux (former president of the Credit Lyonnais Bank, and old friend of Mauroy), directed by Baïetto (former director of the Société Centrale pour l'Equipement du Territoire), and had other influential members. A group of banks, SNCF, and the local chamber of commerce were convinced to take part in this exploratory venture and subscribe to the partnership.

The first decision of the study partnership was to construct a second station for the international TGVs, essentially for technical reasons. It was also decided to use the areas between the projected and the existing station to build the new 'citadel' of Lille. On the whole, the areas available for development were in excess of 100 ha: 70 ha immediately, 50 ha in the longer term. Virtually un-developed because of pending military rights, the land was donated by the state to the city of Lille for the symbolic amount of one franc (here also, the influence of Mauroy was crucial). The new station was to be called Lille-Europe; the old was re-christened Lille-Flandres. Between the two stations – between the Flandres and Europe – an international business centre was to rise. To avoid 'a Défense between stations', a diversified programme was suggested, consisting of offices, services, shops, culture, housing, public facilities, and open spaces. On the basis of this programme, eight architects of international reputation were invited to present their ideas. They were asked to make an oral presentation. Thus it was not a design competition. In the words of Baïetto:

> It is nonsense to try to achieve an urban project by means of a design competition: an urban project implies multiple aspects and actors, and thus you have to choose a person rather than a project. (Treiber, 1995)

The contest, held in the autumn of 1988, was won by Rem Koolhaas: 'He was chosen because he had a vision of the city, not just of a project.' The key to his proposal is the notion of interconnectivity – functional, spatial, and visual.

From that point on, the story of the project, with the exception of a brief intermission for public consultations, could be described as an interplay between the mayor (Mauroy) and the master architect (Koolhaas), mediated by the executive director of Euralille (Baïetto). Each of the players was responsible for (including feedback into the project) a portion of relationships with the outside world: respectively political (both the institutions and the local population), technical (essentially the great number of consultants), and operational (investors, developers, and users). In the course of 1989, the exchanges between the three (and indirectly between the constituencies they each represented) became intense. The result was a simplification and clarification of the concept initially proposed by the architect. Streamlining was necessary in order to reduce costs and increase continuity between the new district and the existing city. In the meantime, Baïetto untiringly searched for investors for each element of the programme, one by one. The influence of Mauroy was repeatedly called into service. It was through his efforts that the personal support of President Mitterand was obtained for a European Foundation of the City and Architecture. Private investors, after some initial reluctance, were gradually drawn in. But they imposed certain conditions. For example, they asked for – and got – a reduction in the proportion of office space, which they felt would reduce risk.

In the second half of 1989, the project was presented in two rounds to the local council. At the end of the same year, a phase of public consultation was started. That phase was to end in April 1990 with an open discussion forum. The most important amendment to the original plan in this phase was reinforcement of the physical integration of the complex, both internal and with the surrounding area. After these changes, the positive results of opinion polls taken among the population were adduced as evidence that sufficient consensus had been reached. In the meantime, intense negotiations with and between different agencies (such

Table 5.1 Euralille: summary of the main phases

Phase 1: strategic key decisions, 1986–1987

January 1986	Channel Tunnel
October 1987	North-European HST: regional mobilization
December 1987	HST stop in the centre of Lille

Phase 2: planning, 1988–1990

February 1988	Establishment of the Euralille study partnership (local and regional governments, banks, SNCF, Chamber of Commerce); discussions; programme
Autumn 1988	Urban design competition (closed, oral). Rem Koolhaas wins
1989	Three-way discussions: Koolhaas (technique), Baïetto (management), Mauroy (politics)
Mid-1989/mid-1990	Public consultations and council votes; presentation to city council, districts and metropolitan government; public discussion forum, population poll, etc.

Phase 3: implementation, 1990–1995

June 1990	Foundation of the Euralille SEM: local and regional governments 54%, banks 40%, SNCF 3%, Chamber of Commerce 3%
June 1991	Start construction
23 May 1993	First TGV Paris–Lille
29 May 1994	First TGV Paris–(Lille)–London
1994	Opening of Lille-Europe station, Lille Grand Palais, Centre Euralille
1995	Opening of office towers, Credit Lyonnais and World Trade Centre

as Euralille, SNCF, other transport companies, and the metropolitan government) were also undertaken and successfully completed. It should be noted that, because of the forming of a new governing coalition, in 1989 Mauroy also became president of the Communauté Urbaine.

On the whole, opposition to the project was weak. In Lille, it mostly coincided with right-wing political opposition to the mayor. The other key actors and the rest of the local population – when they were originally indifferent, sceptical and in a few cases explicitly hostile (notably among environmentalists and small retailers) – were gradually won over to support the initiative. The main themes of criticism by the political antagonists of Mauroy were doubts about the financial feasibility of the plan, and objections to the choice of an architectural style that departed with local tradition. However, a viable alternative – a study trip to the London Docklands notwithstanding – did not arise. Criticism along different lines, and more consistent, was voiced by environmentalists and small retailers, but the argument put forward by the former that development would destroy an existing park was too weak. The existing park attracted few visitors, and a new

10 ha park was to be part of Euralille. The retailers of the city centre were afraid of competition from the new shopping centre. Euralille addressed their fears by reducing net shopping floor space (from 65 000 m² to 31 000 m²). At the same time Euralille introduced measures to avoid direct competition between shops in the new complex and shops in the adjoining historical city centre (for example, orientation of Euralille on innovative, specialized products, and reservation of 37% of the shopping floor space as a second location for local businessmen).

Phase 3: implementation, 1990–1995

In June 1990, right after the plan was approved by the metropolitan government, the Euralille study partnership transformed itself into a public–private development partnership, a *société d'économie mixte* (SEM; see section 5.1), presided over by Mauroy and directed by Baïetto. The planning framework is provided by a special development zone known as a *zone d'aménagement concerté* (ZAC; see section 5.1). The SEM Euralille was granted authority in the ZAC by the Communauté Urbaine (the metropolitan government) for a 15-year period (until 2005). Construction was launched in June 1991. Since then, the progress of Euralille can be read through the succession of the opening dates of its various elements (Table 5.1). The most notable setbacks in this period were due to vicissitudes in the financing (both public and private) of single elements, which forced the project managers to delay the realization of some of them. The basic elements, however, were not affected.

5.4 Property development at Euralille

In the words of Rem Koolhaas, Euralille is

> based on the hypothesis that the perception of Europe is going to change completely under the dual impact of the trans-Channel tunnel and the extension of the high-speed train network. If this hypothesis is borne out, Lille, as the receptacle of a great many typically modern activities, will gain considerable importance. The TGV high-speed train lines will take the place of the old fortifications that have been eaten up by a sprawling periphery. And with the hybrid and timely presence of a gigantic futuristic project a stone's throw from the historical centre, activities formerly considered to be peripheral will move towards the heart of the city. Working within the existing context our task is to make a quantum leap towards a radical future as exotic as it is imminent. (*l'Architecture d'Aujourd'hui*, 1992)

What are these 'typically modern activities'? And what sort of development organization and marketing strategy do they require? These points will be discussed in the following sections.

5.4.1 Functions

The list of functions of Euralille included in the now concluded first development phase, on an area of 70 ha, is as follows (see also Figure 5.4).

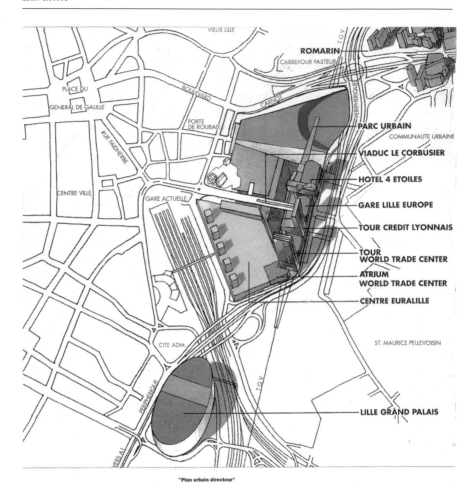

Fig. 5.4 Euralille: the elements of the programme. (Source: Euralille)

In the *Centre Euralille*, the triangular prism connecting the new station to the old one, there may be found:

- commercial areas covering 92 000 m^2, of which an area of 31 000 m^2 is net shopping floor space;
- leisure accommodation (5900 m^2);
- a multifunctional space for performances, expositions and other events (2200 m^2);
- catering in various forms (5250 m^2);
- higher education (international business school, 18 570 m^2);
- public services (4000 m^2, including post office, municipal office, daycare centre, and a 'silent place' for spiritual meditation);
- housing for sale (6377 m^2, 168 units);
- temporary housing (11 216 m^2, 407 units);
- a hotel (2350 m^2, 97 rooms);
- private services (in a first phase 5821 m^2; an additional 11 717 m^2 are planned);
- parking spaces (81 600 m^2, 3500 places).

The shopping centre contains one 'Carrefour' hypermarket (12 000 m^2), seven mid-sized premises, and 130 boutiques. The food sector represents 20% of the supply, personal equipment 16%, cultural and leisure products 11%, restaurants 6%, and home appliances 5%. One-tenth of the retailers are foreign; a third are, by contract, regional. Fifteen million visitors per year are expected. There are long daily opening times, but on Sundays the centre is closed. The housing programme includes 168 up-market flats, 198 serviced student flats, 12 temporary flats for researchers, 52 lodgings for travelling railway employees, and a self-catering hotel with 143 flats.

The *Cité des Affaires* encompasses the new TGV station and the three towers above it. There are:

- 39 720 m^2 of offices in the World Trade Centre and the Credit Lyonnais towers;
- 15 449 m^2 of restaurants, business services and other (temporary) offices, exhibition rooms, and shops in the base of the WTC tower and directly adjoining the TGV station hall;
- a four-star hotel (11 000 m^2, 204 rooms, not built yet);
- parking (32 880 m^2, 1370 places, 250 of which are reserved for users of the station).

The World Trade Centre is a crucial element in the development strategy of Euralille. As an authentic global communication node (including advanced telecommunications), it 'will allow firms to meet their partners, present their products, and establish business relationships with the whole world.'

In the *Lille Grand Palais*, the oval congress centre at some distance from the stations, there are:

- 18 000 m^2 of diversified congress space (12 meeting rooms, three auditoria for 1500, 500 and 350 people, and a subdividable space for up to 400 people);
- 20 000 m^2 of partitionable exhibition space;
- an event hall with a capacity of 5500 people (7500 m^2);
- catering facilities.

The catering sector includes a banquet hall for 1600 guests, a cafeteria for 400 meals, an à la carte restaurant for 80–100 meals, and parking (29 520 m^2, 1230 places).

To these should be added:

- the European Foundation of the City and Architecture (FEVA, 8500 m^2, not built yet);
- a park of 10 ha;
- another 400 housing units (25% as social housing, not built yet);
- a tertiary complex of regional scope located in the bordering municipality of La Madeleine and associated *ex post* to Euralille (74 500 m^2, of which 45 000 m^2 is for offices).

All the functions listed above belong to a 'first phase'. Provisions have been made for future expansion, most notably of the office content. The row of towers, for instance, could be extended along the TGV line in a southerly direction. The total cost is estimated at Fr 5300 million, of which Fr 3700 million (70%) comes from private sources, Fr 500 million (9%) comes from semi-public sources, and Fr 1100 million (21%) is publicly funded. The great majority of this programme was completed by the summer of 1997.

Euralille also has a specific job-creation programme. An 'economic and social accompaniment mission' has been established. Its task is to train and place the local unemployed (528 persons had been employed through the programme as of September 1994). In 1996, 2800 were employed at Euralille, of whom 1530 were in the shopping centre. Of the total number of jobs, about 2000 are said to be new. In the long term, 2000–3000 employees are expected to be working in the office buildings, and a total of 5000 in the area. The hope is that 40% of these will be new jobs.

5.4.2 Organization

The Euralille SEM combines the functions of promotion (one-third of the budget in the first two years), global coordination and management of the operation, and the direct development of single elements of the programme, such as parking spaces and the congress and exhibition centre. For the remaining parts, development rights are sold to public and private developers, which in turn sell the buildings to investors. These new owners either use the premises themselves (for example, 40% of the Credit Lyonnais tower) or rent out the space (such as the remaining 60% of the Credit Lyonnais tower). In the case of the shopping centre, the developers themselves are also investors and users. The initial capital of the SEM was originally fixed at Fr 35 million and later at Fr 50 million. As prescribed by law, local authorities hold the majority of shares. In 1994, the government participants represented included:

- municipalities (Lille with 16.5%, and La Madeleine, Roubaix, Tourcoing, and Villeneuve d'Ascq, each with 2.5%);
- the metropolitan government (16.5%);
- the province (5.5%);
- the region (5.5%).

The private investors, many of whom were already represented in the study partnership, included:

- regional banks (Scalbert-Dupont 7.3%, Banque Populaire du Nord 7.3%);
- national banks (Caisse de Dépôts et Consignations 7.3%, Crédit Lyonnais 7.3%, and Indosuez 4.4%);
- international banks (National Westminster Bank, Bank of Tokyo, Banca San Paolo di Torino, Générale de Banque, each with about 1%);
- the insurance company Lloyd Continental.

SNCF (represented by its subsidiary SCETA) has a 3% share, the same as the local chamber of commerce. Part of the contribution of the city of Lille is in the form of land.

Financial feasibility has been a leading criterion in setting up the project organization. In the words of Baïetto:

> I think our work prior to start-up was fundamental. We gave ourselves the time to think about the financial set up, to see what was possible and what was not, to consider what we could get from the collective bodies and private partners concerned, and what this would mean in terms of overall financial balancing. (*l'Architecture d'Aujourd'hui*, 1992)

Euralille can be seen as

> a mixture of smaller projects funded by private investors within a master plan defined by the public sector and coordinated by a nominally mixed, though public sector controlled, management agency. (Newman and Thornley, 1995, p. 242)

These smaller, independent projects include (infrastructure not considered) the World Trade Centre, the Credit Lyonnais tower, the hotel tower, the Centre Euralille (shopping centre), the Lille Grand Palais (congress and exhibition centre), complementary programmes (park, parking, FEVA), and an associated tertiary programme (le Portes du Romarin).

5.4.3 Marketing

Unlike other examples of great urban projects in Europe, little if any of the property supply in Euralille is purely speculative. Rather, a dialogue has been sought with the market to work out specific hypotheses. It is not generic *functions* that are planned in Lille, but rather *initiatives*. In other words, the mix of functions of Euralille has grown along with its marketing (the search for developers, investors and users). The property marketing strategy is geared towards maximum use of the exceptional qualities of the location, but the objective is to be reached without disrupting the metropolitan real estate markets.

In 1996, the average office prices at Euralille were Fr 11 314 per m^2 for sale and Fr 1044 per m^2 per year for rent. It is contended that prices were about a third of what could be found in London, Brussels or Paris, and 10% higher than elsewhere in the metropolitan area. Offices have been put on the market gradually, not to exceed 20–25% of the local annual supply; in a metropolitan market of 90 000–100 000 m^2/year, not more than 20 000–25 000 m^2/year have been offered. Furthermore, it is argued that this supply is very specific (prestigious address, floor space of more than 1500 m^2, 'smart buildings', etc.), and more complementary than concurrent to that of the rest of the metropolitan area. The aim is to make a new offer on the metropolitan market primarily to attract companies trading in Europe's north-western markets but who have not yet set up in the region, together with regional companies seeking an international showcase. Before March 1995, 45 000 m^2 were put on the market. Part of the new space was already reserved by the developers and investors: for example, 40% of the Credit Lyonnais tower. Also, the property market of the Lille region has been hit less hard than markets elsewhere by the property crisis. In 1993, for instance, there was 300 000 m^2 of empty office space in Lyon (a metropolitan area of similar size), compared with 36 500 m^2 of vacant office space in Lille.

Starting in 1994, various elements of Euralille have come into use. In subsequent years, some preliminary evaluations were also made. Of course, these are only very early appraisals. They were carried out when several of the conditions on which the marketing formula was based (such as the existence of a north European HST network) were only very partially realized. Also, the European and especially the French economy have been going through a difficult period. The economic slump discouraged new initiatives, and constrained public and private spending. Nevertheless, the emerging picture already revealed what the most and the least successful aspects of the project were to be. The conclusion drawn in several studies (Agence de développement et d'urbanisme de la métropole lilloise, 1996; Menerault and Stissi-Epée, 1996; Observatoire des bureaux de la métropole lilloise, 1996) and confirmed by our interviews in Lille is as follows.

The position of Lille as a service pole in the region has been strengthened. Even nationally, Euralille seems to have helped the city to hold onto its share. However, the international tertiary centre, which was fervently desired, has not yet materialized. Detailed information on the commercialization and performance of the various components supports this conclusion (Agence de développement et d'urbanisme de la métropole lilloise, 1996). The shopping complex, including the hypermarket, is doing fairly well: with a few exceptions, the premises have all been let. As a consequence, the centre of Lille as a whole has reinforced its role among metropolitan consumers, stretching across the Belgian border. As envisaged, Euralille appears to be developing in a fashion that is complementary rather than concurrent to the historic city centre, reminiscent of the function of Hoog Catharijne in Utrecht (Chapter 6). But the ambition of creating a different, high-profile supply, geared to the international consumer, has not yet been realized. The data on the use of the cultural, entertainment and congress and exhibition facilities are also encouraging. Lille here had to fill a gap in the supply, and the new facilities have been used to capacity. The apartments have been absorbed by the market; they are fully occupied by the special target groups that they were built for. Finally, accommodation facilities are also performing well, even though the four-star hotel is still on the drawing board. (This is not the only part of the plan still awaiting construction. The architecture centre FEVA has been put off indefinitely, and the social housing is planned for the near future.)

The weakest point of the entire operation appears to be the office element, despite all the caution and the limited quantities built. Of the total of 63 395 m^2 of offices, only 30 983 m^2 or 49% was in use as of April 1997. Even in the current modest upturn of the market, locations on the periphery appear to be doing better than those in Euralille (Observatoire des bureaux de la métropole lilloise, 1996). Several explanations have been offered. Of course, the economic downturn weighed heavily. Second, the various properties have very different appeal. The Credit Lyonnais tower was 64% let, the Atrium 89%, and Eurocity 77%. The real problem was the 25 100 m^2 of the Lilleurope tower, which was 100% empty. The tower is owned by a national consortium of banks. For them, the tower is just a marginal asset. Until recently, they had tried without success to find one single large user. According to sources in Lille, the current (summer 1997) more flexible

Table 5.2 Property development at Euralille[a]

Surface area	70 ha
Area ownership	SEM Euralille (City of Lille)
Total floorspace	273 710 m^2 (28 220 uncertain)
Offices	45 720 m^2
Private services	22 290 m^2 (8720 uncertain)
Congress/exhibition space	38 000 m^2
Permanent housing	6380 m^2 (168 units)
Temporary housing	11 220 (407 units)
Leisure	15 600 m^2
Shops	31 000 m^2 net
Hotel, restaurants, cafes	18 600 m^2 (11 000 uncertain)
Education	11 400 m^2
Public services	4000 m^2
Foundation for Architecture	8500 m^2 (uncertain)
Parking	6100 places
Costs (including railway infrastructure)	Fr 5300 million (70% private, 21% public, 9% semi-public)

[a] To this, 74 500 m^2 of floor space in the adjacent development of Le Portes du Romarin may be added, including offices (45 000 m^2), a hotel, housing (160 units), services, and shops.

marketing approach might bear fruit. Third, and perhaps most interestingly, the difficulty of letting the office space casts doubt on some of the basic assumptions of the initiative. In particular, it erodes the belief that Euralille could become a hub for international firms operating on the European market. Again, there might be some change on the way. But there is still a risk that Lille will simply be bypassed. Instead, it is quite conceivable that the vertex points of the golden triangle of Paris–London–Brussels will continue to attract the internationally oriented activities

Table 5.2 provides a summary of the key data of property development at Euralille.

5.5 Euralille: evaluation

The redevelopment of the railway station in Lille is perhaps one of the best-known redevelopment projects in Europe. Although the widespread enthusiasm about this project has inspired others (especially governments and developers elsewhere in Europe), some critical comments have also been heard. Reviewing the redevelopment of the railway station area in Lille, four observations can be made.

The first two concern the actors and the process. The municipality has been the mainspring of the initiative. The mobilizing and binding role played by Pierre Mauroy epitomizes the process. Mayor for more than 20 years, president of the

Communauté Urbaine (the metropolitan government), former prime minister, senator and president of the Société d'Economie Mixte (SEM) Euralille, Mauroy has been the physical link between different levels of public decision-making, the private sector and the local population. Thanks to his multiple roles and political influence, he has been able to put together and maintain a solid coalition involving a broad spectrum of the local and regional élites, both public and private. This group first lobbied successfully to have the TGV stop in the city. Then they formed the study association Euralille, which later turned itself into the public–private partnership of the same name. To guarantee this cohesion as well as support and acceptance by outside interests, innovative negotiation and communication tools were conceived and applied. These innovations include Japanese-style quality circles, opinion polls among the local population, discussion forums, and public conferences with experts. On the side of the private sector, a particularly important factor has been the involvement since the outset of regional, national and international banks. Without their commitment, it would have been difficult, if not impossible, to carry the project through the difficult economic period. In contrast, the railway company SNCF had an essentially reactive role, limiting its action to the transport sphere. As in Zürich (Chapter 8), it can be argued that by so doing they may have reduced their risk, but they may also have missed the opportunity to profit fully from the development.

With regard to the process (the second observation) it was noted that the dimensions and the content of the project have been adapted many times in response to changing economic and political circumstances. The elements giving identity to the new parts of the city were, however, firmly committed at the outset. The ensuing flexible implementation mainly concerned the commercial parts. What has been finally built is impressive. But it is also important that allowance for future growth has been explicitly included in the plan and provided for in its implementation (for instance, office towers could still be added). The programme, while adhering to a strong overall concept, was conceived as a collection of independent and manageable projects to be implemented by autonomous agencies. For each project, specific investors and users have been sought. The vision (an accumulation of high-profile urban functions around the transport node and the related decisions and investments) is 'hard'. The way in which it materializes is 'soft': for instance, the amount of office floor space was reduced after negotiations with investors; amendments to the shopping content were made to protect the existing local businesses from competition; and project elements were transferred to adjacent municipalities to ensure their support.

The third and fourth observations deal with the concepts of *node* and *place*. As far as the node is concerned, the third observation focuses on the acquired nodal position within the north European high-speed train system. The increase in the accessibility of the station area in Lille is among the most spectacular. As cited, according to the FAST study commissioned by the European Union (Arenas *et al.*, 1995) Lille will be the most accessible city in Europe by the year 2020, up from eleventh place in 1991. The campaign promoting the project has capitalized on these facts, giving the material improvement a symbolic aura. Lille, and Euralille, have suddenly gained a place on the mental map of Europe. Interconnection is indeed the concept around which the whole plan revolves. It must be stressed, however, that not only the TGV has played a role. The Lille-

Europe/Flandres station complex also enjoys excellent connections to regional and metropolitan transport (TER, metro, tram) systems. Euralille is not just accessible by public transport; it is also directly connected to the motorway bypass (*périphérique*), and 6000 new car parking spaces have been provided. Improvements of all transport levels and modes have thus been an intrinsic part of the development. However, pedestrian connections to, from and through the area do not always make the grade. Neighbourhoods on the eastern side of the TGV tracks are difficult to reach from the station complex, but so also is the new congress and exhibition centre. Furthermore, transfers from one train station to the other are quite complicated and time-consuming, making actual TGV–TER integration difficult.

With regard to the place concept, since the programme was initially circumscribed, the leading idea has been to accumulate a dense 'urban mass' at the point where the degree of interconnection was highest, thanks to the TGV and the local and regional transport networks. The new high-profile functions that have been introduced include an international business centre, an international congress and exhibition centre, and a regional shopping centre. These exceptional elements have been deliberately embedded in a diverse urban district. An important aspect of public investment has been to ensure the diversity of functions. For example, besides offices and shops, other functions such as housing, education, recreation and culture have or will get a prominent place. The rich network of public spaces linking the elements to make a whole must be also seen as part of this 'urban' strategy. However, one question still to be answered in Lille is whether the new and the existing (station and neighbourhood) will develop a positive, dynamic relationship, or whether an island effect will prevail. The first appraisals of the impact of Euralille suggest that complementarity effects are prevailing. However, the current difficulties in marketing the offices raise doubts about the basic assumption that centrality in international transport networks would translate into centrality in international activity networks.

6
Utrecht Centrum Project and the Zuidas

6.1 Preamble: the national planning system

Perhaps surprisingly, Newman and Thornley (1996, pp. 27–76) categorize the Dutch planning system as belonging to the *Napoleonic family*. The basis of the system, from which the characterization is derived, is formed by its broad legal context, which consists of a Napoleonic code and a written constitution. In the Netherlands, there are three levels of government: the national government, provinces (12), and municipalities (572 in 1997). Each level of government has clearly circumscribed legislative and administrative powers. Within those bounds, it is autonomous as long as it does not conflict with the interests of higher authorities. The national government provides a framework (in the Physical Planning Act of 1965) prescribing the procedures for the physical plans of the other levels of government. Additionally, national spatial policy is formulated in Reports on Physical Planning (regularly revised), which run through a special legal procedure, the so-called National Physical Planning Key Decision. The Reports on Physical Planning are meant to coordinate sectoral policies and provide provinces and municipalities with guidelines for their physical plans.

Provinces provide a regional plan (*streekplan*), which is an administrative guideline for municipal plans. Municipalities, for their part, develop two kinds of physical plan: a structure plan (*structuurplan*) and a land-use plan (*bestemmingsplan*). The latter is legally binding for individuals as well as for other parties (including governments). Citizens can oppose any planning proposal at each level of government. Furthermore, developers have to apply for a building permit (which municipalities have to grant if it is in accordance with the land-use plan). Objections can also be raised with regard to building permits (ISOCARP, 1992, pp. 146–153). Compared with other countries, where the implementation of a physical plan is concerned municipalities in the Netherlands are richly equipped. Not only can they make use of public instruments such as compulsory purchase, but they are also actively engaged in the land market (see below).

The Dutch territory is covered with physical plans. These provide a high degree of certainty for developers as well as for citizens. Considering the density of plans, it is not surprising that one of the main points of discussion remains a perceived lack of flexibility (Needham *et al.*, 1993). Furthermore, a distinctive feature of the Dutch planning system is that municipalities have a very active land policy. A government hand in acquiring, servicing and selling land is common practice in most Dutch municipalities (Spit, 1995). This deeply affects the relationships between developers and governments. Of the three levels of government, the local level is by far the most important.

The emphasis in physical planning is on the local level. But, as far as the larger infrastructure projects are concerned, financing and planning is mainly the task of the national government. At the same time, private investors are becoming increasingly involved. The increasing reliance on private funding leads to complex situations when it is part of a wider process of change. Specifically, the complexity arises when private finance is combined with a decentralization tendency in physical planning and a centralization trend in the financing and planning of large infrastructure projects. And this is generally the case with railway station area redevelopment.

6.2 Context: railway station area redevelopment in the Netherlands

The publication in 1986 of the document *Verdichting rond stations* ('Densifying around stations') (Bureau voor Stedebouw Zandvoort, 1986) was a particularly explicit example of many signs that railway station area redevelopment was taking off in the Netherlands. In that document, jointly commissioned by the environment and transport ministries and by the Dutch railways, *densification* of station areas is advocated as the logical corollary of compact city policies and of the promotion of public transport. From that moment onwards, the context has evolved. The mixed success of the projects has forced the sponsors to reconsider the approach repeatedly. Still, the redevelopment of railway station areas has remained high on the government agenda, and is also climbing on the agenda of the market. In 1993 van Nierop identified as many as 50 station area projects in the country (Figure 6.1).

National land-use and transport policy has given strong impetus to the redevelopment of railway station areas in the Netherlands. Its most striking components are:

- *A location policy.* The 1988/91 national *Fourth Report on Physical Planning/Extra* (Ministry of Housing, Physical Planning and Environment, 1991a) pays special attention to mobility and urbanization issues. In particular, it expresses great concern for the negative effects of current transport trends on both the environment (pollution, energy and land consumption) and the economy (road congestion). Among other measures, an answer is sought in a location policy: the so-called ABC policy. Its main thrust is to promote the concentration of activities that generate passenger traffic around public transportation nodes.
- *Investment in public transport.* Based on the same environmental and economic considerations, public transport is strongly supported in the 1990

Second Transport Structure Plan. Accordingly, public transport accounts for a high share of government investment. For rail transport in particular, the aim of doubling the number of passengers in the year 2010 is formulated in the Rail 21 programme. Rail 21 is a countrywide package of projects resulting in the highest investment per kilometre of rail in Europe (*Rail Business Report*, 1994). That trend is reinforced by the special priority given by the current governing coalition to investment in transport infrastructure. Partly thanks to this impetus, the long-awaited construction of high-speed train links to France (HSL Zuid) and Germany (HSL Oost) is finally under way.

- *Urban key projects*. The Fourth Report also advocates reinforcing the competitive position of the main urban nodes, which are seen as the engines of economic growth. Strategic urban development projects promoted by municipalities and involving private partners – the so-called *key projects* – are deemed essential in reaching this goal, and are supported accordingly. In this way, national policy endorses city marketing initiatives of the municipalities, as well as their efforts to strengthen the role of the urban core. Essentially, city authorities are trying to attract service employment, and stem the outflow of middle-class residents. Several of the key projects are railway station area redevelopment projects, as in The Hague, Utrecht, Groningen, and Amersfoort.

While the national government has been defining the criteria for the allocation of subsidies, the initiative for specific projects has been typically taken up by municipalities (in most cases) and/or the railway company (until recently with essentially a transport focus). Relationships between these and other relevant actors (private actors, local transport companies, local interest groups) have not always been smooth. Especially in the more complex projects, this may have been the main stumbling block. One of the most ambitious station redevelopment plans in the country, the Utrecht Centrum Project (UCP, see below), is a good example of how difficulties in building consensus have had a paralysing effect (Bertolini, 1996b), but also of how a working understanding might be now emerging.

The picture is evolving. The Dutch railways (NS) are in the midst of a privatization process, the final outcome of which is still uncertain. NS is moving away from being a state bureaucracy providing transport services. It is moving towards becoming a private-style business, with transport of passengers and goods as its core activities. The commercial exploitation of stations and other property assets is seen as a complementary, profit-generating activity. Accordingly, NS is increasingly active in railway station area redevelopment. The process is slow, however. NS-Vastgoed, the property division of the railway company, was set up only in 1994.

The market sector – and particularly the role of actors as landowners, developers, investors, and their consultants – is gaining importance in railway station area redevelopment in the Netherlands. The financial involvement of these actors has been considered essential since the beginning. However, they have tended to remain sceptical about the potential of station areas. They argued that government policies should have been more selective in order to make private investment attractive. Seldom have private actors taken the initiative. The interesting innovations are projects at locations with both excellent public and

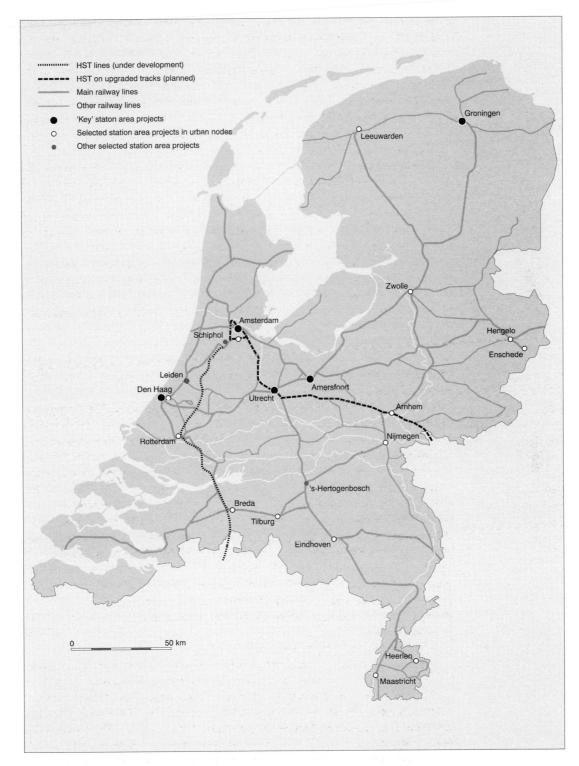

Legend:

.... HST lines (under development)

- - - - - - HST on upgraded tracks (planned)

———— Main railway lines

———— Other railway lines

● 'Key' staton area projects

○ Selected station area projects in urban nodes

● Other selected station area projects

Fig. 6.1 National railway network and main station area projects in the Netherlands.

private transport accessibility: the so-called 'B' locations in Dutch planning jargon. Intense market dynamics may for instance be observed around stations along the Amsterdam southern railway and motorway trajectory, as at Amsterdam Zuid-WTC (see below) and Amsterdam Bijlmer stations.

6.3 The Utrecht Centrum Project as node and place

6.3.1 The node

Because of its central position in the national railway network (Figure 6.1) Utrecht Centraal is the second biggest railway station in the country. About 110 000 passengers make daily use of the interchange (1997). An additional 65 000 leave or take buses or trams to or from this point. It is a node with intense growth prospects: the expectations are that by 2015 it will handle around 205 000 passengers a day, or almost double the present amount. The through station was already radically transformed in the 1970s by adopting a 'bridge over the tracks' design. Within the framework of the Rail 21 national investment programme, other ambitious infrastructure works have been completed more recently. For instance, there has been an increase in the number and multilevel branching of the tracks, and an adaptation of existing road underpasses. Other changes are planned for the near future. These include an extension of the platforms, a new car and bicycle tunnel, a new 'compact' bus station, new parking spaces for cars and bicycles, and rationalization of car access. Further expansions and adaptations will be required by the envisaged connection to the HST to Germany and to the new Randstad regional railway network.

Most importantly, following a recent joint initiative of all the transport operators active in the node, these and other new projects have been brought under the unifying plan for a Mainport Utrecht (GVU *et al.*, 1996). A one-terminal concept for the interchange will be applied (Figure 6.2). Here 200 000 passenger movements (exchanges) per day will take place. The same level of quality for all transport means must be obtained, and this quality must extend into the surroundings. Accessory commercial services (essentially shops) in the station will complement the transport services. Interchange will be the central concept. Priority will be given to the integrated logistics of the user, instead of that of autonomous transport companies. International, national and regional trains, and buses, trams, taxis and innovative forms of collective transport will all be accessible from a single 'station balcony'. This will require, among other measures, re-routeing bus and tram lanes next to the railway tracks, digging an east–west tunnel for local transport, and providing operational space underground – all under an enormous, futuristic station roof spanning 230×360 metres.

6.3.2 The place

The station area of Utrecht Centraal (Figure 6.3) has already been radically restructured once before. In the 1960s and 1970s, the congress and exhibition centre of the Jaarbeurs, then on the city side, was moved across the tracks to the west, peripheral side. Then Hoog Catharijne was built between the station and the historical city centre. This giant shopping and office complex, which also contains

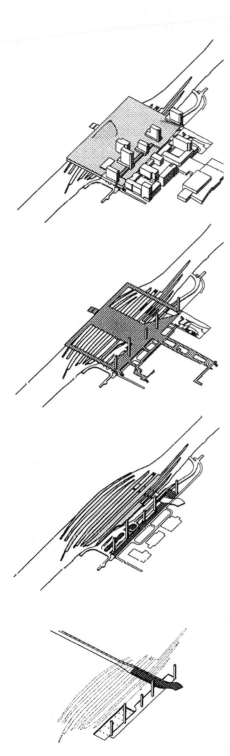

*Fig. 6.2 Utrecht Centraal, the
one-terminal concept. Levels from top
to bottom: roof; passenger hall;
north–south tracks and lanes
(HST, train, tram, and bus); east–west
tracks and lanes (tram and bus).
(Source: UCP)*

Fig. 6.3 UCP, the place. To the left of the tracks, the multifunctional complex of Hoog Catharijne and the historic city. To the right of the tracks, the congress and exhibition centre of the Jaarbeurs. (Source: UCP. Photo: KLM Aerocarto)

cultural and sports facilities and housing, was erected progressively. Details of this transformation are discussed below. In short, the balance of the operation was essentially positive in economic terms, though much more controversial in urban design terms. On the one hand, Hoog Catharijne has provided the centre of the economically dynamic city of Utrecht with the space it needed for the expansion of tertiary activities. This has been accomplished in conjunction with the provision of a highly accessible public transport node. On the other hand, the new shopping and office complex has severed the existing city from the station and neighbourhoods on the other side of the tracks. The location forces all pedestrian flows through a labyrinth of shops, and pours heavy traffic into the surroundings. Today, Utrecht is faced with a new round of similar issues. Following a leap in scale, tertiary activities demand yet more space and greater accessibility. This in turn exacerbates the unsolved difficulty of reconciling the concentration of functions and the growth of transport flows with the liveability of the area and its surroundings. However, this time the integration of these different dimensions is, at least in intention, being faced head on.

6.3.3 The process

Before embarking upon a discussion of the current development process, an account is needed of the previous round of area renewal. That is, it is necessary to review the process by which the Hoog Catharijne (HC) shopping and office complex was built next to Utrecht central station.

HC entered the Utrecht scene in 1962. At that time, a property developer approached the municipality with an integral restructuring plan for the central station area, next to the historic centre. The plan entailed moving the Koninklijke Jaarbeurs (KJ, the congress and exhibition centre) to the peripheral west side of the railway tracks. It also proposed the construction of Hoog Catharijne on the central east side, alongside an envisaged inner motorway ring. This modern complex was supposed to contain shops, offices, and cultural and recreational facilities. Visitors would enter HC from a raised, entirely pedestrian 'ground' floor connecting the station and the city centre, while motorized traffic would be segregated at street level. An ad hoc company, wholly private, would take charge of the design, construction and management of the complex.

The municipality responded enthusiastically. HC appeared to be a brilliant answer to the perceived shortage of space for tertiary development in the historic centre. Furthermore, it seemed to offer a way of adding value to the point of maximum accessibility of the national railway network. A contract with the developers was signed on 25 February 1964. These developers immediately started the implementation of the first phase. However, houses scheduled for demolition were occupied by students and homeless people, who claimed the premises for accommodation. Local groups, later supported in their claims by central government, also opposed filling in the historic canals to make way for the motorway. At the end of the 1960s, the opposition, structured in a multiplicity of interest groups, succeeded in having the canals as well as some residential buildings put on the list of protected monuments, thus forcing some amendments to be made to the plan. Also, local small businesses contested the plans, demanding better integration of the station, HC, and the existing city. The private partners of the municipality, however, remained inflexible. They felt unassailable, since their contract left little room for renegotiation. Construction thus started in 1968. In 1970, part of the complex was inaugurated, including the congress and exhibition centre, a hotel and a sports hall on the west side of the station. The other elements followed. The opposition had to gradually accept the facts. On 23 September 1973 Beatrix, then princess, opened the main component of the plan: a 75 000 m^2 shopping and office centre.

UCP, first round: towards the master plan
The linearity with which expansions of Hoog Catharijne follow one another from 1973 onwards is, however, only apparent. Its proven economic successes notwithstanding, there was growing criticism of the failure of the complex to integrate with its surroundings, of the resulting severance of the links between city and station, and of the insecurity of the public spaces. Also, from this evolved perception, in 1986 a new initiative was launched for the restructuring of the area, the Utrecht City Project (UCP). The new plan was promoted by the municipality, which was also the main landowner, in partnership with the other owners of land or buildings. These include the pension fund Algemeen Burgerlijk Pensioenfonds (ABP, since 1982 owner of HC), the congress and exhibition centre Koninklijke Jaarbeurs (KJ), and the national railway company Nederlandse Spoorwegen (NS). The initiative responded to several demands. It was partly an effort to solve the cited architectural and urban design shortfalls of the station area through the abatement of barrier and island effects. At the same time, the initiative sought to improve the quality of the public spaces and to diversify the functions. It further sought to reduce car dependence, which was a precondition for obtaining central government funding. But a central objective was also to strengthen the position of the station area and of the city as a location for high-profile tertiary activities.

In 1988 an agreement in principle was reached by the four partners, and a master plan was expected to follow. The reality proved to be much more complicated. Before the master plan, many other plans had to be made, including two interim reports in 1989 and 1991. The most important cause of the delay was the inability to reach firm agreement within the partnership, but there was also increasing pressure on the public actor from local interest groups. In February 1990 inhabitants and environmentalists joined forces in an umbrella group, the Bewoners Overleg City Project (BOCP), to challenge the plan. Once again, their example was followed by small businesses of the central city. The main issues brought forward by BOCP were the traffic impact, the volume of offices, the disappearance of existing green space, and the feared adverse consequences for municipal resources and services. In 1990 a discussion platform was started by the municipality to deal with these concerns. After alternating fortunes, the platform was definitively stopped in 1992. An independent consultancy (Agora) was then commissioned by the municipality to organize the public debate. They too had only partial success. From the discussions, it emerged that two quite distinct interpretations of the UCP existed. On the one hand there was the view held by the partnership, led by compact city and economic policy objectives, with liveability as a by-product. On the other hand there was the vision of the politically active part of the population, centred around liveability and environmental issues. From the latter viewpoint, the development of activities around the station was essentially seen as a way to pay for the measures to improve liveability.

While public discussion continued, plan-making proceeded, without much interaction between the two processes, within the public–private partnership. A master plan was finally presented in May 1993 (Gemeente Utrecht *et al.*, 1993; Figure 6.4). It was an ambitious plan, envisaging far-reaching intervention in the infrastructure, around 300 000 m^2 of offices, 25 000 m^2 of shops, and almost 1000 apartments. However, it was also a weak plan. In the first place it was not signed by ABP. Furthermore, support by other partners – NS, the Jaarbeurs – was either partial or passive. In particular, as would emerge later, each of the partners had some fundamental reservations about the plan. ABP was afraid of competition for its indoor shopping centre from the envisaged new shopping developments at street level. NS was not convinced by the financial calculations. And the Jaarbeurs did not see the added value of an active involvement. All three, it must be said, were also in the process of more or less extensive reorganization. This implied that company objectives and approaches had to be redefined before firm commitments could be made. New discussions with local interests followed the publication of the master plan. Among these, the prevailing feeling was that to the injury of being excluded from the real negotiations was added the insult of being consulted only when decisions had already been taken. Objections were answered with rather vague statements such as 'will be researched further', 'will be reconsidered and researched', or 'will be striven for'.

Indeed, the municipality did not appear to be intimidated by local criticism. Rather, it appeared to be more worried by the reservations of the private partners. And it also seemed to be concerned about the queries posed by central government, on which essential funding depended, suggesting that the national authorities were not convinced of the financial feasibility of the project. The picture was

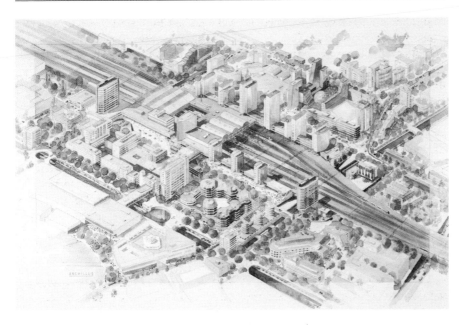

Fig. 6.4 The 1993 UCP master plan; artist's impression. (Source: Stuurgroep UCP)

made more problematic by the uncertainty emerging on the property markets, especially in the area of office development.

UCP, second round: the development company
In December 1993, all of the above notwithstanding, a framework agreement (*raamovereenkomst*) for the establishment of a new public–private partnership incorporating the municipality and three of the biggest property development companies in the country (MBO, Mabon Wilma, and Multi-Development Corporation) was presented to and approved by the city council. The local authority would play a leading role, ensuring that public policy objectives would not be subordinated to business objectives. For this reason, it would participate with 51% of the shares (and financing). But in exchange for their willingness to take on part of the risk, market interests would also get certain guarantees. One was a guarantee of direct involvement in plan-making (the important decisions had to be supported by a 75% majority in the partnership). Another was assured priority in the assignment of future development rights (also an incentive to reach the implementation stage).

The agreement reached with the private developers was cited by the city executive as a demonstration of the viability of the initiative. However, some of the most important interests in the area – the railways, the owners of HC and the Jaarbeurs – were not represented. The dialogue with the railways continued, but no formal agreement was yet possible, mainly because of the uncertain implications of the ongoing reorganization of the company. With ABP (the owner of HC), the arrangement was to 'negotiate further on the basis of additional information'. With both NS and ABP, the municipality would establish a 'structural consultation'. In general, it was indeed recognized that informing and consulting with higher administrative levels, citizens, interest groups and others was one of the primary tasks of the development company. It was also recognized that

95

communication with the local population and interest groups had been insufficient in the past, as opposed to regular contacts with private partners, investors, and higher levels of government. A possible solution was to distinguish degrees of partnership (and the 'selective participation' it demanded), especially where the public responsibilities of the municipality were concerned. The city council were to have the first and the last word at every step with relevant policy implications. These intentions were reinforced by the ascendancy, in the spring of 1994, of a new 'solution- and consultation-oriented' city executive. The name of the

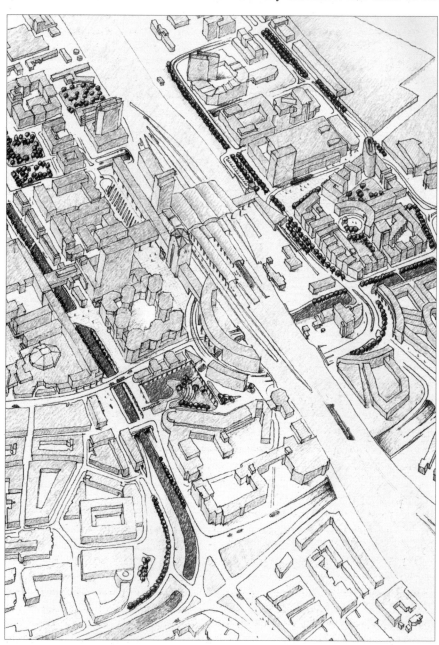

Fig. 6.5 The 1995 spatial functional concept; artist's impression. (Source: Ontwikkelingsmaatschappij UCP)

initiative changed too. It was no longer called the Utrecht City Project but became known as the Utrecht Centrum Project, possibly to avoid reference to a supposed 'Manhattanization' of Utrecht.

The expectation of the development company was that an initial development phase – covering all the steps from research and evaluation to formalization of a development plan in a land-use plan with judicial powers – would take about 15 months. A land-use plan (*bestemmingsplan*) was thus expected by the spring of 1995. However, the first phase of the work (evaluation and research) was not completed until June 1995, when a *spatial–functional* concept was published. The document (Ontwikkelingsmaatschappij UCP, 1995; Figure 6.5) – a rather conventional urban design plan – was seen as a basis for consultation with the local population, potential investors, firms located in the area, higher administrative levels, and other interests. It was determined that, after the consultation, the development company and the municipality 'would decide on the further progress of the plan-making'. The expectation was that construction could start in 1996, and that the plan would be completed in 2004. However, it was also recognized that the document had only a draft status, partly 'depending on the measure of the agreement to be reached with third parties'. And this remained a problem, as uncertainties about central government financing and, perhaps more importantly, structural contrasts with the other long-term interests in the area (NS, ABP and Jaarbeurs) were still in the way.

UCP, third round: the administrative platform

Little progress was made over the following months. It became increasingly clear that direct involvement of the three key actors – the railways (NS), the owners of the shopping complex (ABP), and the congress and exhibition centre (Jaarbeurs) – would be unavoidable. At last, communication channels started working again. In February 1996, after a (negative) joint evaluation of the existing spatial–functional concept, a *bestuurlijk platform* (administrative platform) was put in place, involving all four key actors. For the first time, it seemed, there was enough awareness of how much each one needed the others to pursue its own objectives. And for the first time, it seemed that those individual objectives had been defined clearly enough to allow substantial negotiations.

The results were indeed striking. After only four months of intense discussions, facilitated by an external process manager and assisted by an urban designer, an *oplossingsrichting* (solution guideline) was published in June (Figure 6.6). That document analysed some of the fundamental contradictions, and pointed out some possible solutions. In four months, the area's potential and problems were (once again) surveyed. The survey was based on interviews with residents, public officers, politicians, and property owners. An agreement was reached on a new spatial functional concept, or 'what the ground plan will look like – which buildings will be demolished and where new buildings will come' (*Nspirit*, 1996, p. 19). The development company appeared to have been forgotten. But with a little exaggeration, it can be said that more had been achieved in those four months than in the preceding eight years! The enthusiasm among the four partners was palpable. The general feeling was that the decisive point of no return was about to be reached. Also, other actors, including the local opposition, seemed to share the perception that 'this was the real thing'. They appreciated the declared

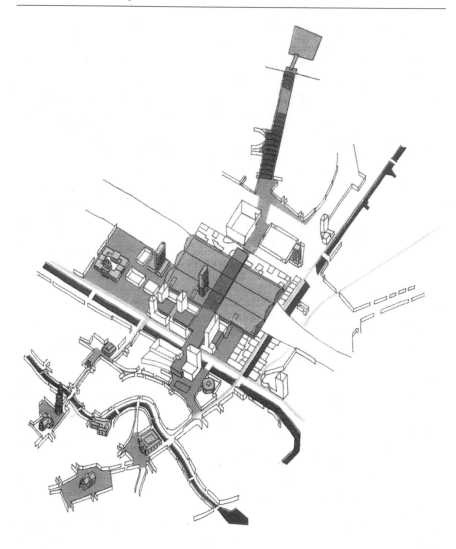

Fig. 6.6 Solution guideline: the system of open spaces, integrating station and city (as elaborated in the VSO). (Source: UCP)

intention of dealing more openly with subsequent stages. In October, NS-Vastgoed (representing NS and the other public transport companies), the Jaarbeurs, Winkelbeleggingen Nederland (representing ABP, owner of HC) and the municipality signed an intentional agreement. That document laid down the results of the negotiations up to that point and, most importantly, defined the financial approach. In essence, each of the partners was to develop its own areas, and the surpluses were to feed into a common purse to finance – together with central government subsidies – the unprofitable elements.

After further elaborations and consultations, a *voorlopig stedebouwkundig ontwerp* (VSO, provisional urban design plan) was presented by the administrative platform in February 1997 (Figure 6.7). The fundamental lines of the guideline were maintained, but there were important emphases that led to some resistance and tempered the general enthusiasm. In particular, a *stadsboulevard* (city boulevard), including a new east–west tunnel and added capacity to radial access roads, was proposed to solve the accessibility–liveability issue (see below). However,

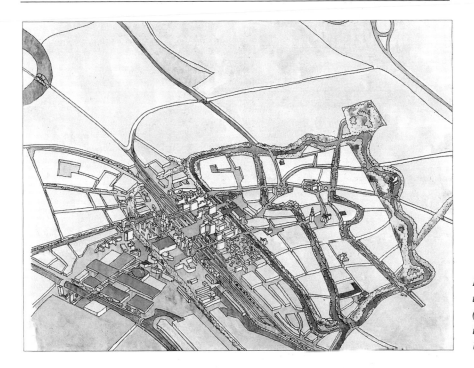

Fig. 6.7 Provisional urban design plan (VSO); artist's impression. (Source: UCP)

local groups and members of the city council contested these accents. They demanded clarification of the impact of what they saw as a new inner ring with access routes through surrounding residential neighbourhoods. Also, the volume of offices and other commercial functions, especially on the west side of the tracks, was considered excessive. Those functions were seen as detrimental to the liveability of the area and a threat to the economic base of the existing city.

The VSO, after consultations and further studies, should lead to (a) a definitive urban design plan (*definitief stedebouwkundig ontwerp*, DSO) and (b) a legally binding local plan (*bestemmingsplan*), which would be submitted to formal consultation and then to debate and a vote in the city council. In the summer of 1997, reactions to the VSO were being considered by the administrative platform. That entity would then propose a DSO to the city executive. This should happen by November 1997, so that before the end of the year it could be presented to the city council, which ultimately has to give the green light. The urban design plan could then be translated into a *bestemmingsplan*, or the point of no return. If the council, as hoped by the four partners, approves the plan by the end of 1997, then construction could start in 1998, and the whole project could be ready by 2008.

Table 6.1 summarizes the main phases of the process.

6.4 Property development at the Utrecht Centrum Project

6.4.1 Hoog Catharijne

There has been no unanimous evaluation of the successive waves of re-development plans for the Utrecht central station area. The different interpretations of the Utrecht Centrum Project (UCP, formerly the Utrecht City Project) can be

Table 6.1 Utrecht Centrum Project: summary of the main phases

---

Phase 1: Hoog Catharijne, 1962–1973

1962	A property developer proposes to the municipality an integral restructuring plan for the station area, to have the name of Hoog Catharijne (HC)
25 February 1964	Contract between the developer and municipality signed
	Public protests
1968	Construction of HC starts
23 September 1973	Inauguration of the main component of the plan: a 75 000 m² shopping centre
	Economic success but public criticism

Phase 2: rise and fall of the public–private partnership, 1986–1993

1986	The Utrecht City Project (UCP), a new initiative for the station area, is launched by the municipality, the Algemeen Burgerlijk Pensioenfonds (ABP), the Jaarbeurs, and the national railway company NS
1988	An 'agreement in principle' is reached by the four partners
	Public concern
May 1993	Master plan is presented. ABP does not sign it; NS signs with reservations
	Contrasts within the partnership

Phase 3: rise and fall of the municipality–developers company, 1993–1995

December 1993	A framework agreement for the establishment of a development company incorporating the municipality and three property development firms is approved by the city council
	Former partners are out of the planning process; public concern continues
June 1995	The development company publishes a 'spatial–functional concept'
	Contrasts with former partners and public not solved

Phase 4: rise of a stakeholders' platform, 1996–1997

February 1996	After a (destructive) joint evaluation of the spatial–functional concept, an administrative platform is started, involving the original four key actors
June 1996	The solution guideline is published
	Elaborations and consultations
February 1997	The provisional urban design plan is presented
	Public reactions
End 1997	Expected presentation of a definitive urban design plan to the city council

Phase 4: implementation, 1998–2008

1998	Hoped for construction start, so that the whole project could be built, in phases, by 2008

---

traced to the different perceptions of Hoog Catharijne (HC), of its economic success as well as its failures in other respects. Thus that is where we shall start our review. In 1991 HC contained offices (149 500 m^2), shopping and restaurants/catering (74 000 m^2), hotels (19 000 m^2), housing (350 units), four cinemas, a sports hall, a music centre with two concert halls, and congress and exhibition spaces (94 500 m^2). All were part of a vast complex stretching along two sides of the tracks and containing the railway station, reconstructed according to a 'bridge over the tracks' model parallel to the development of HC. The impact of HC on the city has been the object of repeated analyses. Reviewing the studies done thus far, Ottens and Ter Welle-Heethuis (1983, p. 393) concluded that HC 'has prevented the erosion of the central function of the historic centre and has determined an increment of the employment.' From these and successive studies, it emerges that the retail (commercial) supply of HC is complementary, rather than competitive, to that of the city centre. A specialization trend can be recognized in the geographical origin of the visitors: mainly internal to the city for the town centre, mainly external for HC. Also, the supply of tertiary space appears to be complementary. HC would function mainly to attract business from outside the city, while the city centre would function as an incubator of new activities. The trade fair has also benefited from the HC operation. Once it had been relocated on the other side of the tracks, it profited from more space and increased accessibility, reinforcing its role as one of the two main congress and exhibition centres in the country. Finally, the interaction with the public transport node has also been reciprocally beneficial. The shopping centre and the station have fed into each other. In 1993, 74% of the people who went to HC that year (approximately 25 million) got there by public transport (Gemeente Utrecht *et al.*, 1993).

More ambiguous or even negative are the effects on the surrounding neighbourhoods. Between 1974 (a year after the opening of the shopping centre) and 1980, the streets connecting HC with the cathedral, which is the symbolic centre of the city, had seen on average a 32% growth in the number of passers-by. Yet the streets that had been 'cut off' registered a 46% decline (Bogaard, 1981). In the areas marginalized by development, negative effects have added to the loss of visitors. These other effects include an increase in vehicle through-traffic and a fall in property values. A similar drain on resources was also felt by the municipal treasury. Given the difference between the variable interest rates applied to the city debts and the fixed rates applied to the rent paid by HC for using the area, the treasury registered an annual loss of several million guilders (Kargadoor, 1979). Another negative point turned up in the evaluation of the architecture and urban design qualities of the complex. HC has deprived the city of a direct relationship with its station, eliminating any alternative to the labyrinthine path across the shopping centre. That shopping centre can hardly be defined as a part of the city. Beyond the shops and the (invisible) offices, there is little else. The residential function has been nearly banned, and the few dwellings that are present are invisible too. The monofunctionality of HC has produced other monofunctionality. Because HC is not a pleasant place to be, hotels, restaurants and cafes have multiplied in the historic centre, as well as specialized shops. There those establishments have thrived, above all at the cost of the residential functions and retail sector serving daily needs.

Master plan (1993)

The programme of the Utrecht City Project envisaged by the 1993 master plan (Gemeente Utrecht *et al*., 1993; Figure 6.4) in response to these shortcomings is ambitious. The UCP foresees extensive infrastructure works. These include the addition and multiple branching of tracks (in the long term, also an extension of the platforms and a second passenger hall); the construction of a new tunnel for cars and bicycles; a dedicated tram line; new bus lines and a bus station; new car and bicycle parking space; and adaptations of the street layout. With regard to activities, it proposes the addition of offices (268 000–332 000 m²), shopping, cafes, restaurants and hotels (23 000–28 000 m²), housing (945–975 units), a third concert hall, a casino, an extra cinema, a theatre, and art galleries. The massive programme is not justified merely by citing urban design insufficiencies, nor by pointing to economic and public transport developments alone. As in other station projects in the Netherlands and elsewhere in Europe (Bertolini, 1996b), financial feasibility calculations weigh heavily. In essence, the profits generated by all the offices are indispensable to cover the high infrastructure costs and the other 'nice things for the city'.

The plan of the public–private partnership is however not the only possible 'definition of reality'. In 1992, the Bewoners Overleg City Project (BOCP, a coalition of local residents and environmentalists active since 1990) published its own analysis of the UCP (BOCP, 1992). This document typifies later local reactions and thus warrants a brief discussion here.

The BOCP chose, provocatively, to base its reasoning on the needs of the user, not on the need to balance the budget. This choice implied a series of requirements:

- The project had to be multifunctional.
- The public spaces must not be dominated by large-scale facilities.
- The plan must reflect the needs of the area, not trade-offs between what is imposed by the central government and what is desired by developers.
- The impact of traffic on the quality of public spaces must be more seriously considered.
- Natural features must be protected and expanded.
- Noise caused by trains had to be controlled at the source so that residential areas would not have to be confined to marginal locations.
- 10% of the dwellings must be social housing, including apartments for disabled persons.
- Existing buildings and structures that were in good condition had to be put to better use and not demolished.

The BOCP also demanded more clarity on the part of the municipality with reference to financial forecasts and deals, as well as regarding the continuation of the project's intentions in future management policy. Finally, the BOCP wanted the local authority to give priority to the unemployed of the surrounding areas in the allocation of jobs, and to provide shelter for the beggars and homeless who have been using HC at night. On the positive side, the BOCP appreciated the intentions of the partnership plan to improve the security of the public space and especially the ground floor, to invest in public transport, and to improve the connections between the railway station and the city.

The BOCP was not the only voice of discontent. The small businesses of the city centre also criticized the UCP. The critique voiced by the small business community was of a rather different nature from that expressed by the inhabitants. The paramount preoccupation was the accessibility of the historic city. Just like 20 years earlier with regard to their demands for HC, they asked for more parking space for cars, a ring road, an underground metro, and more bicycle paths and parking. Fearing overwhelming competition they also opposed the development of new retail and public functions on the west side of the tracks. However, they supported the idea of strengthening the HC shopping centre on the first-floor level (that entailed possible expansion at the ground level), but the business community also called for investment to make the rest of the city centre more pleasant and safe. In general, they were perplexed by the growing concentration of the retail sector in the city.

Spatial–functional concept (1995)

Criticism such as that paraphrased above has been partially acknowledged by the public–private development company that was established at the end of 1993 to turn the master plan into a spatial–functional concept (SFC). The objectives adopted by the SFC (Ontwikkelingsmaatschappij UCP, 1995) reiterated the general objectives of the master plan: realization of high-quality public transport facilities and reduction of automobility; realization of high-quality public spaces, strengthening of the economic structure of the city and region; and concentration of labour-intensive employment around the public transport node. In particular, it stressed how strong the components in the railway station area were (IIC, the Jaarbeurs, the transportation node), but how weak their integration was (as shown in the quality of the public spaces). A bit ambiguously, the poor accessibility of the area by car was seen as a problem as well.

The SFC (Figure 6.5) tried to answer these problems by proposing a spatial structure that could guarantee the functionality of the individual elements, and coordination of the whole. On the functional side, the point of departure is that the UCP must become an integrated element of the city centre. The most important condition for achieving this is the concentration of diverse attractive functions. The mixture of functions will also help to reinforce the economic structure of the area. However, in terms of the quantities proposed, the new plan did not deviate much from the 1993 master plan. There was a little less emphasis on offices (down to 255 000 m^2) and a little more emphasis on housing (up to 1100 units), possibly as a reaction to the prevailing poor prospects in the office property market. With regard to accessibility, a double-pronged approach was proposed: improve access to the area by car, but at the same time give priority to pedestrians. Supposedly, this apparent contradiction could be resolved by bringing as much traffic as possible underground.

In general, the SFC deals more with urban design than with programmatic issues. This should not come as a surprise, as the main functional actors in the area (ABP, NS, Jaarbeurs) were not involved in working out the plan. In trying to overcome this evident lack of external support and consultation, as well as the confusion among the market partners, great emphasis was given to flexibility of implementation. Accordingly, the leading criterion for the approach to financial matters was the ability to deal with changing circumstances. Development was to take place in phases within circumscribed sub-areas. This would make it easier to control the cash flow and allow for the transfer of functions within the project area. It would also make it possible to call development to a halt (perhaps temporarily) after any one of the steps. The idea was that each phase should be self-financing, at least in principle. A land-exploitation budget would be the most important instrument to direct decision-making on financial matters. Also, to increase flexibility, the construction of offices, shops and housing would as far as possible be kept separate from the construction of infrastructure, which would necessarily have to follow other procedures. Behind this separation lies the crux of the matter: the project is feasible only if central government and third parties 'do their part'. But the impression remains that fundamental problems could not be solved because fundamental partners were not involved.

6.4.4 Solution guidelines (1996)

The document entitled *UCP: analyse, diagnose en oplossingsrichting* ('UCP: analysis, diagnosis and solution guidelines') was published in June 1996 (Bestuurlijk Platform UCP, 1996). It shows what can be done if the 'real' interests are brought together. The spatial–functional concept of 1995 was cited as its basis, but in practice that basis seems to have been abandoned. More important is the fact that some crucial dilemmas of the development are finally being confronted. In this document, a way forward is agreed upon by the key actors. Its point of departure is an analysis of the strengths and weaknesses of the area. The strengths are the 'enormous' demand for offices due to the central position in the country, the 'biggest' public transport node, the popularity of HC and of Utrecht's historic centre, and the international reputation of the Jaarbeurs. The weaknesses are the widespread perception of the area as unpleasant and insecure, and the ambiguities in the organization of functions (what is public? what is private?), as well as in the connections between the railway station, HC, the congress and exhibition complex, and the city centre.

The guidelines concentrate on the layout of public space. This is seen as the crucial point of intervention in solving the problems (Figure 6.6). While still allowing for flexibility, the envisaged solutions require radical intervention; and that would never have been possible without the commitment of the four key actors. Parts of the HC shopping centre will be demolished, and others will be drastically altered. The Jaarbeurs will embark on an ambitious programme to diversify its activities in the culture and entertainment sphere. The national railways, together with the local transportation companies, will pursue a total concept for the node, with all transportation flows being handled under one roof.

While much is asked of the partners, the new configuration of the area offers some clear advantages for each of them. The present route from the historic city through the shopping centre and to the congress and exhibition centre is both maintained and reinforced by keeping pedestrians at the first level (a condition posed by HC). However, the labyrinthine shopping centre will be transformed into a true shopping mall, with two spacious and airy cross-axes. It will have no more than four entrances – instead of the 15 it has at present – each abutting on a public square or park. A direct and open link between the railway station and the city is achieved by demolishing part of HC and replacing it by a station square. From the square, people can enter a new railway station balcony, giving access to all the different transport networks. The new 'total' station will also be a link between the city centre and the western districts on the other side of the tracks.

The document (Bestuurlijk Platform UCP, 1996) is more generic on programmatic and accessibility issues. It is said only that the office content will have to be substantial, in view of the great demand (the property market and the economy are picking up), but also to finance the many unprofitable elements. Furthermore, the congress and exhibition grounds are indicated as a good location for large-scale public functions, because of the availability of space and the excellent accessibility by car. Specifically, the location is considered suitable for a casino, a mega-cinema, and event halls, all functions that would be difficult to fit into the old city. Even more generic is the section of the document referring to traffic issues. The need to overcome the barrier effect of north–south rail and road infrastructure is reiterated. But no details are given, as 'it must be further researched and elaborated how the traffic in the future will pass through the area' (Bestuurlijk Platform UCP, 1996, p. 15).

6.4.5 VSO (1997)

Some key choices that were presented in the 1996 guidelines are courageous; they are testimony to a breakthrough. However, as mentioned, some delicate issues still have to be solved. The provisional urban design plan (*voorlopig stedebouwkundig ontwerp*, VSO), which was published in February 1997, was meant to provide answers. The document (Figures 6.6–6.8) begins by restating the general objectives of the UCP (improvement of public space etc.). What follows is more interesting. The main problem, according to the analysis, is the barrier that the area forms between the eastern and western parts of the city. The main objective is to give clarity – and a feeling of security – to the pedestrian public spaces, integrating them into the existing networks (Figure 6.6). The solutions entail reinforcing the axis formed by the city centre and the congress and exhibition centre, improving – with a new station square – the relationship between the city centre and the railway station, and realizing a new station complex, in accordance with the 'one-terminal' concept (Figure 6.2). The key indications of the 1996 guidelines are thus maintained.

There are some important urban design specifications. Possibly the most striking one is the so-called 'city boulevard' (*stadsboulevard*, Figure 6.8). The city boulevard is seen as a means to solve the accessibility–liveability dilemma. Existing roads will be upgraded into a four-lane ring road around the area. They will lead to underground parking garages (for a net total of 11 600 car parking spaces, against a net total of 21 000 bicycle parking spaces). The ring will also provide bus lanes and bicycle paths and footpaths. It will be lined with rows of trees, and will run along the canals. As a result, while performing necessary traffic distribution functions, it will also become an integral part of the network of public spaces. Accompanying measures (such as park and ride, integral parking and accessibility management, detour of through traffic, but also development of attractive alternatives) will help to check traffic flows. Even so, the guidelines state that in the light of the ambitious programme, and all transport alternatives

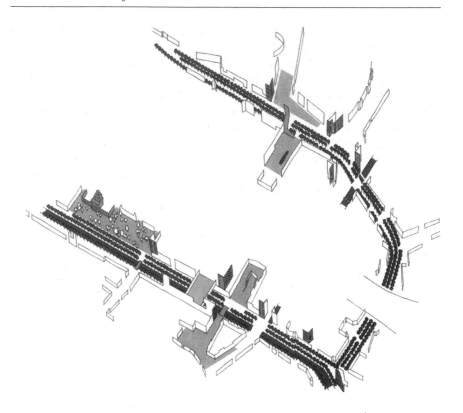

Fig. 6.8 VSO, the city boulevard: solution of the accessibility–liveability dilemma? (Source: UCP)

notwithstanding, car traffic in and to the area will increase. The ambivalent, dilatory conclusion is that

> For the next planning phase the issues will be: 'How can the quality of access to the UCP area for all transportation means be guaranteed, without this being at the expense of both the development of the location and the liveability in the existing city?' (Utrecht Centrum Project, 1997, p. 12)

Besides providing a more detailed approach to traffic issues, a second crucial clarification has been made with respect to the 1996 guidelines. Now, building volumes must be indicated in detail. Compared with previous plans, the programme envisages more offices (around 360 000 m^2), most of which will be concentrated on the west side. Also on the west side there are large-scale urban entertainment functions (including casino, mega-cinema, mega-theatre, urban entertainment centre, and food courts). Most of the new dwellings (of a total of 1845 housing units, or about 220 000 m^2) are concentrated on the east side, where the music centre will be expanded. The new activities are expected to generate no less than 20 000 new jobs. The office supply will be diverse, not only in size and in market segment (about 15% in the most and least expensive segments, about 35% in the two middle segments), but also in the sort of office environments represented. Rather than following actual demand, an innovative product will be created on an already desirable location, including a new business centre on the western station square (about 100 000 m^2, complete with accessory services and possibly a World Trade Centre). Also, the housing supply will be varied, but with a net prevalence of apartments for sale (85%).

An important issue is the financial strategy. It has been decided that each of the long-term partners will develop its own areas, to avoid the complications of redistribution of values. At the same time, the surpluses will feed into a common purse to partly finance – together with central government subsidies – the un-profitable elements. Each partner's share in the common purse will be determined on the basis of the development capacity that the plan allocates to its areas. Phasing will be crucial, with each step seen as a self-supporting (and self-financing) whole. Land development costs are estimated at 1 billion guilders. To that amount 600 million guilders must be added for upgrading of the transport network (also outside the area), and 200 million guilders to renovate the transportation terminal. If construction costs are included, the total amount of investment in the area would add up to 3 billion guilders in ten years (1998– 2008). However, a detailed financial plan will be presented only in the definitive urban design plan, at which point a detailed infrastructure plan will be elaborated. The citizens of Utrecht will incur no costs – or so the planners say – when the plans are carried out. All the investments will be financed by property revenues and by central government subsidies.

Table 6.2 gives an overview of the main structural data.

Table 6.2 Utrecht Centrum Project; main structural data

Area ownership	Mostly Utrecht municipality and NS; ABP and Jaarbeurs have long-term land leaseholds
Total floor area	616 700 m² (net, excluding leisure)
Offices	360 000 m² (30 000 m² substitution)
Housing	221 400 m² (1845 units)
Shops	42 700 m² (5000 m² substitution)
Hotels, restaurants, cafes	9600 m²
Culture	18 000 m² (concert hall)
Leisure	Casino, megatheatre, multiplex cinema, food and leisure court, urban entertainment centre, etc.
Parking	4000 extra (11 600 total) car; 9000 extra (21 000 total) bicycle
Costs (excluding main infrastructure)	3 billion guilders (of which 1 billion guilders land development costs, to be recovered through land rents)

6.5 Utrecht Centrum Project: evaluation

The future of the Utrecht Centrum Project has long been overshadowed by its previous history. In an earlier form it entailed the development of Hoog Catharijne. Essentially, it represents one of the most complex redevelopment processes in Europe. Added to the previous experience, there are numerous constraints and complicating factors in this particular area. Nevertheless, the ambitions of all actors involved are still high. A reconstruction of this particular case as presented above is instructive to anyone involved in redevelopment processes of this kind of area in Europe. Four observations are particularly relevant. The first concerns the actors involved, with reference to their past experiences.

The Utrecht Centrum Project story shows how the quality of the relationships among an array of heterogeneous actors conditions the outcome of station area projects. In Utrecht, no feasible plans were possible until a positive working relationship had been developed between the main actors in the area. Those actors are the municipality, the railways, the owners of the shopping centre, and the managers of the congress and exhibition centre. That paved the way for progress. In a few months, more progress was made than in the years that had passed since the initiative was launched. The breakthroughs demonstrated by the solution guidelines must in the first place be explained by this new quality of the interaction between the actors. It was also important that the internal reorganization processes, in which all the partners were involved, had reached a stage where they could seriously commit themselves to the project. Maintenance of this quality throughout the period of implementation and beyond appears to be a crucial condition in achieving the ambitious plans. By contrast, less appears to have changed in the quality of the communication with local interests. This remains a weak point of the project. The problem is that it is extremely difficult, and not very credible, to involve the population when they are under the impression that the fundamental decisions have been already made elsewhere.

The second observation concerns the node–place concept, and specifically the node element in that concept. The station of Utrecht Centraal has historically been the hub of the Dutch national railway network. This position has meant that, while Utrecht is a medium-sized city of around 230 000 inhabitants and only the fourth largest in the country, its station is the second biggest, just behind Amsterdam Centraal. The Utrecht transport node is in continuous flux. It has recently been expanded and adapted. It is going to be further strengthened by an HST link to Germany and to Schiphol Airport. Most importantly, a one-terminal concept is being pursued by all the transport operators active in the node. The integrated perception of the user, rather than the compartmentalized perspective of the transport operators, will be the guiding criterion. If implemented, the one-terminal concept would redress the present shortcoming of the node: the difficulty of intermodal transfers. The changes foreseen are enormous, not just in physical but also in organizational terms. Once central government financing is definitively ensured, the far-reaching reconstruction of the infrastructure would have to be coordinated with continuing transportation services and with the ambitious urban development programmes also being pursued. Cooperation between transport operators would have to be maintained in the implementation and management phases; and cooperation is imperative in the face of an ongoing privatization process that will affect each and every one of them. In all likelihood, the new interchange of Utrecht Centraal could (and should) be the proving ground for an innovative node-management formula.

The third observation is complementary to the second. It focuses on the place element in the node–place concept. As a place, Utrecht Centraal, including its surroundings, is faced in a particularly explicit way with one of the most difficult dilemmas of railway station area redevelopment. On the one hand, the area is a highly accessible place, attracting concentrations of high-profile functions. On the other hand, it is part of a wider urban fabric, often of a totally different order. In Utrecht, pressures for further concentration of functions come from the market, but also from national and local policies, both economic and environmental. A crucial task of the UCP initiative is to allow both the station area and the surrounding neighbourhoods to develop autonomously while ensuring that complementarity rather than destructive competition prevails. Such a task has many dimensions. These include realizing the quality and continuity of the public spaces, managing traffic to and through the area, and managing spatial competition between economic activities. The current plans for the Utrecht Centrum Project face these issues with more clarity than has been demonstrated in earlier attempts. A great effort has been made to abate barrier effects and provide for pleasant open spaces, to look for ways to neutralize the negative effects of traffic, and to harmonize new activities with existing ones. Some questions are still awaiting answers, however. The envisaged city boulevard solution to the dilemma of accessibility by car versus liveability of public spaces and the surroundings still has to be verified. The enormous concentration of new office and entertainment functions on the west side, combined with the existing congress and exhibition facilities and with much better car accessibility, could result in the emergence there of a sort of autonomous edge city, at odds with the rest of the station area and the surrounding residential neighbourhoods.

The fourth observation deals with the interaction between node and place. Utrecht Centraal is an evolving transport node. Expansion and adaptation of the infrastructure is likely to be a never-ending story. This makes any plan for the area highly dependent on the many uncertainties of financing and implementing infrastructure works. On the place side, the volatility of the property market only makes matters worse. The project is founded on the assumption of a high and growing demand for office space at the station. Also, other elements of the functional programme depend heavily on how the markets respond. In order to deal with this combination of uncertainties, implementation of the UCP will be through independent subprojects, each being as autonomous from the others as possible. Furthermore, 'hard' and 'soft' elements have been combined in the development approach in an attempt to shape certainties while allowing for flexibility. In Utrecht, one of the hard elements is the condition of self-financing of the whole and of each of its parts. Another is the implementation of the traffic distribution scheme and of the open spaces plan. A permanent consultation structure among the main actors is also seen as a hard condition. 'Soft' refers to how all this will be implemented. Accordingly, the planning instrument will be a legally binding local plan (*bestemmingsplan*), but one that would allow 'the possibility of being further specified'(a so-called Article 11 plan). It will have a process orientation, following an 'if . . . then' structure.

6.6 The Zuidas as node and place

6.6.1 The node

At present, Amsterdam Zuid – the main station in the Zuidas development area – is a secondary station located on Amsterdam's southern railway bypass. It is

Fig. 6.9 Amsterdam Zuid and the Zuidas in the metropolitan context. (Source: DRO, Amsterdam)

served by two intercity train services (connecting Schiphol airport with the north-east of the country), local trains (west to Schiphol airport and The Hague, east to Flevoland), a metro line (the Ringlijn, inaugurated in 1997 and connecting peripheral subcentres), and a fast tram line (connecting Amstelveen with Amsterdam Centraal Station). Several buses also stop at the station. An important aspect of its location is that the station area directly connects to the Amsterdam motorway ring, and through it to locations across the country and beyond (Figure 6.9).

As a result of the ambitious plans to reconstruct the national and regional railway networks, the position of the node will drastically improve. It will become absolutely central. The Amsterdam southern railway tangent will get direct connections to southern and northern destinations. More trains will bypass Amsterdam Centraal Station and stop at Amsterdam Zuid instead. In this respect, Amsterdam Zuid is an example of what is happening elsewhere in Europe, with peripheral stations becoming as important as – or even more important than – central stations in congested historic centres (for example the TGV stations around Paris, or the ICE station in Kassel, Germany). As a result of this evolution, Amsterdam Zuid will be an international intercity station by around 2010. It will also be a main node in the envisaged regional rail network (Figure 6.10). As a

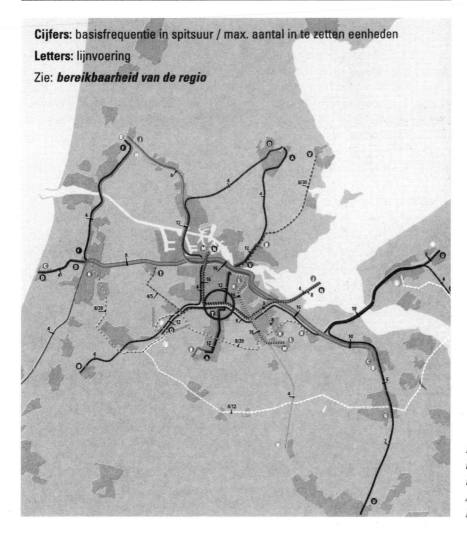

Cijfers: basisfrequentie in spitsuur / max. aantal in te zetten eenheden

Letters: lijnvoering

Zie: *bereikbaarheid van de regio*

Fig. 6.10 Amsterdam Zuid in the envisaged regional rail system. (Source: GVB Amsterdam, NS Reizigers, NZH Groep, Midnet Groep)

result, the station will be directly, rapidly and frequently connected with virtually all important centres in the country and with most locations in the Amsterdam region, including excellent connections with the airport of Schiphol. Furthermore, HSTs from Germany to Schiphol will stop at the station, as well as TGVs from Belgium and France. Connections with Amsterdam Centraal station will also improve when a new north–south metro line is opened (plan finally approved in 1997, construction to start around 2000, inauguration slated for 2005).

The quantitative impact of these developments will be far-reaching. In 1996, the railway station counted 18 000 boarding and alighting passengers a day. In 2010, 125 000 passengers a day (or 185 000 boarding and alighting) are expected, plus 30 000–40 000 HST travellers. All this will of course require radical expansion of the station infrastructure. NS (the Dutch national railway company) plans an expansion from two to four tracks by 2003, and later to six tracks. Other additional tracks are needed for metro and regional rail growth. Qualitatively, just as importantly, the railway station will function increasingly as an interchange between different modes, rather than as the beginning or end point of train travel. Integration of the modes will become central, both in the 'software' (integration of services, rates, management, etc.) and in the 'hardware' (issues of access, orientation, space occupation, etc.). Furthermore, the road infrastructure will also soon be reaching capacity, and an expansion of the motorway from three to four lanes in both directions is envisaged. Several problems connected with these infrastructure requirements still have to be solved, as we shall see when discussing the case.

6.6.2 The place

Amsterdam Zuid station and the surrounding areas (Figure 6.11) are part of what is known as the Zuidas (south axis, Figure 6.9). The Zuidas is the result of the decision taken in 1934 to reserve an area for infrastructure and recreation between the existing city and areas designated for future urban expansion. It was thus conceived as – and has become – both a connection area (in the east–west direction) and a border area (in the north–south direction). From the Second World War onwards, the Zuidas has become the recipient of users of large amounts of space that could not expand in the existing city. These include – not far from Amsterdam Zuid station – the congress and exhibition centre known as the RAI, and the Free University with the university hospital. The station area itself has been attracting a growing concentration of high-profile office space. First came – around 1960 – the offices of the real estate developers' organization NMB, followed in 1972 by the county courthouse and in 1985 by the World Trade Centre. Later also the 'Assurantiebeurs' moved to the area. In the 1990s the head office complexes of the Atrium and the Twin Towers were completed. More recently, developments have crossed over to the south side of the station and the ring, where the headquarters of the ABN-AMRO bank are currently under construction. New projects are continually launched: at the end of 1996, a 40 000 m² expansion of the World Trade Centre was announced.

The Zuidas occupies a strategic position in the wider region. It lies on the transport corridor that links the rapidly growing east – that is, the eastern parts of the Randstad and the eastern part of the country – with the country's main airport of Schiphol and the booming areas surrounding it. Furthermore, the adjacent neighbourhoods are among the most sought-after areas for working and living in the city, and the historic centre of Amsterdam is within easy reach. The area has the highest office rents in the country, with the exception of Schiphol Airport. A job growth rate of 22%, compared with 13% for the city as a whole, was registered between 1985 and 1995; in 1995, there were 22 100 jobs in total (Nagengast, 1997, p. 75). According to developers (Van Nierop, 1993, p. 94; Nagengast, 1997, p. 76) the success of the area may be ascribed to the availability of a large amount of office space and the excellent accessibility by car, with the necessary parking facilities, all absent from the central city. In addition, the appeal of the area is enhanced by its international allure, which is lacking in other peripheral locations, the concentration of law firms (a by-product of the move of the tribunal to here), and the vicinity of the airport. Nevertheless, prestigious occupiers notwithstanding, the general quality of the urban environment and especially of the public spaces is mediocre. The building complexes and the area

Fig. 6.11 Amsterdam Zuid and the Zuidas viewed from the air. The station is at the centre left of the picture, in between the two motorway lanes and spanning the rail infrastructure bundle. A cluster of office towers is next to it. (Photo: Aerofoto Schiphol)

as a whole are badly severed from their surroundings. The railway and above all the motorway ring form a huge barrier to neighbourhoods on the south side, and there are hardly any functional or visual links with neighbourhoods on the north side. These environmental limits, together with a transport infrastructure approaching saturation, are seen by many as heavy constraints on further development.

6.6.3 The process

Until recently, developments around Amsterdam Zuid railway station have been of an incidental nature. In the late 1980s, while the municipality was struggling to attract investors to the IJ-oevers area next to Amsterdam Centraal station, an intense, spontaneous market dynamics was taking place at peripheral locations along the motorway ring. The traditional orientation of the city on its port on the north side, which the IJ-oevers project tried to continue, was thus being subverted by an orientation of new developments towards the south side, better connected with the airport and the rest of the Randstad. In 1988 an exhibition and publication (ARCAM, 1988) first gave a synthetic, and to many a shocking, impression of the new spatial reality taking shape. Putting together information on plans and projects until then only fragmentarily available to the general public, the independent ARCAM foundation showed how peripheral developments were turning Amsterdam 'inside out'.

The answer of the municipality to this evidence has for a long while remained ambiguous. The official policy was that the IJ-oevers was the most important location to develop, in order to reinforce the economic base of the city centre, and that developments along the ring were not to be allowed. But the risk that firms might leave or bypass the city – which desperately needed both the jobs and the land rents they carried with them – altogether was too great to adopt a hard stance. Thus, one after the other, exceptions to the policy were made to allow companies to remain or locate at least within the city boundaries. Nothing more, though: in 1993, an officer of the municipality still declared:

> An integral vision [for peripheral developments] has no priority. You just have to allow sometimes something in order to avoid that firms escape to competing locations. (Van Nierop, 1993, p. 95)

However, this approach was meeting growing criticism. Market actors lamented that an urban design framework and coordination of development would boost property demand and values in the area. Also, concerned local district authorities (these are the lower-level municipal governments installed in 1990 and responsible for, among other things, spatial planning at the neighbourhood level, with the exception of projects of broader, 'big city' significance) remarked that transformations were happening without reference to each other and to the context, making local impacts difficult to identify and to manage. Quite strikingly, the big transport infrastructure providers and operators – the department of public works, the national railway company (NS) and the local transport company (GVB) – were at this point not participating in the debate. However, ambitious interventions and plans to boost the accessibility of the area were, quite independently from the urban development debate, following each other (section 6.6.1).

In the early 1990s, events were making the position of the municipality increasingly difficult. While little happened at the IJ-oevers, exceptions continued to accumulate along the ring: in a later stage, the municipality itself estimated the amount of office space thus developed at around 300 000 m^2! Also, the large bank concern ABN-AMRO demanded authorization to build its headquarters next to Zuid station, exacerbating tensions that were also maturing inside the municipality. Then came the proverbial last straw: in February 1994, the private partner of the IJ-oevers initiative withdrew, not believing in the financial feasibility of the operation. A policy U-turn appeared inevitable.

In the spring of 1994, following the local elections, a programme agreement was voted by the new council, in which a new policy was indeed agreed. On the IJ-oevers, rather than an office concentration, a mixed living–working area would be aimed at, anchored to activities in the cultural and tourist spheres, and thus continuing the character of the historic city centre. Along the Zuidas, an office district of international standing would be promoted, bringing together in an integrated plan developments that were then happening piecemeal. Contradicting what had been affirmed only a year earlier, the city council stated that

> For the Zuidas, the area for large-scale offices, an integral plan will be prepared in order to avoid that the development continue to happen incidentally. (reported in Gemeente Amsterdam, 1996)

Also, the method would change: a 'Zuidas coalition' was formed, on which not only the aldermen for urban planning and for economic affairs of the central city were represented, but also their colleagues at the local district level, and representatives of the other main interests in the area: the department of public works of the central government, the national railway company (NS), the congress and exhibition organization (RAI), the World Trade Centre (WTC), the Free University, and the ABN-AMRO bank. The last four are all large space users located in the area. Political decision-making would happen within an 'Administrative Conference Zuidas', composed of the central city and local district public officers already referred to. When a set of decisions was sufficiently mature to be translated into a development plan with legal force (*bestemming splan*), this would happen according to the usual procedure. Each operational subplan would thus eventually have to be approved by both the central city and the local district councils. Finally, to 'prepare decision-making' a 'Zuidas nucleus' of civil servants was put in place under the direction of an external consultant. A communication team would support the whole organization in its relationships with the wider public.

The whole organizational construction, which had evolved from dissatisfaction with conventional, more bureaucratic approaches, was quite new for Amsterdam. In particular, the external consultant (who had in the past held a leading post in the city) had an unprecedently high degree of responsibility and autonomy. Important also was the decision that the partners would continue to work together after translation of the master plan into plans with a legal status. The belief was that the complexities of implementation, and of monitoring progress and quality, require continuous active participation.

The coalition defined the objectives of the plan as: to exploit the Zuidas to give an impulse to Amsterdam; to re-organize parts of the area; to 'heal' the urban fabric along the rail and motorway rings; and to pursue a positive financial result from the whole operation. In implementing this vision, the first task of the executive nucleus, which started working in January 1995, was the realization of a series of studies, preparing the way to an integral master plan, which was to be ready by mid-1996. A first urban design study was presented in July 1995; a second urban design study and a development strategy were presented in December 1995. The latter advanced the crucial idea, endorsed by the administrative conference a month later, that rather than define a final state the master plan should identify a global vision and the steps needed to reach it.

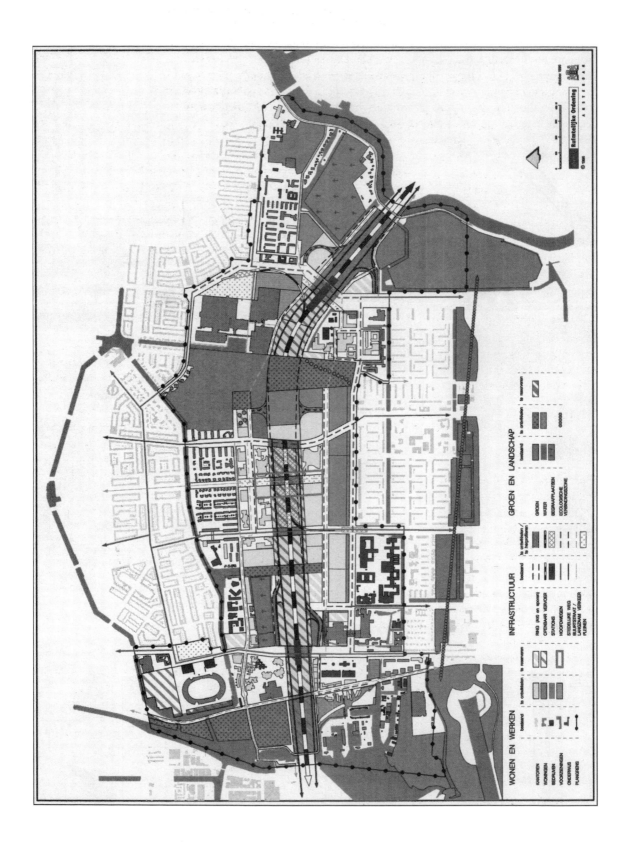

In October 1996 a draft version of the Zuidas master plan (Bestuurlijk Overleg Zuidas, 1996a, 1996b; Figure 6.12) was presented to the public. The usual information and consultation meetings were held, but less conventionally the plan was also publicized in the local media: newspapers, radio, and TV. Furthermore, bilateral discussions were organized with sport clubs, schools, churches, environmental groups, businesses, and other interest groups in the area. In this period other main actors also made their move. Most importantly, in February 1997 the transport operators presented their common vision of the future node of station Zuid, the heart of the Zuidas (Gemeentevervoerbedrijf Amsterdam *et al.*, 1997), denouncing insufficiencies of the master plan in allowances for infrastructure growth and change. Leading the group was NS, the Dutch national railways. Quite interestingly, and differently from other situations in the country, the approach of the NS appeared here strongly oriented towards its core transport business and its passenger subsidiary, and less towards its emerging property and station exploitation interests.

In March 1997 the consultation period ended, and critical points were elaborated inside the master plan organization. In the summer a set of amendments to the master plan were being prepared by the administrative conference, with the intention of submitting a definitive text to the city and district councils for final approval in the autumn. Controversies and uncertainties, especially around infrastructure issues (see below), did not however appear to be entirely overcome.

Table 6.3 summarizes the main phases of the project.

6.7 Property development at the Zuidas

6.7.1 Objectives

The central objective of the Zuidas development, of which Amsterdam Zuid station and the areas around it are the core, is an economic one: to reinforce the economic structure of the Amsterdam city and region in general and of the Zuidas in particular through an integrated approach to its development. There is, however, a more ad hoc motive. Far-reaching transformations in both the property and transport domains are already on their way, despite this planning initiative. In the last 25 years 350 000 m^2 of offices have been built in the area, mostly in an 'incidental' way. Also, the need to expand the road and rail infrastructure is a result of exogenous developments. The Zuidas plan tries to make sense of all this in order to realize, largely a posteriori, wider urban development objectives. The most delicate point, and indeed the heart of the problem, is thus how to integrate in a limited space these already intense transport and property dynamics.

Central elements in the development strategy are a further strengthening of the accessibility of the location, the achievement of a functional mix, high densities, a concentration of economic activities in the core of the area around Zuid station, high-quality open spaces, and the enforcement of a selective allocation of parcels. The instrument chosen to implement these objectives is an integrated master plan.

Fig. 6.12 Masterplan Zuidas. (Source: Bestuurlijk Overleg Zuidas)

Table 6.3 The Zuidas: summary of the main phases

Phase 1: the municipality against market trends, late 1980s/early 1990s

End 1980s/beginning 1990s	While the municipality struggles to attract investors to the central IJ-oevers area, an intense, 'spontaneous' market dynamics takes place at peripheral station locations along the motorway ring

Phase 2: the municipality with market trends, 1994–2000

February 1994	The private partner of the IJ-oevers initiative withdraws
Spring 1994	Following the local elections, a new policy is started: on the IJ-oevers the objective will be a mixed living–working area; along the Zuidas, an office district of international standing will be promoted. The Zuidas coalition and the Zuidas administrative conference are installed
January 1995	The operative 'Zuidas nucleus' begins its work
	Studies
October 1996	Draft version of the Zuidas master plan presented to the public
	Information and consultation campaign; bilateral discussions
February 1997	The transport operators present their vision of the future node of Zuid station
March 1997	The consultation period ends, elaboration of critical points begins
Autumn 1997	Expected submission of a definitive text to the city and district councils for final approval
1998–2000	Completion of legal procedures, locally and nationally; detailing of plans

Phase 3: implementation, 2001–2022

2001	Implementation expected to start. Four stages will then follow, length depending on absorption of offices by the market: provisionally first up to 2008, second up to 2013, third up to 2017, and fourth up to 2022

Integrated' means here based on studies covering environmental, property market, infrastructure, financial, phasing and other issues. The master plan entails a vision of the future of the Zuidas, or an urban design framework, agreed upon by the administrative conference of the central city and the local districts: a sort of spatial contract between administrations. It has an orientating and tutoring function, and it allows changes. It indicates what is essential and what is flexible. It has no legal status, and must thus be eventually translated into detailed plans (*bestemmingsplannen*) with legal force.

6.7.2 *Programme*

Development of the Zuidas in general and of the area around Amsterdam Zuid station in particular is seen by the municipality as a move to improve the position of the city among European office locations. This is also consistent with the national urban nodes and location policies, and is needed to create employment in the city: in the long term 40 000 jobs could be realized here in the office sector and supporting services. Its promoters contend that the Zuidas is the location in the country with the best potential to become a European office centre. This would be confirmed by the record office rents already exacted in the area. However, and here may lie some ambiguity, multifunctionality is seen as necessary in a high-profile office complex. The creation of an office environment will be sustained by the international image of the already expanding cluster of congress, exhibition, and hotel activities. Housing and the university would provide the required liveliness and hospitality. In the areas to be developed, multifunctionality concretely implies a mixture of houses, shops, hotels, restaurants, sports facilities and, above all, high-quality public spaces: squares, parks, boulevards, and natural elements.

Market research shows that a potential for 600 000–900 000 m^2 of offices exists in the area, over a 30-year period. The targets of the Zuidas are offices for banks, international trade, services, and administration. Both private firms and public institutions are welcome, both large and small – provided they can afford the high rents. It is, however, still under discussion whether offices will be speculatively built or whether users will be sought in advance. A total of about 660 000 m^2 of offices and 1560 housing units in 20 years is envisaged by the master plan, of which about 195 000 m^2 of offices and 595 houses respectively will be built in the first phase, stretching over about 6.5 years. In the first two decades, space for development will be found by intensifying or transferring low-density activities (essentially sport and recreation). After that, further air-rights development will be possible if the infrastructure has been brought underground. Development will start from the heart of the Zuidas: the areas around Amsterdam Zuid station.

The emerging vision for the south axis has far-reaching implications for potential developments elsewhere, and most importantly for the IJ-oevers, next to Centraal station and the historic city centre. Here no office concentration will be promoted, but rather continuation of the character of the inner city, and cultural and tourism functions. Also, other subcentres, most of them also at stations along the motorway ring (such as Zuidoost at Bijlmer station, and Teleport at Sloterdijk station), are seen as complementary rather than competitive. The same applies to Schiphol Airport, possibly the fastest-growing property location in the country. Public policy will, if necessary, reinforce these trends. Not everybody agrees, however, with this confidence in a more or less self-regulating regional office market; some think that there is still a risk of oversupply and destructive competition between locations (Nagengast, 1997, p. 77). A study by the Free University (Rienstra *et al.*, 1996) confirms that, in the light of a historically strong demand reinforced by the current office market revival, realization of a top office location is a real possibility, but the envisaged yearly average of 30 000 m^2 of offices would mean attracting more than the whole top segment of the most optimistic market projections for the Amsterdam region. The Zuidas has this potential, but this would be at the expense of locations elsewhere in the country, unless international firms were to locate in the area from abroad. This is not easy to achieve, given Amsterdam's relatively weak position in the European office market. The same study argues that the Zuidas plan's potential for job creation is well grounded, but this could accelerate the abandonment of the central city by economic activities.

6.7.3 Urban design principles

A first principle is multifunctionality. The plan envisages a concentration of offices on and around the main infrastructure, a concentration of houses further away, and a concentration of services around the station. Nevertheless, a functional mix is considered desirable in all sections, and essential around Amsterdam Zuid station. Public consultation has reinforced this point, and in the amendments currently being considered, multifunctionality has been better specified. Target percentages for secondary functions have been identified in both the office and housing concentration areas, ranging between 10% and 25%. However, no details have been given of financial measures to support the percentages of less profitable or unprofitable activities in office parcels, in contrast with what for instance has been done in Zentrum Zürich Nord (Chapter 8). Also, the quantity and quality of services around the station have been better defined: a total of 6500 m², aimed partly at the daily users of the transportation centre and office complex, and partly as image strengtheners. The location of public facilities poses a dilemma: how to attract them without weakening other areas, and particularly the city centre?

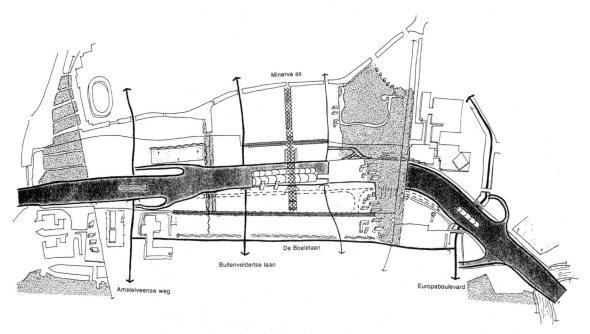

Fig. 6.13 Masterplan Zuidas: the system of public spaces integrating the transportation infrastructure in the surroundings. (Source: Bestuurlijk Overleg Zuidas)

A further constraint on multifunctionality, in the event that the dock model (see below) is not chosen, is that noise levels, especially of car traffic on the motorway, will not allow housing near the infrastructure bundle. In an open-air infrastructure layout, the problem of the risks associated with the transport of dangerous materials would also have to be dealt with.

'Healing' of the urban fabric is a second guiding concept that emerged from the urban design studies. Important tools here are the implementation of a more consistent network of open spaces, and the overcoming of the infrastructure barrier. The network of open spaces includes a hierarchical grid of roads (main traffic roads, urban streets, and neighbourhood streets), pedestrian and bicycle paths, green and water elements (Figure 6.13). In particular, it is felt that the achievement of a high-quality public domain requires improved north–south links, including bicycle and pedestrian routes, improved access to Zuid station, and priority given to the pedestrian in the whole central area. The station will become a wide passage bridging (above or under) the infrastructure, and connecting station squares on both sides. Open spaces are assigned a strategic role in the master plan: they would ensure the desired environmental quality, regardless of the uncertain evolution of labour and housing markets, and of changing financial and political perspectives.

A third and core issue is how to integrate a dynamic bundle of road and rail infrastructure into a dynamic urban environment. Three integration models have been identified (Figure 6.14):

- A *dike* model, in which the infrastructure runs, as at present, on raised ground, and cross-links are passages through or over the dike's body;
- a *deck* model, in which the infrastructure stays where it is now, but construction entirely envelops it;
- a *dock* model, in which all the infrastructure is brought underground, allowing a continuous urban fabric at ground level.

The third option is the preferred one, in the light of the much higher development potential that it offers. Its main disadvantages are, not surprisingly, its much higher costs (approximately 1975 million guilders, in contrast to 575 million guilders for the dike option, and 1000 million guilders for the deck), but also its relatively greater constraints on expansions and adaptations of infrastructure capacity.

In order to realize the dock model, the decisions and actions of the main infrastructure operators and providers – largely outside the influence of the Zuidas promoters – have to work towards that solution. This also applies to the imminent decisions concerning expansion of the rail capacity from two to four tracks and of the motorway from three to four lanes in each direction. This has raised two issues. The first is the demand from the transport world for more flexibility. The transport operators do not see in the master plan a strong enough concept for the node (Gemeentevervoerbedrijf *et al.*, 1997); they doubt that an underground terminal could achieve the high quality desired, and they denounce the insufficient space allowed for operational needs (including two missing regional rail tracks, and garaging and turning space in the event that Zuid should become the last stop of the HST). Furthermore, they do not consider it possible to fix all future

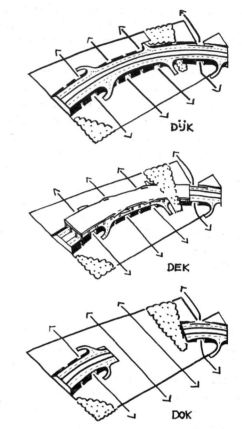

Fig. 6.14 Masterplan Zuidas: the infrastructure integration models. From top to bottom: dike, deck, dock. (Source: Bestuurlijk Overleg Zuidas)

needs now, and want more flexibility. Reinforcing a point already made in a study presented by NS a year earlier, they conclude that a mixed, layered or 'stacked' infrastructure integration model, with the infrastructure partly above and partly below ground, and appropriate land reservations, would offer the needed extra capacity, flexibility, and an adequate image and compactness of the node.

Revisions of the master plan following reactions to the draft version are currently (summer 1997) being considered. Perhaps the most important points concern the infrastructure, following these critical reactions of the transport operators. Further study will be undertaken of a stacked infrastructure integration model as proposed by the transport operators, with roads underground and rail infrastructure partly at and partly above ground level. Studies will also be made of the suggested need for additional rail infrastructure, of the possibility of realizing the station in phases, and of the layout of bus, tram and people-mover lines and station. Other spatial claims of transport operators have been rejected, including those of the railways for permanent space above ground for accessory and operational needs and facilities, and for car parking space for HST passengers.

The second issue resulting from the choice of the dock model is the need to convince central government of the worth of the extra investment. In order to secure sympathetic decision-making around infrastructure issues and the vital extra investment that this requires, the city needs central government to choose the Zuidas as a national office location, following the example of La Défense in France or Docklands in the UK. The promoters of the master plan argue that the plan is consistent with national policy objectives of reinforcing the Netherlands' competitive position as a location for international firms and decision makers, and of increasing the share of public transport by concentrating activities around stations. However, Amsterdam has to show that, unlike previously, it can both reach and maintain internal agreement and work together with external public and private partners. Perhaps more importantly, the plan demands a hard choice in favour of one location and one city, which is not usual in the Dutch political context. Such a choice would be a break with the Dutch tradition of distributing the benefits, in this case among all the four big cities, and will certainly meet resistance. Indeed, the other big cities are developing locations that will be at least partly competitive: Nieuw Centrum in The Hague, the Utrecht Centrum Project in Utrecht (see earlier), and Kop van Zuid and possibly the area around the central station (a future HST stop) in Rotterdam. The government has 'appreciated the proposals', and is studying them. A crucial decision is expected in the spring of 1998.

6.7.4 Development strategy

At the core of the development strategy for the Zuidas is the decision not to draw up a final state, but rather to work by means of process planning. This important decision is grounded on the belief that a blueprint approach in the Zuidas is neither possible, nor desirable, nor necessary. Decision-making should concern only what cannot be decided later, so that key choices are made at the most appropriate time, and real problems are dealt with as they arise. Furthermore, future social, financial or other changes may be better accounted for, as each step can be fine tuned along the way. Possibly the most important argument is that a crucial aspect of the development strategy is the effort to coordinate infrastructure and property developments both in space and in time. In addition to spatial issues, as discussed above, integration raises also time issues: time for technical construction, but also time for political procedures. The latter, especially for major interventions in the infrastructure, are complex, and contain many uncertainties.

In practice, a step-by-step plan stretching over 20 years is envisaged, which keeps options open as long as possible (among others, on the infrastructure integration model), and which allows under any condition a maximum of development. The first step is defined in detail, but the following steps are progressively more of an outline. Each step is identified by a set of key political decisions and actions, concerning principally the infrastructure, but also such things as land takes and transfers of functions. It is made up of subprojects, which are as far as possible independent from one another, and it takes up as much time as absorption by the market of the planned offices and housing will take. The latter, especially as far as offices are concerned, is the most important phasing criterion. The length of each phase is calculated on the expectation that the Zuidas could on average absorb 30 000 m^2 of offices in the top segment each year, providing the plan with the necessary cross-financing of less profitable or non-profitable elements.

6.7.5 Financial framework

Infrastructure investments (rail, motorway, bus station) are left out of the calculations for the plan, and are seen as a central and/or local government responsibility (possibly with private involvement), largely independent from the Zuidas property development. If the operations of private actors are omitted, then the costs are essentially those of preparing the land for development (654 million guilders), plus the above-average investment in creating and maintaining open spaces and natural elements (531 million guilders). Incomes are essentially the land rents. Rents are in turn calculated on the basis of an average of 440 guilders/m^2 rent for office spaces, and a 3250 guilders/m^2 sale price for housing. Both amounts belong to the very top section of the Amsterdam and Dutch markets. The fundamental assumption is that the Zuidas could absorb 30 000 m^2 of that top office segment per year. With these assumptions a slightly positive balance of 73 million guilders over 20 years can be achieved: 1190 billion of costs and 1425 billion of income, unevenly spread over time (Bestuurlijk Overleg Zuidas, 1996b, pp. 49–51).

It is, however, acknowledged that the assumption of 30 000 m^2 offices per year in the top market segment is optimistic. This figure depends on the Zuidas being the only top location in the country. Historically, the absorption has been around 15 000 m^2 per year. Also, implementation of the plan as envisaged requires extra investment in all categories of infrastructure. This has yet to be secured, which explains the importance of convincing central government, in particular, of the worth of the plan. However, the vast land holdings of the city of Amsterdam (the actor assuming most of the risks) provide some crucial flexibility in dealing with delayed incomes.

The financial framework for achieving environmental quality has been better detailed after the consultation phase. The required extra investment in open spaces and natural elements (partly due to compensation for disappearing features) has been quantified, with special attention given to the need to preserve the quality of the public spaces throughout the very long development period.

Table 6.4 The Zuidas: main structural data

Surface area	37.5 ha
Area ownership	Mostly municipality of Amsterdam, but several long-term land leaseholders (in addition, infrastructure providers could possibly exploit air rights)
Total floor area	863 700 m^2 (offices and housing)
Offices	648 000 m^2 (total)
Housing	215 700 m^2 (1438 units total)
Public functions (shops, culture, leisure, etc.)	6500 m^2 (in the first step)
Research and development	7250 m^2 (in the first step)
Costs (land development costs, excluding main infrastructure)	1190 million guilders (to be recovered through land rents)

Two innovative instruments will be used to finance them: a 'quality' and a 'green' fund will be started, fed by special development fees.

Finally, an overview of the main structural data of the Zuidas is given in Table 6.4.

6.8 The Zuidas: evaluation

The Zuidas represents a different kind of development process. Not only does the location differ from railway station areas in central cities, but it is also still in an early stage of development. Against this background, four observations are particularly relevant. The first has to do with the actors involved.

A rich but fragmented picture characterizes the actors' landscape of the Zuidas development. Dynamic realities are present, but a common vision and a cooperative working relationship are only very recently being built. This last is, needless to say, an absolute precondition for any of the ambitious plans to be realized. The Zuidas is a new initiative. Many of the mistakes of other projects could thus be avoided. It has been essential to recognize the relevant actors (partners) and promote early contacts, with the objective of creating a cooperative working atmosphere and a joint approach to development. The organizational structure is innovative in several ways. An administrative platform ensures communication across local government levels and sectors. The executive group of civil servants making the plans is led by an external consultant. A Zuidas coalition, in which all the relevant interests are represented, regularly discusses progress. Possibly the most crucial challenge for this initiative, led as it is by the local authority and the property market, is to develop through increased interaction a better understanding of the issues posed by transport operators and infrastructure providers.

A second observation deals with the node–place concept, again starting with the node element in the concept. Amsterdam Zuid station is in many respects very well placed in both the local and supra-local transportation networks. Its peculiarity is that accessibility is not only excellent by public transport, but also by car, given its location on the Amsterdam motorway ring. Reorganization of the national and regional railway networks will further and radically improve its position in public transportation networks. A new metro line connecting it with Centraal station and in the future with Schiphol Airport has received the final green light. The station will be a stop for the HST both to Germany and to Belgium and France. The capacity of the motorway will also grow. However, at present there are still many missing links. The maximum effort must be made to provide not only good national and international transport connections, but also good regional and local connections. The integrated terminal concept being promoted goes in this direction, but a crucial prerequisite is that the model for integration of infrastructure and urban development integration that is eventually chosen should allow enough flexibility for future expansions and adaptations of the infrastructure and the services.

Complementary to the node development, the place element also shows potential. This is the third observation. In many ways, locations such as the Zuidas can be considered the locations of the future. Like other peripheral station areas, Amsterdam Zuid station and its surroundings present an intense spatial–economic dynamic. However, also like other peripheral station areas, its place profile, while containing strong elements, does not have an all-round, complete, and thus self-sustaining character. More importantly than with other more traditional locations appears the need to devise strategies to make currently separate activity blocks into an integrated urban district. For example, prestigious office buildings are already present, but internal integration and, most importantly, integration with other functional elements in the surroundings is very poor. There is still a risk that the area could be trapped in a monofunctional character. An entire range of functions (including housing, shopping, culture and recreation) is either absent or under-represented. The current plans recognize both the original strong and weak points of the location. Diversification and integration of functions are being pursued down to the building parcel level. The task is a difficult one, as historical separation and the presence of massive infrastructure barriers pose many constraints. Also, the issue of complementarity versus competition with other locations in the city, and particularly with the historic centre, is still open.

The fourth and last observation has to do with the context of the development process. In a highly dynamic, rapidly changing context such as that of the Zuidas, it is vital to be aware of the temporal dimension of development. This has meant identifying transformation processes already largely under way, both in the property and the transportation sphere, and producing a planning framework to allow for increased integration and a flexible evolution. Inevitably, together with opportunities, conflicts will intensify in the area. Extensive dependence on infrastructure investment and on market demand produces uncertainties. Reciprocal dependence between the far-reaching transformations envisaged in both the node and the place dimensions increases them. In answering this, the Zuidas master plan will provide a 'hard' framework binding the choices of public administrations and shaping guarantees for market actors. At the same time it will have a step-by-step character: combinations of subprojects that are, as far as possible, autonomous will eventually lead to legally binding local plans. Key decisions on infrastructure and land-use issues structure the development process. The need to keep options open for as long as possible has been a guiding criterion. Crucial, but not yet fully achieved, is agreement on a model for the integration of infrastructure and urban development that allows sufficient autonomy to both transport and property developments, while exploiting the possible synergies.

7

Stockholm City West

7.1 Preamble: the national planning system

Sweden belongs to the *Scandinavian family*, according to Newman and Thornley (1996, pp. 27–76). This family differs significantly from the British family, but less so from the Napoleonic and Germanic families. The influence of the Germanic family is particularly obvious in the system, with its emphasis on written law. Yet the Scandinavian legal system has adopted its own style, avoiding the precision and codification of the German system. A complete legal code has never been formulated; the Scandinavian legal system seems to be more pragmatic. Administratively speaking, the Scandinavian family is something of a hybrid. As with the Napoleonic family, there is a strong relationship between national and regional governments. The central government has agencies operating at a regional level, trying to implement national spatial policy; this may be regarded as a strong tendency towards centralization. At the same time, local governments are getting organized at a larger scale for reasons of efficiency. The dual development of centralization versus decentralization is prominent within the Swedish system.

In contrast to the Swiss planning system (Chapter 8), the regional level of planning is very weak in Sweden. The emphasis in the new legislation for planning is clearly at the level of the 286 municipalities (1992). The Swedish system has thus been called a 'planning monopoly' (Newman and Thornley, 1996, p. 66). The central government can intervene in municipal plans only if manifest national interests are involved, or if there is some danger to health or safety. The Building Act of 1987 requires all municipalities to make a comprehensive plan (*översikts-plan*) for the whole territory. This plan has also to incorporate the national interests. The most important planning instrument, however, is the detailed plan (*detaljplan*), which is legally binding. It is prepared when change is expected or developments are due. Negotiation and consultation take place with the developer during the formulation of the plan. Finally, it has to be ratified by the municipal council. Detailed plans can vary in form but must always specify intended land use, public space, building lots, and implementation period. Interested parties as well as public bodies must be consulted. Appeal can be made to the county board and, if unsuccessful, to the national government. Public control is also exercised through the media. According to Swedish law all documents kept by the national or the municipal governments are public (ISOCARP, 1992, pp. 204–218). Based upon the detailed plan, the developer can apply for a planning permit, which is automatically granted if the proposed development conforms to the plan.

In order to resolve problems in areas with several landowners, the new Act for Joint Development provides new planning instruments to assist private developers and the municipality, whenever the latter does not have an economic stake in the development.

Financing of urban development operates primarily through developers and other private parties, although it is not uncommon for local governments to participate in spatial projects. Compared with other municipalities in Europe, the Swedish municipalities are more powerful and independent.

7.2 Context: railway station area redevelopment in Sweden

The main players in railway station area redevelopment in Sweden are the national railway company (SJ) and the municipalities. In this respect, Sweden does not differ much from the other countries in Europe. However, the leading role taken by the railways, following a consistent national programme and approach, is comparatively striking. SJ is ahead of most of its European counterparts with regard to the way of restructuring, and its market orientation. Since SJ was privatized in 1988, it has successfully introduced its own version of the high-speed train (HST), the X 2000. Furthermore, it has been able to gain market share in the face of dwindling subsidies and growing competition. In the process, it has become one of the most productive railways in Europe (*Railway Gazette International*, 1994; *De Volkskrant*, 1996). However, SJ has been pursuing a rather different model than the radical fragmentation that has been most notably applied in the UK. Integration and coordination among the different business units, including a newly founded property division, appear to be (still) high.

The real estate division of the Swedish railways was created in 1988, as a spin-off from the privatization policy. Its core business is the redevelopment of land holdings at stations in central locations. Property development has two main functions: it is a potentially important resource in financing investment, and it provides the chance to make stations centres of urban activity once more. The first, largely completed, step in this direction was the Station Environment Programme, a massive investment entailing the refurbishment and modernization of some 100 stations. The second, current stage is the Travel Centres Programme, which forms the core of SJ's property development strategy. The aim of the programme is to turn stations into complete, modern travel centres at locations where train travel has potential. From a comparative European perspective, it is particularly important to underline the strong guiding role of this transport-centred concept. It applies to the *whole* development strategy of railway station areas in Sweden. Thus it also includes the land not directly required for transport-related uses; compare, for instance, the very different guiding philosophy in London during the 1980s, sketched below in Chapter 9.

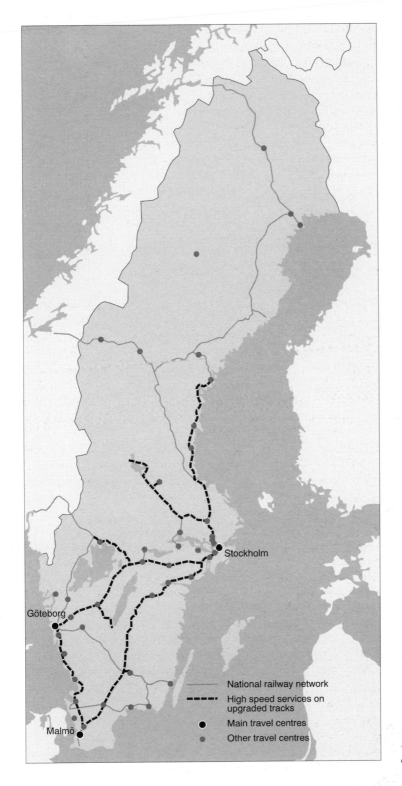

National railway network
High speed services on
upgraded tracks
Main travel centres
Other travel centres

*Fig. 7.1 National railway network
and travel centres in Sweden.*

The municipality is seen by SJ as the most important partner when developing a travel centre. Accordingly, travel centres and the surrounding areas are being developed in close cooperation between the railways and the municipalities concerned. At present, about 50 plans for railway station areas in Sweden are at different stages of development (Figure 7.1). As of 1996, cooperation agreements with the local authority had been signed in 25 municipalities; in another 20, negotiations were in progress. Travel centres in connection with property development have been implemented in Ånge and Nässjö. Similar projects are being developed in Skövde, Södertalje, Linköping, and Hässleholm, while negotiations in Göteborg, Malmö, and Västerås are at an advanced stage. The development at Stockholm Central station, while having been initiated before the official launching of the Travel Centres Programme, is a telling example of both the Swedish approach to station area redevelopment and its evolution through time. In many ways, it can be said to have been, and to continue to be, a test case for SJ property strategies. SJ expects that the whole travel centres programme will run on into the first years of the second millennium before it is completed, but there are uncertainties. Since the property boom went bust, and throughout the present period of recovery, SJ and the municipality have had to adopt a more proactive stance, taking on some of the initiative previously left to market actors. On the other hand, even in the midst of the property crisis, the real estate division of SJ was one of the few property companies in Sweden with confidence in the future: 'It is the sheer location of these properties and the renovation of the railway system that makes SJ's properties so attractive for investors' (*Sweden Today*, 1994).

7.3 Stockholm Central station as node and place

7.3.1 *The node*

The location of Stockholm Central station is excellent with respect to both node (accessibility) and place (adjacent land uses) aspects. The station is the focal point of train services to the rest of the country (Figure 7.1). Long-distance connections are increasingly being run by the high-speed X 2000 tilting trains. In 1996, there were 13 HST services a day to Göteborg (3 hours 15 minutes) and seven a day to Malmö (4 hours 50 minutes). A high-speed regional train service is to be developed in the densely populated Mälaren valley, east of the city. Meanwhile, a rail link with the airport of Arlanda, currently under construction, will open in 1999.

The urban and regional transport systems also converge at the station, where the underground and a regional rail system meet (Figure 7.2). A new track should add to the capacity of existing southbound regional services. A new bus terminal is also connected to the station. It is the departure point for national long-distance routes, for buses to the ferries that sail to the island of Gotland, and for buses to the airport. The station also enjoys very good car access, as it is directly linked to an urban motorway bypass.

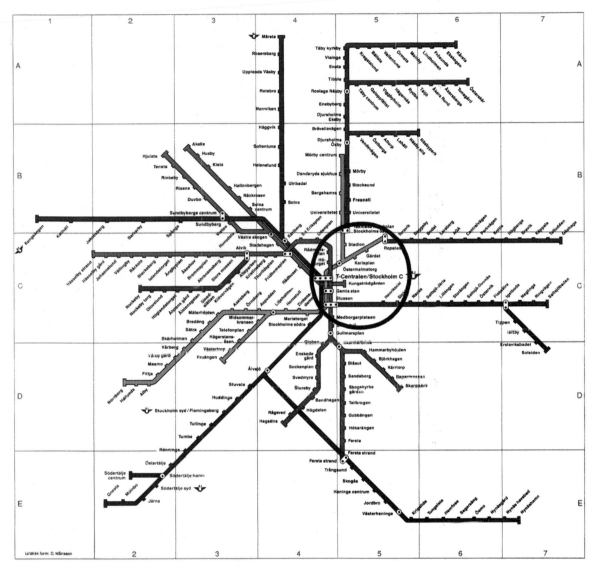

Fig. 7.2 Stockholm Central in the urban–regional public transportation networks.
(Source: SL. Map: Panorama Press AB Stockholm)

7.3.2 The place

The station lies next to the Norrmalm district (Figure 7.3). This is the business and shopping core of the Swedish capital and of the surrounding city region. It was extensively redeveloped in the 1950s and 1960s. In Stockholm's draft structure plan of 1996, the station area is indicated as a 'strategic area for urban multi-purpose redevelopment', the only one in the whole inner city. Furthermore, a comprehensive rehabilitation of the adjacent central business district (CBD) is also planned. In the rest of the inner city, the existing amenities will be 'enhanced

131

Fig.7.3 Stockholm Central and its surroundings. The station is at the top centre of the picture, the terminal–WTC complex is below, the Norrmalm district to the left. (Source: Stockholms Stad, SJ. Photo: Staffan Trägårdh)

and maintained'. The station will be developed into 'an entrance and portal to central Stockholm, a meeting point and a travel centre' (SJ and Stockholms Stad, 1997, p. 4). It should be noted, however, that while the CBD is within walking distance of the station, actual pedestrian connections are not always good, as traffic arteries and dead ends impede a free flow. Additionally, on the south and west sides of the area, the motorway bypass blocks access to the waterfront. There is little scope for change in this situation in the near future. The accessibility of the area could thus remain essentially dependent upon the transportation networks. As a consequence, it is unlikely that the central activity areas (such as shopping) will expand towards the station and link up directly with developments there.

7.3.3 The process

Stockholm City West is a development that is taking place in stages. The first completed phase was the Vasa Terminal–World Trade Centre. This building complex contains a bus terminal and offices. It was erected next to the station on land obtained by covering over the rail tracks. The second phase, an international congress and hotel centre, is currently under discussion. In the third phase, housing, shops and offices should set the tone. All is to be built by further bridging over the tracks.

The first phase: the Vasa Terminal–WTC, 1979–1989
The project was triggered by the need for a bus terminal next to Stockholm Central station. Various proposals for building it on a deck spanning the tracks

had been examined many times. Each time, the idea was set aside because no one was prepared to pay for it. Interest was reawakened at the end of the 1970s. The new concept was to build offices above the bus terminal so that the land values generated could finance construction. A first appraisal showed that the plan was feasible. On that basis, the Swedish railways (SJ) agreed to explore the possibility jointly with the City of Stockholm. A cooperation agreement between the two was signed. Once a programme was defined, the city–railways partnership organized a land-use competition. The winner would be awarded an option on site leasehold for commercial development. The aim of the competition was to get imaginative ideas for a plan, a design, its architecture, and its engineering. At the same time, the proposal should be financially realistic and economically viable. The competition was held between the autumn of 1982 and spring of 1983. Consortia of aspiring developers, contractors, and multidisciplinary teams of experts were formed to participate. The programme they had to interpret contained:

- a bus terminal for the buses to Stockholm Arlanda international airport, SJ's coach services, and buses to the Gotland ferries in Nynäshamn;
- at least 40 000 m² of office space;
- construction of a new viaduct (Kungsgatan) crossing the tracks, and enlargement of an existing one (Klarabergsgatan);
- a deck for taxis and short-term parking.

Participants were also asked to provide information on how much rent they were willing to pay for the leasehold of the office block.

After an initial examination of the competition entries, the jury – led by the director of SJ and the city housing and town planning chief officer – designated Vasaterminalen (a consortium of Fastighets AB Hufvudstaden, L.E. Lundberg-företagen AB, and SIAB AB) as the preliminary winner. Confirmation of the award would take place only after negotiations had been held and agreements had been reached on the leasehold and tenders. A financial review had been provided with the competition documents, but it was only 'morally binding', as many details still had to be worked out. In the first half of 1984 Vasaterminalen under-took preliminary design work at their own risk. Meanwhile, negotiations on and detailing of the planning framework also took place. Only then could the actual 'first prize' be finalized. This entailed acquisition of the leasehold rights to the site on which the office blocks were to be built. Thereafter, construction could begin, against payment, of the bus terminal, the street viaducts, and the other public facilities. The negotiations were complex. The parties involved (SJ, the City of Stockholm, and the Vasaterminalen consortium) had to deal with multiple issues that required detailed and extensive agreements. For example:

- The project was technically complicated. It had to be constructed above the tracks without serious disruption of rail traffic.
- The project was administratively complicated. Apart from the partners and the developers themselves, the national government was also directly involved through a subsidy to the city.
- The project was financially complicated. The programme was conspicuous, while neither SJ nor the City of Stockholm had the liquidity to pour into the

project. Furthermore, as landowner, SJ was looking for an acceptable return on its property. The deal also had to be financially acceptable to the developers' consortium.

In the late summer of 1984, after six months of negotiations, the partners signed a package of contracts containing eight intermeshed agreements. The substance of the package is schematically depicted in Figure 7.4.

Basically, a new property was being created on part of the railyards of Stockholm Central station. The land would remain the property of SJ, and would

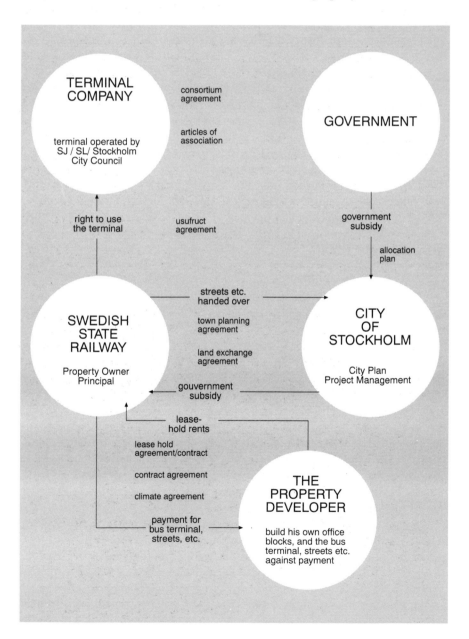

Fig. 7.4
Vasaterminalen: the
network of contracts.
(Source: P.H. Westin)

be rented out on a leasehold basis to Vasaterminalen AB. The first 25 years would be rent-free for the developers. In exchange, at their own expense, they would build the bus terminal and the other public facilities. The City of Stockholm would pass the government subsidy onto SJ in exchange for the transfer of the new streets and public spaces from SJ to the city. Terminal facilities would be leased free of charge for 20 years to an ad hoc 'terminal company', which would be a joint venture of SJ, the city, and the regional transportation authority SL. The railway area beneath the terminal would be used exclusively by SJ. In short, the revenues acquired in connection with the new building rights – that is, the 20-year yield on the land generated from 45 000 m^2 of new city offices – would finance the public facilities.

In June 1985, after the agreements had been signed and the detailed development plan had been adopted by the council, construction could begin. After four years of construction work, the complex was opened in 1989–1990. The central location, and the booming property market and economy, meant that finding tenants was not much of a problem.

The second phase: a congress centre, 1994–2004
The success of the Vasa Terminal concept prompted interest in the possibility of further covering of the tracks. In May 1986, the city and the railways jointly presented a development concept for the whole area for public consultation (Figure 7.5). A hotel complex (35 000 m^2) and a congress centre (25 000 m^2) were proposed next to the WTC, and developments, consisting mainly of offices (a total of an additional 125 000 m^2), on adjoining sites. The total cost was estimated at around SKr 4.5 billion (SKr 2.2 billion for the sections under construction, and SKr 2.3 billion for those proposed). Soon afterwards, the railways and the city

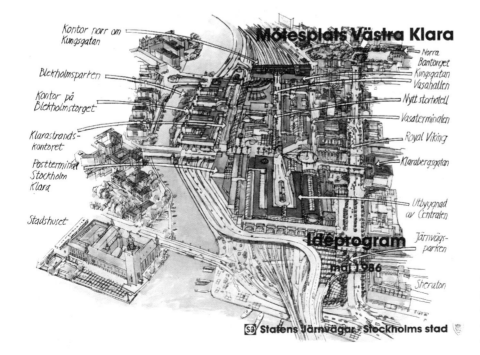

Fig. 7.5 *The concept plan of 1986. (Source: Stockholms Stad, SJ. Drawing: Christer Hagman)*

signed cooperation agreements on future development. Some preparatory work (foundations, for example) was done in combination with construction on the Vasa Terminal– WTC. It was expected that the whole site could be fully built up by 1994. However, these high hopes were dashed by the economic recession and the ensuing slump in property prices. Thus little of this programme has been implemented. Only some of the offices above the motorway (seen at the left in Figure 7.5) have been built. Next to these premises some houses also appeared, though the plan originally called for offices. They were made possible by an amendment to the original plan, a change that was essentially politically motivated. An interesting outcome is that, once completed, there was no problem in finding tenants for the dwellings, while the offices remained empty for a long period, thanks to the sudden downturn in the market.

The entire planning and development process thus came to a halt at the beginning of the 1990s. All related actions were postponed indefinitely. The same thing was happening everywhere in the metropolitan area. Only in 1994, in a slowly improving property market, was interest revived in the project, which had been renamed Stockholm City West. The approach had changed, however, as management of uncertainty had become a major concern. While the plan was still seen from a wider perspective, attention was turned to the parcel of land next to the already developed terminal–WTC. The rest was considered as mere 'future hypotheses'. Once again, the initiative was promoted jointly by SJ and the city. Their relationship was as good as ever. Per-Hakan Westin, the City of Stockholm's project manager in the Vasa Terminal project, had become director of the real estate division of the Swedish railways. A city-wide brainstorming session was held to confirm and redefine the content of the next development stage. Prominent representatives of the business, political, cultural, scientific and media communities were engaged in an informal consultation exercise. In the end, it was decided to go ahead with the idea of a congress centre. It was conceived as an international facility, with a range of services (such as advanced telecommunications and hotels) and a capacity (up to 4000 visitors) that was unmatched in the city until now. The initiative would have been given a boost if Stockholm were to have won the competition to host the Olympics in 2004. In that event the congress centre would have been launched as a media centre. In September 1997 a further brainstorming session was to be held with organizations and individuals active in the field of conferences. Discussions are currently (1997) being held with the Stockholm conference committee. They are worried about competition with the existing congress and exhibition centre, which is peripherally located. Hotel companies have also been contacted; some of the firms interviewed could possibly become partners in the development (Figure 7.6).

No public consultations have taken place so far, but they will after some decisions have been made. Little opposition has emerged, simply because 'there are no neighbours'. The interviewed participants believed this could change in the future. For instance, opposition might arise if the project gets involved in the impending discussion about building new rail and road infrastructure to the south across the lake. Alternatively, objections might be raised if it goes further north along the water, 'taking away the view' from adjacent property. Reaching the greatest degree of consensus is seen as a high priority. Both market actors and the local population appear cautious. They are only slowly recovering from the

Fig. 7.6 Completed and planned components of Stockholm City West: in the centre the built terminal–WTC complex, on the right of it the congress and hotel centre under development, above and under it future developments. (Source: Stockholms Stad, SJ. Photo and drawing: Boris Culjat/HJS Arkitektkontor AB)

property crash and some unhappy public–private deals of the 1980s. Meanwhile, the project has been presented to the building board of the city for review. Building features have been discussed, and work on a detailed plan has started. This is taking place in close collaboration between the planning and real estate departments of the city. At a later stage the appointed developer will be drawn in. In March 1997, three multidisciplinary consultant groups (selected from an initial round involving 22 Swedish and foreign groups) were asked to subject their suggestions for the congress and hotel centre to detailed feasibility studies. In the invitation they received to submit a more detailed plan, they were told that integration with the existing city and local traffic plans was an area of major concern. They were also asked for an implementation method that would not disrupt existing rail traffic. In the same period, the plan was presented at the MIPIM real estate exhibition in Cannes. In June, the three consultants presented their plans; if shown to be feasible, development will take place in the form of a leasehold, or the land could be sold.

It has not yet been decided whether the same partnership model (a competition to identify an architectural plan and a developer-partner) will be applied as was used for the terminal–WTC. Market conditions are totally different from what they were in the 1980s. The private sector is no longer in any rush to compete. More preparation time is needed. After approval by the building board, the search for financing will start. The congress and hotel centre would have to cover its own costs; no public investment is envisaged there. However, things could change if some clear benefit to the city is shown – for instance, in the area of tourism (an increasingly important economic sector). The parties are confident that they will be able to interest private investors in the project, and that they can open its doors in 2004.

Table 7.1 summarizes the main phases of the project.

Table 7.1 Stockholm City West: summary of the main phases

Phase 1: planning and implementation of terminal–WTC, planning of whole station area, 1979–1989

End 1970s	Idea: (airport) bus terminal plus offices above the tracks; cooperation agreement between the City of Stockholm and the Swedish railways; feasibility studies; definition of the programme
End 1982/beginning 1983	Development competition: negotiations with the winning consortium
1984	Elaboration of the development plans and the land-use plans (*detaljplan*)
June 1985	Start construction
Mid-1986	Public consultations on the area plan
1989/1990	Opening of terminal–WTC complex

Phase 2: planning and implementation of congress centre, 1994–2004

Beginning of 1990s	Planning and development process of the station area is interrupted because of the property market crash
1994/1995	Planning and development process of the station area starts again: advice rounds
1996–1997	Elaboration of the land-use plan; feasibility studies
2004	Opening?

Phase 3: planning and implementation of following stages

Still unknown

7.4 Property development at Stockholm City West

The already built terminal–WTC complex (Figure 7.3) contains 45 000 m² of office space, hotels, restaurants and shops. Together, it is a place of work for 2000 people. In addition, it is a terminal for local, airport, and long-distance buses. The complex occupies an area of 1.5 ha, providing a total of 60 000 m² of space. The total cost of the complex has been estimated at around SKr 1400 million. The key figures are summarized in Table 7.2. The office complex is organized according to the World Trade Centre concept. It provides offices for rent (for a total of 1500 workers; short-term leases are also possible) and 300 parking spaces. On the fourth floor, there are a number of ancillary facilities. These include a conference complex, containing an auditorium with seating for up to 180 persons and meeting rooms for 8–50 people. An exhibition hall of 850 m² and a World Trade Centre Club complete the list. Elsewhere in the building there is a 160-room hotel (with a 'budget-business' formula), a restaurant with banquet room, a cafeteria, and body-care facilities. Administration and management are centralized, and access to the building is restricted.

The management of the World Trade Centre had no problem in finding tenants

Table 7.2 Property development in Stockholm City West: main structural data

Surface area	40 ha
Area ownership	Swedish railways (mostly)
Total floor area	220 000 m^2
Offices (World Trade Centre)	45 000 m^2 net (developed)
Congress and hotel centre	60 000 m^2 (planned)
Housing, shops and offices	100 000 m^2 (proposed)
Parking	975 places (plus 650 in a 300 m radius)
Cost	SKr 4.5 billion (1986 estimate, total); SKr 1.4 billion (actual, terminal/WTC, 100% private)

in the booming markets of the late 1980s. It came on the market at the right moment, just before the crash. The offices have been occupied by the same sort of firms that can be found elsewhere in the central business district; the rents are comparable, too. Since then a lot has changed, however. The Stockholm property market has undergone a deep depression. The World Trade Centre, however, performed better than other properties. Essentially, this appears to be due to its unique combination of high accessibility (by all modes: road, rail, and indirectly air) and high general standards. However, many believe that further expansion of the office content requires a different approach today. There are no prospects for an office-only formula, whatever the quality. A more specific and exceptional attractor is needed. Consequently, after a brainstorming session, which involved several central actors of the city, the idea of an international congress centre gained support (Figure 7.6). In a space of around 60 000 m^2, the centre would cater for up to 4000 visitors. It would be equipped with the latest telecommunication technologies, and it would be connected to facilities such as hotels and shops ('shopping on the ground floors will make the streets lively'). The area will offer 'the best possible opportunities for establishing national and international organizations in the fields of commerce, science, culture and politics' (Stockholm City West brochure).

Given the unique nature of the development, no competition from other locations in the metropolitan area is expected. Some congress facilities are being developed around the airport of Arlanda, though on a much more limited scale. Rather, the existing peripheral congress and exhibition centre at Alvsjo might suffer from the development of Stockholm City West. Central properties are in fact already performing better than peripheral motorway ones (such as along the E4 corridor, for example). However, some worries persist: integration with the immediate surroundings, and local traffic issues.

Finally, thought is being given to the following stages (for a total of 100 000 m^2), which are still in the hypothetical stage. It is possible that houses will be built over the tracks, perhaps mixed with some commercial functions, but the idea of locating a shopping centre at the station is not being taken seriously. Competition with the existing shopping area of Norrmalm, which is presently undergoing a facelift, has to be avoided. On the other hand, the poor pedestrian links with that same central shopping district (as described in section 7.3.2) would impose a major constraint on the success of such a development.

In discussing the development strategy of Stockholm City West, it is crucial to consider the transport facilities and the new bus terminal (about 500 buses and 20 000 passengers a day). The main concept of the interchange is that the length of time for which passengers are neither inside a bus nor in the terminal building should be as short as possible. As at an airport, they board buses directly from gates a few minutes before departure. The scheduled departure and arrival times are displayed on electronic boards and monitors inside the hall, along with other travel information. This hall is a pleasant, ample and light space covered by a glass vault. It boasts a variety of small shops and a cafe, alongside some other services. The main hall is connected by corridors, both above and below street level, to taxi stands and the train and underground stations. Additionally, while the terminal–WTC complex was being developed, the central railway station underwent thorough renewal. It now extends its high level of comfort and functionality to the whole transportation interchange. Without a doubt, the re-modelling has been crucial to the success of the development.

7.4.1 Background information: the reorganization and investment programmes of the Swedish railways

In order to fully appreciate the Stockholm City West development, as well as any station development in Sweden, it is essential to know something about the current reorganization and reorientation of the activities of SJ (the Swedish railways). Furthermore, the Swedish approach to market orientation of the railway business appears to be particularly successful, at least relative to that adopted by many other countries in Europe. Some insight into that approach, particularly for the property issues that are concerned, is certainly worthwhile. Its most relevant features are: the establishment of a property division; the travel centres and the environmental programmes; and the development of high-speed X 2000 services.

The property division is one of the four divisions into which SJ was split in 1988. The other three are passenger transport, freight transport, and engineering. At the same time, track construction and maintenance became the task of a fully separate, government-owned company called Banverket (BV). The objective of the property division of SJ (with 300 employees, one head office, and four regional offices) is

> the continued development of attractive and new travel centres and development of adjacent real estate . . . increasing the value of and activating SJ's real estate holdings, and at the same time coordinating all SJ's interests, both internal and external, in questions related to physical planning. (SJ Real Estate Division, n.d, p. 3)

In 1994, real estate management accounted for 4% of SJ's revenues. About one-third of SJ's real estate holdings are externally leased, and the percentage is growing. In 1994, the real estate division had an operating revenue of SKr 1.008 million and an income after depreciation of SKr 412 million. These figures correspond to respectively 9.7% and 248% of the parent entity's revenue.

The emphasis on travel centres is important, as the travel centres programme embodies the essence of SJ's property philosophy. Real estate development next to stations and promotion of train travel are seen as complementary; these goals are pursued accordingly. Travel centres are to be developed as 'transportation interchanges with an urban location'. A travel centre is not just a railway station. It includes the surrounding areas, access roads for buses and cars, and parking spaces for cars and bicycles. The travel centre should also act as a commercial centre, providing services to passengers and other visitors. Development plans call first of all for eliminating the run-down image of railway stations. This entails turning them into centres offering a wide range of goods and services to make train travel more convenient. This must provide good parking facilities, easy access to local buses, car hire agencies, shops, banks, post offices, and possibly hotel and office space.

> What could be better for a company whose business involves travelling than being located close to or even on top of a railway station? As we see a greater number of high-speed rail connections in the upcoming years this of course will be of great importance. For those who have their offices in a station complex the journey time from city centre to city centre is approximately the same by rail or air and on the train travelling time is not wasted. You can work on your computer, make important phone calls, hold meetings, eat or just relax. (The director of SJ property interviewed in *Sweden Today*, 1994)

Four actors are identified by SJ as important players in the process of station development: SJ; the local authority (main resource: planning instruments); the national rail administration, Banverket (controls infrastructure, is controlled by the state); and the regional transport company (controls local networks, is controlled by the local authorities, is financed also by the state). External financing is vital. But the problem is the present oversupply of office space. An increase in demand is not expected. The reverse is more likely. Rationalization of administrative work means that less space is needed. This is why the fifth actor – the developer – is scaling down its activities. Investors arc very cautious. The expectation is that they could be interested only in very special locations like Stockholm City West and a few others. Essentially, they would consider only the central locations in the three biggest cities.

Particularly important for the development of travel centres is the relationship with the other key actor, the municipality. In Sweden (comparable to, for instance, the situation in the Netherlands) the municipality plays a particularly strong role in urban development. The typical development approach entails making early contact with the local authority and developing a common vision on the site. Signing a cooperation agreement is typically the first step. Thus established, the cooperation is extended throughout the development process. It begins with the joint definition of a programme. Once in place, that programme constitutes the basis for relationships with third parties, such as consultants working out alternative solutions or developer consortia bidding for contracts to carry them out. Later in the process, and after several rounds of negotiations, an implementation agreement is signed with the winning developer consortium. At the same time, a development agreement is signed between the railways and the municipality. The preparation and approval of a detailed development plan, which will give the development proposal legal status, run parallel to this process. The detailed development plan is the responsibility of the municipality.

In recent years, slack property markets have made it harder to get projects off the ground. However, the director of SJ Real Estate is optimistic (unlike many others in the troubled Swedish property industry), because 'we own some of the most attractive real estate in Sweden'. The approach has been amended to give higher priority to marketing and an early search for potential tenants. A more active role and direct involvement in the planning process appears to be required. The traditional tactic of 'wait and see' is no longer possible. Under changing market conditions, efforts have been concentrated on the more important travel centres. Moreover, implementation of the major projects (those at Stockholm, Malmö, and Göteborg central stations) is to take place in stages.

According to SJ:

> In the future real estate market, good locations will be of decisive importance. SJ's real estate holdings, in attractive locations close to communications, are considered to offer interesting investment potential, and are likely to be even more attractive in the long term. The current recession is being used to prepare for our development and travel centre projects. The time-consuming planning process means that it normally takes 2–5 years to produce definitive plans and sign a final implementation agreement. These activities tie up a relatively small amount of capital in relation to the increase in value the planning process is expected to generate once the real estate market has recovered. (SJ Real Estate Division, n.d., p. 6)

The travel centres programme must be seen as part of a wider strategy. In particular, it must be connected to the expansion of X 2000 services and the environmental programme. Together, these two innovations have boosted the use of stations and trains.

The Swedish version of the HST, the X 2000, started service in 1990, running between Stockholm and Göteborg. The X 2000 resembles the Italian Pendolino in that both trains – thanks to a tilting device – can reach high speeds without needing special track. Maximum speeds (~200 km/h) are lower than those possible on the French TGV (~300 km/h), but the great advantage is that existing track can be used (if sufficiently improved). Furthermore, like the German ICE, the service has relatively high frequency and a high level of comfort (conference rooms, comfortable seats with tables, coat hangers, telephones, faxes, on-line information, etc.). Rather than just providing fast point-to-point connections (like the TGV), the system should be seen as a diffused network interconnecting multiple centres (like the ICE; see Figure 7.1). An adaptation of the X 2000 is being developed as a fast regional transportation system for the greater Stockholm region. Unlike Italy, Sweden does not plan to switch to a dedicated HST network in the future. Given the country's low urbanization densities, the traffic potential does not justify the investment. Since 1996, high-speed trains have run regularly between the capital and all the major urban centres. In 1994, for the first time, the train surpassed the aeroplane in market share on the Stockholm–Göteborg route.

SJ's goal is for the train to become the fastest means of transport between destinations at distances between 100 km and 600 km. HSTs are part of a system that includes intercity (same routes with more stops), interregio (high-speed cross-connections bypassing Stockholm), and night trains. Furthermore, combinations of train, air, ferry, bus and car services are being developed. The whole range of travellers is important. Special facilities are available on board and in stations for each of the categories identified by SJ: commuters, business travellers, parents with children, students, teenagers, retired, and disabled persons. The special facilities include wheelchair seats, family carriages, sockets for PCs, and so forth. The overall market share of SJ, as measured in passenger-kilometres, rose from 5.4% in 1976 to 6.1% in 1990. In 1994 it was 13% for trips longer than 100 km. The train has a 35% share of all commuting traffic in the Stockholm region.

A second important element of the modernization of the Swedish railways is the environmental programme. Between 1989 and 1993, around 100 stations were completely refurbished. Not only were their functional standards raised significantly, they were also equipped with a diverse range of services. The improvement is evident: visiting railway stations in Sweden today provides an experience that has little to do with earlier feelings of shabbiness and insecurity, still so common in stations around the world. Interior improvements include better waiting rooms, new lighting, customer services, a new system of signs, and doors that open automatically. Outside, station buildings and their surroundings have been given a facelift, platforms and entrances have been upgraded, and stations have been adapted to the needs of the disabled. An interesting feature is the frequent choice for restoration of the historical station building, possibly as a sub-element of a new complex. Besides providing an appealing image, this choice has enhanced the physical relationship with the existing urban centres. As part of this programme, a completely modernized Stockholm Central station was reopened in August 1994.

7.5 Stockholm City West: evaluation

As elsewhere in Europe, the redevelopment of Stockholm City West took a long time. Therefore it is not surprising that the first observation made in any evaluation of the process usually has to do with the stages of development.

Since its outset, Stockholm City West has been conceived as a stepwise development. The bus terminal–WTC complex was completed a few years ago, while the congress centre is in the planning phase, and successive expansions are still only hypotheses. At the same time, a vision for the whole area was made explicit early on. Provisions to allow future expansion have been made (technical ones, such as foundation work, but also political ones, such as consultation on and approval of the development principles). The vision and the procedure to define each implementation phase (city–railway cooperation, competition among developers, public participation) could be considered 'hard' elements; the 'soft' elements would be the documents interpreting the global vision for each implementation section (what exactly is to be done and how to do it in each phase). The ongoing articulation of the goals is the way the project can adapt to changing circumstances (such as demand from the market and/or society).

The second observation made in an evaluation is closely related to the first. As development processes take more time, interests tend to shift. The commitment of the (initially willing) participants tends to shift accordingly. In Stockholm City West, however, a good working relationship between the railway company and the city was maintained throughout the whole process. Together, they initiated and managed it, and now they are preparing the future stages. Of all the cases analysed, this is the one where the city–railway relationship seems to have worked best and to evident reciprocal benefit. The roles have been interpreted straightforwardly. The railway and the city have jointly taken both the initiative and the successive key decisions, while private consultants and developers (on a competitive basis) have further defined and implemented them. One reason why this partnership has been so successful is the fact that the municipality has a long-standing tradition of urban development as well as a broad view and ample resources. But even more remarkable is the degree of vision and professional expertise that the railway company has on property issues. The Swedish railways have a clear business philosophy. Most importantly, they are consistent in their implementation of it. They invest in their core activity (transport), and property development is seen as an integral part of this strategy (as a financial resource, but also as a direct contribution to the upgrading of the station environment). Conversely, the overall improvement in transport services makes station areas more attractive objects for property investment.

Our third and fourth observations deal with the node–place concept. As for the node, the Stockholm case shows well how better accessibility has more than a quantitative component. The station has been the object of the environmental programme, a nationwide effort of the Swedish railways to enhance the experience of train travel. Once an unappealing place, Stockholm Central station is now a pleasant public square enjoyed by a diverse public. The same level of quality is to be found in the adjacent bus terminal, a new facility that could be easily mistaken for an airport lounge. These qualitative improvements are actually just as important as the quantitative ones, which are also notable. The latter include the development of national high-speed train services and the expansion (reach and capacity) of the regional rail network. Both these national and regional systems are centred on Stockholm Central station, as is an extensive underground network. A direct rail connection to Arlanda international airport will be added in the future, and frequent rapid bus connections are already available. Furthermore, the station area is directly linked to an urban motorway. However, as in Lille, pedestrian (and bicycle) connections to and from the surroundings are weak.

The development was triggered by the realization that a combination with office space would have made it possible to construct a long-awaited bus terminal next to the railway station. This is the fourth observation, and refers to the place concept. From this initial idea, a vision for the whole station area gradually emerged. By covering and building over the tracks, a fully fledged urban environment could be progressively developed. Next to the completed World Trade Centre/(airport) bus terminal, an international congress and hotel centre is also planned. In successive stages, the accent will shift to housing, further adding to the functional mixture. For the definition of the programme, innovative tools have been employed. For example, a city-wide brainstorming exercise was held, involving representatives of the most diverse fields, from business to politics to culture. Furthermore, the successful insertion of additional outstanding functions to the area cannot be separated from the simultaneous upgrading of the whole station environment. Together, these efforts form an extensive programme of the Swedish railways to improve the overall quality of the 'train experience'. One problem is that while Stockholm is very well connected in terms of transport networks, the station area is not yet completely integrated with the existing city centre. That problem is manifest in the many obstacles that impede a free flow of pedestrians (and, consequently, functional continuity) between the station and the city.

8

Basel EuroVille and Zentrum Zürich Nord

8.1 Preamble: the national planning system

According to Newman and Thornley (1996, pp. 27–76) Switzerland belongs to the *Germanic family* from both a legal and an administrative perspective. Planning systems in the Germanic family have firm roots in the Enlightenment, implying systematic order and codification. They are not based on the ideology of change, which is associated with the French code. An important characteristic of the Germanic family is its foundation in basic laws (including the constitution). This legal foundation clearly defines the responsibilities and powers that are delegated to various levels of government. The basic design is a federal body. Switzerland has three levels of government: the *national or confederation*, 26 *cantons*, and over 3000 *municipalities* (communes). Each level is involved in physical planning, but the main planning activities are at the level of the canton (ISOCARP, 1992, pp. 219–229).

The national spatial strategy Guidelines of Swiss Spatial Development provides a framework for plans prepared by the other governmental levels. Thus it can be seen as a reaction to the increasing competition between regions and cities in Europe. The strategy aims in particular at improving public transport between cities, trying to prevent congestion, and contributing to the attractiveness of Swiss cities. The settlement pattern in Switzerland is decentralized, which corresponds to the Swiss federal political system. It is thus not surprising that one of the main objectives of spatial planning is to maintain this polycentric urban pattern. The projected linkage of existing cities in an efficient manner by a new railway system known as Rail 2000 is a key element in this plan. As Switzerland is also fiscally highly decentralized, the financing of infrastructure must be raised not only by the national government but also (and especially) by the cantons and communes.

The federal guidelines leave room for the cantons to formulate their own laws regarding building and planning. Thus the cantons produce their own spatial plans to reflect their specific circumstances. Once approved by the Federal Council, the spatial plans (guiding plans) are binding upon all levels of government. These plans are the main instrument of spatial coordination in the country. Based on the guiding plans, the canton can give directives to communes and approve their plans. The communes, for their part, regulate spatial development through zoning plans (including building codes), which have to apply to the entire area. The zoning plan is binding upon landowners. However, landowners can challenge a zoning plan in a court of appeal and, if necessary, present their case to the Federal Court of Law.

At the local level there is a unique role for the (local) referendum. It may constitute a conservative element of some relevance. Though the planning literature does not consider it to be very important (ISOCARP, 1992, pp. 219–229; Newman and Thornley, 1996, pp. 62–63), for projects such as railway station area redevelopment the local referendum appears to be a significant tool, typifying the decentralization of the system. Such projects are only partially subject to opportunities and restrictions imposed by the national planning system. It is especially the negative effects of redevelopment that are most acutely felt at the local level. Therefore it is not surprising that, next to the instruments derived from the national planning system, a local referendum can be of additional importance.

8.2 Context: railway station area redevelopment in Switzerland

Railway station area redevelopment in Switzerland has a relatively long history. The first projects were launched at the beginning of the 1970s. In March 1991, the magazine *Hochparterre* counted some 40 railway station area redevelopment initiatives in the country, ranging from major projects at Basel's and Zürich's central stations to more modest projects in Locarno, Lucerne and Neuchâtel (Figure 8.1). Some of those ventures began to stagnate in the 1980s and 1990s. New ones have since been started. Most notable among these is the ambitious plan to redevelop the industrial areas north of Zürich's Oerlikon station.

A favourable context for station area projects in Switzerland has been stimulated by at least three developments (CEAT, 1993):

- national programmes to modernize, coordinate and integrate rail and public transport – in particular Rail 2000 at the inter-urban level and new S-Bahn systems at the intra-urban level (as in Zürich, Basel, and Bern);
- a growing awareness of the environmental costs associated with road congestion, and especially of its negative impacts on the quality of life in the main urban centres (again, as in Zürich, Basel, and Bern);
- the persistent financial difficulties of the railway company (as well as looking for ways to cut costs, the company is searching for new sources of profit, which include the valorization of its property assets at stations).

The actors involved are national and local railway companies, local governments and other institutional bodies such as the post and telecommunication company, private professionals, developers and investors, environmental and local interest groups, the media, and the general public. For the national railway company, railway station area redevelopment is essentially a way of improving the

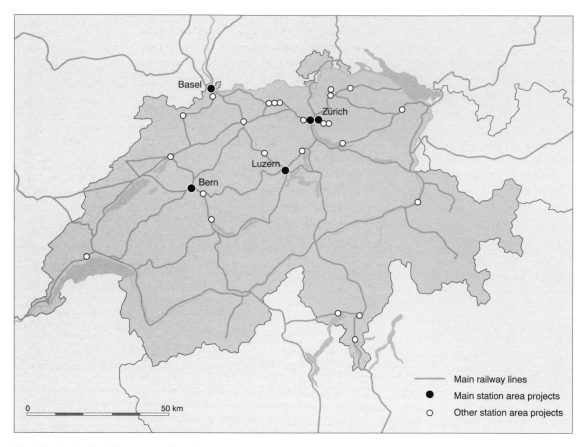

Fig. 8.1 National railway network and main station area projects in Switzerland.

performance of transportation nodes and of valorizing its property assets. Other interests may coalesce around the goals of promoting public transport (the station area as transportation interchange and traffic generator), restructuring the urban fabric (creating/reinforcing an activity centre, diminishing barrier effects), and placing activities on national and international networks (the station as node of material and immaterial flows). Next to this general framework, individual plans might have been triggered by local singularities. Local governments might have been actively promoting a project as part of a city marketing strategy, as in Basel. Or property owners might have made a concerted effort to replace obsolete functions, as at Zentrum Zürich Nord. In all cases, there seems to be a prevailing belief that a general shift towards train and public transport will make, at least in the long term, stations favoured locations. This belief appears to be increasingly shared by most actors, including market parties.

In 1993, Decoutère and Rey concluded their extensive review of station projects in Switzerland with the admission that 'we are still in a learning phase' (CEAT, 1993, p. XVIII). In their opinion, over the past 20 years we have seen the 'emergence' of the issue. For two decades, the railways and the municipalities have been 'throwing the hot potato at each other' in an effort to avoid responsibilities. At the same time they observe a rising interest on the part of the confederation and several cantons (namely Bern, Zürich, and Basel) in the context of policies combining public transport provision (S-Bahn) and urban development at stations. Other positive signs are the growing media coverage of mobility and urbanization themes, public reflection on the potential roles of station areas within a metropolitan Switzerland, and the accumulation of experience by actors involved in concrete station plans. However, there are some persistent signs that things are not all going well. The limited interest shown by private investors in general, the ambiguity of political expectations *vis-à-vis* the railway company, and the insufficient awareness of the many conditions required by a successful implementation, are some of the less promising signals. In that light, Decoutère and Rey reached some mixed conclusions in their analysis of the Swiss case. As important explanations they cite: the novelty of positive evolution; a too technical and functional perception of the transport and mobility issue; and the incremental, non-revolutionary nature of rail innovation in Switzerland. Most importantly, a too 'localistic' approach has failed to capitalize on the specificity of railway station areas. The drawback of that approach is that it does not take their supra-local 'interface' potential into account (as opposed to the French approach).

8.3 Basel EuroVille as node and place

8.3.1 *The node*

The importance of Basel is historically connected with its central position in the European transport networks. It lies at the intersection of the north–south Rhine axis (from northern Europe to Italy) and an east–west axis connecting France, Switzerland, southern Germany, and Austria. Not only the Swiss but also the French and the German railways have a station in Basel. While being relatively marginal in the national rail system, Basel HauptBahnhof is a major hub of international traffic (Figure 8.1). ICEs already stop at the station (2 hours 30 minutes to Frankfurt), and TGVs will soon do the same (1 hour to Strasbourg, 3 hours to Paris). In the near future, high-speed connections through Switzerland into Italy will be provided by tilting trains of the Pendolino type. Like several other railway station projects, the redevelopment of Basel HauptBahnhof and its surrounding areas were initiated in the transport sphere. But Basel has a specific problem. Although it is an important national and international node, the station is not the main node of the local transport system (Figure 8.2). Since the 1970s, the creation of a complete, multimodal transport interchange has been an objective of the municipal government.

8.3.2 *The place*

The city of Basel (Basel Stadt) has a limited area. The French and the German borders, on the one hand, and the separate administrative territory of the county of Basel (Basel Land), on the other, leave very little space for growth within the municipal boundaries. The city accommodates 190 000 inhabitants in an area of 37 km². The urban agglomeration on Swiss territory has about 500 000 inhabitants. The broader urban region stretching into Germany (Freiburg) and France (Mulhouse) has about 2.1 million. An informal association, the Regio Basiliensis, has existed since 1963 to promote an integrated transnational

Fig. 8.2 *Basel SBB station in the local public transportation networks. (Source: Tarifverbund Nordwestschweiz)*

Fig. 8.3 Basel SBB and its surroundings: the city centre on the right of the tracks, Gundelingen on the left. (Photo: Marc Eggimann, Basel)

development of the region. The organization has been an active promoter of the EuroVille initiative. The site of the railway station (Figure 8.3) is offset relative to the old city centre and the adjoining central business district, on the north side of the tracks. A sketchily defined zone separates the station from the city. On the other side of the tracks (on the left in Figure 8.3) is the neighbourhood of Gundelingen. This area has a mixture of middle-income and moderate-income housing, shops, and light manufacturing.

8.3.3 The process

Plans for the railway station area of Basel have been in the making for a long time. More than 10 years elapsed between the first discussions and the start of construction. In this period, a number of objectives have repeatedly been amended. The plans themselves have taken on a life of their own, becoming increasingly detached from the political arena. Three planning phases and one multiple implementation phase can be distinguished in Basel. In the first phase, the basic concepts were defined through an open process in which the public participated. In the second phase (detailed planning) and the third phase (operational planning), the goals were translated into concrete actions, while the degree of participation was progressively reduced. A fourth phase – implementation – got started before the planning process was completed, though in a fragmentary way.

Phase 1: concept planning, 1983–1986

At the beginning of the 1980s, within a context of globally expanding but locally contracting property markets, the risk that new development could 'leapfrog' the city gradually became apparent to the local government. Economic activity, especially in the growing service sector, had to be kept within the municipal borders, and potential new activities had to be attracted. The railway station area seemed to be the only part of the city offering the space that was needed. The development of a service centre at that particular location would make a direct contribution to the local economy, with an expected creation of 4000 jobs. These could offer local firms expansion possibilities, thus keeping them in the city. It was hoped that some of the new premises could be occupied by external firms, or could offer development opportunities to sectors complementary to the strong core of Basel's economy (essentially the chemical industry). An additional benefit of the project would be relief of the pressure on residential neighbourhoods, halting conversion of dwellings to offices for tertiary-sector activities. This would help to stem the outward flow of population (4000 inhabitants per year lost in the 1980s). Development of a service centre would be connected to and would benefit from the long-needed regional transport interchange that would be integrated with the railway station.

In the same years, SBB (the Swiss railways) was redefining its programmes for Basel HauptBahnhof. The station would be developed in the framework of Bahn 2000, the extensive (estimated at SFr 5.4 billion) national development and investment programme of SBB. The already strong position of the station on international transport routes (Germany and France) would be reinforced, as would its role within regional and local transport networks. On the whole, a doubling of the transport capacity was envisaged. But transport development was not the only important area for SBB. Like many of its European counterparts, the Swiss railways were reorienting their activities towards the market. Among other things, they were looking for better ways to exploit their property assets. The redevelopment of areas next to the centrally located railway stations appeared to be an obvious choice.

Some common ground between the objectives of the city government and the railways was clearly emerging. The two parties were contemplating the possibility of a joint development of the area. Also, the Swiss Mail (PTT) was showing an interest in a transformation that could provide it with a new distribution centre and the possibility of exploiting its own property. The county administration (Basel Land) had shown its readiness to collaborate on the realization of the transport interchange. The final impetus for the initiative was provided by the discussion, at the beginning of the 1980s, about extension of the N2 motorway into the city to connect with the railway station. As a precondition for considering the road project, the city council demanded that a global plan for the station neighbourhood be made. In 1983, the city council voted in favour of a credit of SFr 1 million to finance the planning studies in preparation of a master plan for the area. In a referendum, the population approved the measure by a 60% majority. The rest of the funding for the study, which cost a total of SFr 2.5 million, was provided by the other institutional partners: Basel county, SBB, and PTT. The goals of the study were to clarify the objectives, verify feasibility prospects, reach agreement among the partners, and prepare the following phases.

From the outset the promoters opted for an open and participatory definition of the programme. An underlying reason for this choice is that in the Swiss political system – which is characterized by decentralization and extensive forms of direct democracy – no major initiative can succeed without a high degree of consensus. The political system has checks and balances at each step of the process. Any change in a zoning ordinance would have to be voted on by the city council and could be subjected to a popular referendum. The same applies to budget claims, even if it is just for funding of the planning studies.

The three-year planning process resulted in the document Konzept 86 (Figure 8.4). Konzept 86 has been defined in three steps: initially, an inventory of the key problems; then a comparison between alternative development options; and finally an elaboration of guiding development principles. During this period, the population and other interested parties have been kept informed. Meanwhile, the planning process has been open to suggestions from outside. In 1986 the document was approved by the governments of Basel city and Basel county, as well as by the executives of SBB and PTT. In the course of the discussions and consultations, some of the initial objectives were adapted and others were added. Following negotiations with local residents, additional priorities were set: the mitigation of traffic impacts, and the control of development pressure in residential areas.

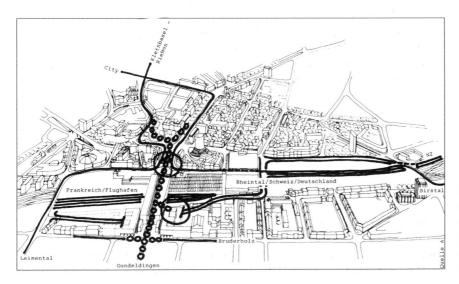

Fig. 8.4 Konzept 86, a transport interchange and a service centre. (Source: Projectleitung Masterplan. Drawing: V.Martinec)

153

The main goals of the development were identified as the realization of (a) a transport interchange and (b) a service centre. To achieve the first objective, a complex package of measures was put together:

- Two tram lines would be diverted to the station, and one that already stopped there would be extended to the suburbs.
- A new bypass road on the south side of the station would provide better accessibility by car to the area, and would free the neighbourhood of Gundelingen from through traffic.
- 650–750 parking spaces would be created.
- The N2 motorway would be extended to the railway station.
- The station square would be remodelled to better serve public transport, pedestrians and cyclists.
- Additional rail tracks would be provided, in order to expand existing national train services, and to allow connection to the French TGV system, the development of a transnational regional S-Bahn network, and a possible rail link to the international airport of Basel-Mulhouse.
- Pedestrian access to and within the station area would be improved.
- A new postal station would be built.

A further improvement of the already excellent accessibility of the site was seen as the main asset for achieving the second objective, the realization of a service centre. Areas for development were already available, and others would be freed. First, new sites would be opened up by moving technical facilities to more peripheral locations. Second, other areas would be made available by redeveloping the parcels currently occupied by artisan workshops along the tracks on the south side. The idea was to attract to the area service firms with a high added value. This would give substance to the hope of developing a business pole, which would make the city of Basel more attractive to investors, both local and foreign.

Phase 2: detailed planning, 1987–1991
In 1987, the council and the population (through a new referendum) voted for the second time in favour of a study credit, this time in the amount of SFr 4.5 million, to continue the planning process. Other successful referendums were held on the construction of underground parking next to the station, and the rezoning of an area owned by the French railways to allow tertiary developments. The rezoning of two other railway areas was approved by the council in 1990, completing the redefinition of the legal framework for land-use regulation. Further elaboration of the plan was commissioned to a private firm specializing in the management of large projects. Its task was to direct the process and coordinate the partners. Special attention had to be devoted to the complex web of infrastructure works, including diversion and extension of the tram lines, pedestrian and bicycle access, a bypass round Gundelingen, and accessibility to the south side of the station. The technical elaboration of the principles defined in Konzept 86 resulted in a new document, Projekt '91. In September 1991, this was adopted by the partners as a basis on which to go further. No fundamental changes were made in the basic contents of the plan in this phase. Most amendments stemmed from feasibility considerations. One notable amendment was presented on financial grounds (insufficient

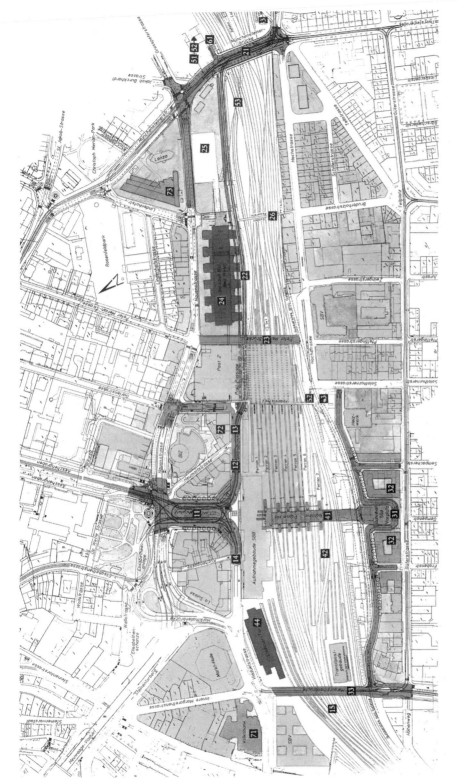

Fig. 8.5 EuroVille: the subprojects. (Source: Koordinationsausschuss EuroVille)

exploitation margins): this was a proposal for a less ambitious passage connecting the north and the south sides of the station, in place of the originally envisaged station bridge. However, the most important changes were not so much in the content as in the process, which became less open to participation and more technocratic. The issues will be examined in some detail in the following sections.

Phases 3 and 4: operational planning, 1992–1995, and implementation, 1994–2005

After 1991, the planning activities moved into an operational phase. Impact studies were carried out, and documentation was prepared for the council vote on the plan. Meanwhile, detailed negotiations between the partners continued in order to hammer out bilateral contracts. Implementation of Projekt '91 had to take place in a context that differed significantly from that prevailing when the plan's basic principles were formulated in 1986. One of the most significant changes was that the real estate market had entered a crisis. Another was that the geographical mobility of firms and workers had grown further. In addition, the financial situation of the public authorities had worsened, while environmental conscious-ness had increased. The translation of the project into actions had to take all of this into account. As a consequence, the motorway link was abandoned in 1992 (officially, it was delayed for 30 years). That decision was made both for financial reasons (a projected cost of SFr 350 million francs) and political reasons (priority given to public transport). Plans for other road infrastructure were also abandoned or delayed. An integrated approach to implementation seemed even less practical than ever. A subdivision of the plan, along the lines anticipated by Projekt '91, into 21 autonomous subprojects was then adopted (Figure 8.5). Changes were also made in the image and the role of the project. The name was changed from 'master plan' to EuroVille, and the project became the main component of an emerging city marketing strategy for Basel.

Fig. 8.6 Bahnhof Ost Basel: new postal station and offices for the market. (Source: Projektgruppe Bahnhof Ost)

Around 1994, while several elements of the package were still awaiting final approval, implementation of individual parts began. Construction of the sub-project Bahnhof Ost (new postal station and offices for the market) began in January 1994 (Figure 8.6). Construction of a signalling post, a locomotive depot, new tracks, reconstruction of the Münchensteiner bridge and of the Nauenstrasse started at around the same time. In the meantime, in 1995, financing of the main infrastructure package was finally approved by a large majority vote, both in the city and the county council, and no referendum was called. Soon afterwards, the board of directors of the PTT and of SBB also approved their share of investment. The task of creating the financial and planning framework for the development of EuroVille could be considered a closed book. In 1996 and 1997, construction of Bahnhof Ost (opening expected in 2000) and of the central parking lots progressed, while plans for the tram lines and the station passage were further elaborated. Five of the six buildings of the office complex had already been rented. The new tenants were the Swiss telecommunications and Swiss mail companies, a software firm, and a business school. The sixth building was reserved for smaller prospective users.

8.3.4 The actors involved

A complex galaxy of actors has been involved with the different phases of EuroVille. The project was initiated by the city of Basel. The idea of combining a transport interchange with a service centre emerged in debates inside the council at the beginning of the 1980s. Basel county got involved essentially because of its interests in the regional transport components (suburban extension of the tram lines, S-Bahn). SBB owns 90% of the areas covered by the project, and Basel HauptBahnhof is crucial to both its transport and property development strategies. For these reasons, its participation in the project was particularly active, often more than that of the city itself. On the other hand, contradictions between the transport and the property dimensions of the operation do not appear to have been entirely solved within SBB. These contradictions crop up in repeated internal discussions. The objectives of the PTT are more limited. Essentially, it is interested in expanding its distribution and administrative facilities in the area, and in developing part of its property commercially.

After the publication of Konzept 86, a partnership (*Immobilien Bahnhofost-gesellschaft*, IBO) was formed between PTT, SBB, and a private consortium led by architecture/development firms on the initiative of the latter. In 1986, these private interests 'knocked the door' of PTT and SBB. The objective of the partnership was to develop the first of the elements of the service centre to be built, Bahnhof Ost (postal station, offices for PTT, and offices for the market). Their main worry was incurring delays in the process; their interest was strictly limited to the perimeter of Bahnhof Ost.

A multifarious range of local interest groups have been involved in or have been otherwise affected by the planning process. *Gruppe Bahnhof* is a political cross-party lobby formed in 1982 to promote the development of the station and its surroundings. This group is connected with employers' and employees' organizations, and to Regio Basiliensis (an informal, cross-national regional political association). At the beginning, in particular, it had played an important role in shaping the discourse around the development and in identifying some of the key slogans, such as 'transport interchange' and 'service centre'. To this group, the project was essentially an opportunity for the city, spanning the economic, urban planning and transport domains. The role of Gruppe Bahnhof could be defined as that of a facilitator, both external (as in communication with the public) and internal (as in mediation of conflicts).

The *Arbeitsgemeinschaft Gundeli-Quartier* represents the local residents and small firms of the neighbourhood south of the station. The group took an active part in the elaboration of Konzept 86. However, their request to participate in the second phase was refused, on the grounds that the neighbourhood was not included in the perimeter of the development. They were instead assigned a diminished role as a discussion partner. Originally, they had a meeting every two months; later the frequency was reduced to one a year between 1992 and 1995. One issue that was important to the group was the negative impact of the project on the neighbourhood south of the railway station. On their request, impact studies were made. However, they have seen little evidence that the results have been taken into consideration.

Finally, an *Interessengemeinschaft Master Plan Bahnhof SBB Basel* (IGMP), a coalition of private interests (banks, insurance firms, artisans, construction firms), was formed to give a voice to the potential investors and users in the area.

Table 8.1 summarizes the main phases of the project.

Table 8.1 Basel EuroVille: summary of the main phases

Phase 1: concept planning (1970s); partnership City of Basel, County of Basel, Swiss Railways, PTT, 1983–1986	
1983	The council approves funding for planning; cooperative plan definition
June 1986	Konzept 86 published
Phase 2: detailed planning, 1987–1991; feasibility and impact studies	
September 1991	Projekt '91 published
1987–1992	City council votes on planning funding, zoning station area, bridge construction
1987–1992	Population votes (referendum) on planning funding; construction of Münchensteiner bridge, construction of Centraalbahn parking
Phase 3: operational planning, 1992–1995; internal discussions in the partnership	
1995	City and county councils vote on financing infrastructure
Phase 4: implementation, 1994–2005	
Beginning of 1994	Start construction of Bahnhof Ost (first market element)
March 1996	EuroVille participates in the MIPIM in Cannes; official start (international) marketing
October 1996	Results of the competition for the station bridge are made public
2000	Expected opening of Bahnhof Ost

8.4 Property development at Basel EuroVille

8.4.1 Functions

The final product of the planning phase was the document Konzept 86 (Figure 8.4). This document identified the main goals of development. These entail the realization of (a) a transport interchange (better transport integration between public transport at an international, regional and local level) and (b) a service centre (expansion of the business district centre in the direction of the station). Complementary measures (such as speed limits, and minimum housing percentages) should protect the surrounding neighbourhoods from traffic and development pressure.

The *transport* objectives (node) include:

*   Public transport:
    an attractive transport chain (SBB, DB, SNCF, suburban trains, tram, bus and taxi);
    improving the modal split;
    tram links between the suburbs and the centre through the station;
    increased station capacity (ICE, TGV, Bahn 2000, S-Bahn);
    reconstruction of the postal station;
    better connections between the central city and the station.
*   Private transport:
    improvement of pedestrian access;
    improvement of motorcycle and bicycle access and parking;
    park and ride facilities;
    accessibility of the south side;
    relief of Gundelingen from through traffic.

The *service centre* objectives (place) include:

*   Urban development/form:
    renewal of the station square and the south station;
    activation of the station as a working and living district;
    promotion of the development of the CBD in the direction of the station;
    better integration of the suburbs;
    relief of the residential neighbourhoods from tertiary conversion pressure;
    spatial orientation of the demand for space;
    a contribution to the ecological balance (4500 workplaces next to the station).
*   Commercial:
    more efficient exploitation of the areas around the station;
    renewal of the postal station;
    construction of Bahnhof Ost with PTT, Telecom and private services.

A total of about 300 000 m^2 is envisaged. The main elements are: Bahnhof Ost, with 180 000 m^2 of mainly office space; Bahnhof Süd, with 80 000 m^2 of mixed uses (housing, offices, shops); and Elsässer Tor, with 18 000 m^2 of services.

To facilitate implementation the plan was subdivided into subprojects. The most important of these are the following (public investment is mentioned when present; the numbers refer to Figure 8.5):

- new, re-localized, signalling post and locomotive depot (51, 52);
- Bahnhof Ost – postal station, PTT and telecom offices, private services (24);
- reconstruction of the Münchensteiner bridge to provide more space for bicycles and cars, three tram tracks, and headroom for trains running beneath (21);
- diversion of two tram lines through the station – implementation 1998–2001, cost SFr 58.2 million, 50% Basel city, 50% Basel county (22);
- underground parking for 400 cars and reorganization of access in the station square (12);
- tertiary development in the SNCF area – rezoned in 1987, architectural competition in 1990, construction not started as of summer 1997 (44);
- remodelling of the station square – architectural competition in 1994, project approved in 1997, completion in 2001, cost SFr 40.3 million, of which SFr 35.1 million Basel city, SFr 5.2 million Basel county (11);
- station north–south link and related infrastructure works – implementation between 1997 and 2000, cost of link SFr 42.4 million, of which 33% Basel city, 67% SBB (41, 42, 43);
- renewal of the station's south entrance and development of the surrounding areas – implementation 1997 onwards, 80 000 m² of non-transport uses, at least a quarter housing, 700 spaces underground parking (31, 32);
- bicycle paths and parking – construction 1998–2000, cost SFr 9.3 million, 100% Basel city;
- road access south side – implementation 1997–1999, cost SFr 37 million, of which 43% Basel city, 57% SBB;
- accompanying measures to include 30 km/h maximum speed zones – implementation 1996–1997, cost SFr 1 million, 100% Basel city – and a *wohnanteilplan* (minimum amounts of housing) in Gundelingen.

Construction of the first market element, Bahnhof Ost, began in January 1994. Completion is expected around 2000. The building under construction (Figure 8.6) has a basement containing an underground postal station with customs offices and parking facilities, surmounted by six five-floor office buildings. Two of these will be occupied by administrative offices of the national postal and telecommunications companies. The remaining four (for a total of 24 700 m²) are being marketed to private firms. Flexibility is maximal. The six superstructures were brought under an independent organization so that they could be constructed at different times, as funding becomes available. The land is leased for 99 years from the SBB and the PTT by the PTT (60%) and IBO (40%). IBO is a partnership of SBB, PTT and a consortium of architects/developers plus a bank. The architects/developers own the majority of shares, and have taken the technical and financial leadership of the operation.

All in all, investment involved in projects under construction or in preparation amounts (1994 data) to SFr 650 million. Public and para-public investment amounts to about SFr 200 million (SFr 87 million Basel city, SFr 34.3 million Basel county, SFr 47.8 million SBB, and SFr 20.5 million the federal state).

8.4.2 Organization

EuroVille is a complex venture. This is primarily because of the extension of the project's perimeter, but it is also complex because of the networks connecting in the station; the number of actors involved, often with contradictory objectives; the level of political and technical interdependence between several sub-elements and decision processes; and the political uncertainty connected to the long time span of the initiative.

Examples of these political–technical interdependences are numerous. For instance, according to a survey made in 1991 (CEAT, 1993), they include the following:

- Once approved by the council, the realization of the parking lot of the station depends on the availability of private investment.
- The realization of the tram lines (city government) is dependent on approval of the Münchensteiner bridge project (city council) and on the realization according to plan of the motorway link (city government, federal government).
- The realization of the postal station (PTT) depends on the construction, out of the perimeter, of a new locomotive depot (SBB) and the removal of the freight facilities (SBB).
- The realization of the tertiary centre south of the station (SBB) depends on the departure of the post (PTT), on the realization of the pedestrian passage (SBB), and on the southern bypass (city council).

In view of this complexity, the adopted organizational structure entails:

- a project direction, with the task of coordinating the actions of the different institutional partners;
- a technical team with six members (two from Basel city, two from Basel county, one from the SBB, and one from the PTT) to act as interface between the four organizations and the elaboration of the plan;
- a high-level delegation of the institutional partners, which meets every six months to discuss and endorse the progress made;
- consultants on specific issues;
- accompanying teams (for example, with the task of informing the population).

This structure significantly changed its identity in moving from the first to the second phase. In the first – political – phase (1983–1986), the project was directed by city officials. Priority was given to openness of the decision-making process and involvement of all the interested parties. The population was regularly informed, and organizations and individuals were formally invited to react. At the same time, a participatory planning process was started in the neighbourhood of Gundelingen, on the south side of the tracks. That process led to a set of planning guidelines (*richtplanung*), which were approved by the city government in 1986. Interaction between the two planning processes was high.

The second – technical – phase (1987–1991) and subsequent phases were of a completely different nature. The development perimeter was divided into four sub-areas, inside which subprojects were identified and developed autonomously. Technical and financial issues dominated the discussion, and only those parties who were directly responsible were involved in the process. Whenever a subproject was ready, implementation could in principle start. There was no need to wait for the picture to be complete. This strategy was justified by several actors as the only one by which such a complex programme could be implemented in the fragmented organizational context of Basel. One consequence is that the public has been progressively excluded from the planning process. Information got scarcer, while opportunities to interact disappeared. The local groups of Gundelingen have been especially critical of this change. Others have pointed out that a global view may have been lost, and with it the meaning of (and thus public support for) the individual elements. For instance, unexpected opposition was encountered with regard to the reconstruction of the Münchensteiner bridge. That opposition almost closed down the project. Debates ensued, concentrating on the increase in car lanes. That focus emerged because other aspects of the infrastructure had fallen out of public view (such as the realization of bicycle paths, the opening of a third tram line, the allowance for construction of additional tracks, and the passage of double-decker S-Bahn trains underneath).

8.4.3 *Marketing*

The marketing strategy of Basel EuroVille, integrated in the city marketing of Basel, has been summed up in a *unique selling proposition*. The assets of the City Centre Basel EuroVille are:

- tri-nationality (multicultural community, internationally oriented business);
- transport position (transport interchange in the middle of Europe);
- urban economy (excellence in the chemicals, banking, insurance, commerce, and distribution sectors);
- personnel (good educational level);
- political acceptance (both the city executive and the city council support EuroVille);
- security (political stability, property security, low crime levels);
- quality of life (intact environment, space for leisure time, high-quality housing, lively cultural scene).

The institutional partners are optimistic about the market response. They see their investment as strategic and long-term. They are not looking for immediate profits, and they are confident in the future performance of the area. The site does not face competition within the urban region. As the argument goes, other big projects in the city (such as renewal of the trade fair) are more complementary than competitive. Vacancy rates in peripheral locations are much higher than in central locations. This is a sign that the attractiveness of the city centre is still great. It would also suggest that public transport accessibility is increasingly seen by investors as an asset rather than a constraint. The additional strength of EuroVille, conclude the partners, is that it offers premises of a size and quality that are absent from the existing property supply of the city centre.

The current marketing campaign of the first private element, Bahnhof Ost (marketing started at the end of 1995, building will be ready in 2000), stresses the 'total' and internationally oriented accessibility of the location and its proximity to the traditional city centre as its strongest points. The city of Basel is advertised as a major international communication node, the seat of multinational (chemicals) companies, banking, insurance, transport and world trade. At the junction of three nations, it 'provides, in a complex way, an obvious impetus for international trading and patterns of thought'. The availability of high-quality, flexible, expandable space within this locational context is seen as the unique asset of the building complex of Bahnhof Ost:

> The layout of spaces as well as the design of the rooms facilitate a broad range of uses, from single office and group rooms to cubicle offices within one large room, and conference spaces between the size of a small conference room and the size of an entire learning centre.
>
> (Bahnhof Ost Basel brochure)

However, the target group appears to remain quite generic. Indeed, any use ranging from education to research, health care, insurance, financing, accounting, law, high-tech, marketing, administration and 'headquarters of international firms and organizations' is seen as possible. Indicative prices are SFr 300/m^2/year; prices in comparable peripheral office locations are SFr 180–200/m^2/year. A particular characteristic of the building is the strong integration of art and architecture, with the involvement of artists of international renown (such as Donald Judd, Vito Acconci, and Maria Nordman). Environmental aspects have also enjoyed special attention (natural lighting, climate control devices, and energy-saving measures, for example). Exceptional provisions have been adopted to protect the offices from noise and vibrations (such as separate foundations and sound screens). According to the developers, all these extra efforts are justified by the need to improve upon the image of the railway station, which they see as 'the main problem of this location'.

The main structural data of the EuroVille development are presented in Table 8.2.

Table 8.2 Basel EuroVille: main structural data

Area ownership	Mostly Swiss railways
Total floor space	About 300 000 m^2
Offices	198 000 m^2
Mixed: housing + (work)shops + offices	80 000 m^2
Parking	About 1600 places planned
Costs	SFr 650 million (projects under construction or in preparation in 1994; 22% is public investment)

8.5 Basel EuroVille: evaluation

EuroVille is an initiative with distinct approaches to the node and place dimensions of the station area. There are two objectives: the creation of a transport interchange, and the creation of a service centre. The first objective is being pursued through a package of infrastructure investment, and the second through a collection of autonomous subprojects. The particularly high internal articulation of the plan is both its specific strength and its weakness. Single projects, tasks and responsibilities are defined more clearly than elsewhere, but an overarching, integrated vision of the node–place and of its role in the agglomeration is largely missing. In more detail, four observations can be made.

A first observation is that the initiative has a solid foundation in an overall improvement of the transport node. Rail services calling at Basel HBF will be improved within the framework of Bahn 2000, the extensive, country-wide investment programme of the Swiss railways. The station is peripheral in the national railway system, but is an international node of growing importance: ICE services to and from Germany (and in the future the Netherlands) already stop in the station, while TGV connections to and from France are planned. The development of an RER/S-Bahn network including the German and French parts of the agglomeration is also envisaged. The EuroVille initiative has capitalized on these programmes, and has amplified their impact by extending the scope of the improvement to urban and local connections. To enhance the station's transport centrality at the urban level, two tram lines will be diverted, and a third, already connected, will be extended into the suburbs. Upgrading of the transportation node also includes a rationalization of pedestrian and bicycle accesses and connections. A new road bypass on the south side of the tracks and new underground parking facilities complete the picture. A direct link to the motorway system is also planned, but construction has been postponed for a combination of financial and political reasons. Funding for all these infrastructures – with the exception of the motorway link – has been secured, and a detailed implementation schedule has been agreed upon. The degree of certainty and consistency of this infrastructure package is remarkable, and is the product of a carefully articulated and patiently constructed decision process.

The solid framework of transport and infrastructure programmes shapes an essential condition for achieving the second part of the station area development strategy, the realization of a service centre. The 'enabling' approach to investment does not stop at the node level, but is extended to the place, or station neighbourhood, level. An important aspect here is the improvement of connections across the tracks, and the upgrading of the entrance to the station on the south (non-city) side, in order to open up property development opportunities in areas until now virtually cut off from the historic centre. In developing these and other non-transport parts of the plan a project-by-project, building-by-building approach has been adopted. For example, all attention is being focused on Bahnhof Ost, the first stage to be put on the market. This sort of approach leads to a second observation. While reducing risks, such a fragmented property development strategy could rebound. A strong overarching concept connecting developments in the transport and activity spheres, both within and between each other, seems to be lacking. As a result, while the transportation interchange is gradually taking shape, the nature of the service centre is still permeated by uncertainty.

The third observation concerns process aspects. The initiative was taken by a partnership of the local and regional government and the federal railway company. They promoted together an open planning process, which resulted in Konzept 86, a broadly discussed document fixing the key spatial and functional guidelines of the project. A second (1986–1991) and a third (1991–1995) more 'closed' planning phases followed, during which the programme was translated first into a technically and financially feasible plan and then into a set of independent but coordinated implementation projects. The whole package was repeatedly submitted to political scrutiny, and was finally approved by the city council in 1995. The early, broadly shared agreement on the basic concepts embodied in Konzept 86 has been a key element in ensuring acceptance of and commitment to the project during the subsequent stages. However, the virtual cessation of public consultation in the latter stages has been the object of repeated criticism from the local community, and may have weakened public support and momentum. This could prove especially problematic in view of the absence of a strong, integrated vision for the place, as mentioned above.

The fourth and last observation stems from the recognition of the exceptionally high degree of flexibility of the urban development plan, both in space and in time. The market components are being developed in stages. Bahnhof Ost, the first of them, is under construction; other sections of the area are still in a planning phase, while the remaining sections are set aside as reserve. In order to make it more manageable, implementation has been considered in terms of financially and functionally independent subprojects. All decisions regarding the infrastructure have been defined in detail, and related financing has been secured, so that there is an accountable framework for the volatile private investment. The infrastructure, the related public investment and the land-use plan could be considered the 'hard' elements, shaping conditions for the progressive definition of the associated commercial components, seen as 'soft' elements. Flexibility of the latter is extreme, and goes down to the building level. Bahnhof Ost is conceived as a building made of sub-buildings. A two-floor basement is being constructed, on which autonomous mid-rise office segments will be added when and if investors and users are found. Risk is thus greatly reduced. But again, such an extreme fragmentation in the implementation may also have its flip-side in the loss of global coherence, and ultimately of the appeal of the area.

8.6 Zentrum Zürich Nord as node and place

8.6.1 The node

Essentially a regional station, Oerlikon, adjoining the development site of Zentrum Zürich Nord, is the second station in the Zürich metropolitan area for passenger flows. It is served by six regional S-Bahn lines (an average of 20 trains per hour), but by only 30 intercities a day (Figure 8.7). Bahn 2000, the development programme of the Swiss railways does not foresee an increase in the national or international capacity of the station. However, it must be stressed that the S-Bahn gives fast and frequent connections both to Zürich's main station and

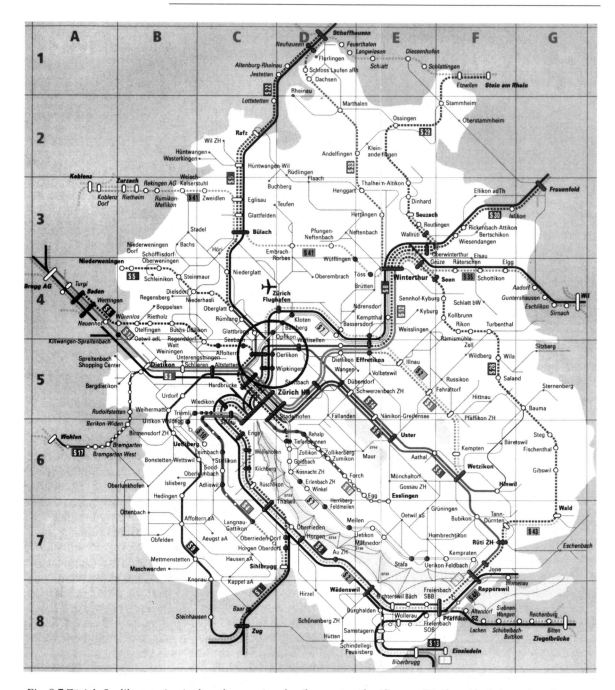

Fig. 8.7 Zürich Oerlikon station in the urban–regional railway networks. (Source: Zürchner Verkehrsverbund)

historical city centre (in 7 minutes, an average of 10 trains per hour), and to the international airport of Kloten (in 5 minutes, an average of two trains per hour).

Furthermore, another S-Bahn station, Seebach, is in the north of the site, and the area is well served by Zürich's local transport system. New bus lines, a proposed tram line and possibly a monorail would provide radial and tangential links, and would interconnect at Oerlikon station.

8.6.2 *The place*

The project area is a partly obsolete industrial site on the north side of the railway station of Oerlikon (Figure 8.8). On the southern side of the tracks is Oerlikon district, an important secondary centre in the Zürich agglomeration. Oerlikon is home to 50 000 people and workplace to 30 000.

With the neighbouring Glattal and Furttal municipalities it is part of Zürich Nord, an area of 120 000 inhabitants and 90 000 workplaces. Zürich Nord is the section of the agglomeration that has grown the fastest in recent years. It has witnessed both heavy restructuring and loss of jobs in its traditional industries (including sites next to Oerlikon station) and a development boom of high-tech

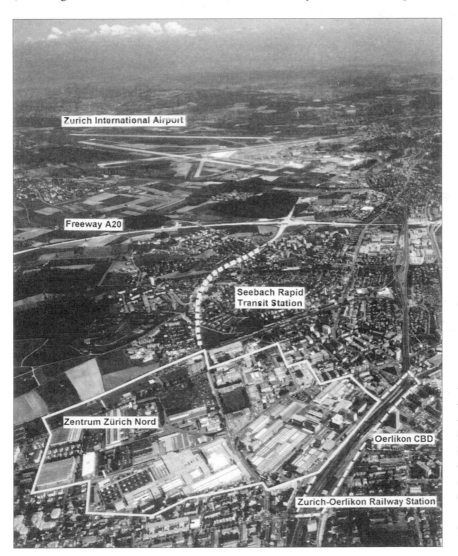

Fig. 8.8 Zentrum Zürich Nord: the project area. In the background are the A20 motorway and the international airport, on the right of the tracks is Oerlikon city centre. (Photo: Swissphoto Vermessung AG. Graphics: UR architects & planners)

and international service firms on more peripheral locations, particularly in the vicinity of the international airport of Kloten.

8.6.3 The process

The plans for the redevelopment of the railway station area of Zentrum Zürich Nord are of a more recent period than those for Basel EuroVille. The first initiatives only started between 1988 and 1991. But here also the translation from initiative to plan, programme and implementation took a rather long period. At least three stages can be distinguished, as follows.

Phase 1: from the initiative to the programme, 1988–1991
The trigger for the urban redevelopment initiative was the de-industrialization and production reconversion processes in the areas north of the station of Zürich Oerlikon. As in many other areas in the city the restructuring of production made industrial land and buildings redundant. In Zürich Nord it was Oerlikon Bürle, a weapon factory, that at the beginning of 1988 approached the major landowner in the area, Asea Brown Boveri (ABB, machine construction), to agree on a common redevelopment strategy. Together they controlled a strategic majority of the land north of the station. Advised by a planner, Ueli Roth, they contacted the city of Zürich and the Swiss railways (SBB). They needed the cooperation of the city as the areas were zoned as industrial, and a change of the land-use ordinance was a precondition for any redevelopment. In the absence of a new municipal plan the legal framework had to be provided by an amendment to the existing plan in the form of special building prescriptions (*sonderbauvorschriften*). These had to be approved by the city and the canton executives, by the city council, and – if a referendum was called – by the population of Zürich. The negative experiences of other big privately initiated projects in the city (such as HauptBahnhof Südwest) were evidence to the landowners that attuning with the public actor must be sought from the outset. SBB was seen both as an important landowner in the area (about 10% of the land) and as the major transport provider: frequent connections to the city centre and the international airport make the station of Oerlikon exceptionally accessible.

The landowners, the city and SBB agreed to form a partnership for the redevelopment of the area. The initiative was labelled Chance Oerlikon 2011. The name alluded to the 'chance' that the freeing of space from industry offered, an opportunity that could be realized by the year 2011. Negotiations began. The main problem was to reach agreement on the percentages of different land uses between the landowner and the city. The industrial firms intended to keep some production in the area, but for the rest strived for reallocation to the most profitable use – offices. Unlike other landowners in the metropolitan area, however, they seemed ready to discuss other possibilities. The worsening conditions in the property market and a management 'with broad views' (ABB is a multinational, innovation oriented company) were among the explanations given by actors and analysts for such a relative openness. The city's policy was to guarantee that, in the conversion, space was retained for production (including small-scale firms), and that a diverse area of the city, including housing and public spaces, was achieved. For the municipality, an important element was the charismatic leadership of

Ursula Koch, the influential alderwoman for urban development. She kept her post during the whole planning process, thus guaranteeing continuity and public accountability in the negotiations. In 1990 definitive agreement was reached on a *struktuurkonzept* that fixed the quantities and percentages of land use for the site. A total of 820 000 m² would be developed (including the renewal of existing industrial buildings); 10% would be reserved for public uses, and the rest would be allocated equally between housing, services, and industry. Average densities would be 160%: 120% for housing, 250% for services, and 165% for industry. According to all the actors this was the turning point in the negotiations, as thereafter 'we knew we could trust each other'.

Phase 2: from the programme to the plan, 1992–1994
Until this point nothing had been said on the form that the development would take. To this end it was decided to launch an open international urban design competition. After two rounds a local team of young architects – Ruoss, Schrader and Siress – was appointed. Public reactions to their competition entry were positive. Above all, two features of their project struck the jury (Figure 8.9):

- The project envisaged a gradual, flexible transformation. Respect for the existing street grid and building masses allowed for maximum discretion in the implementation. A full range of possibilities was accounted for: buildings could be maintained in their present form and function, or just the function could change with few adaptations, or new buildings could be built, though consistent with the masses and the uses of the existing buildings.
- There was a clear concept of how global urban design quality was to be achieved. A diverse and articulated presence of green and open spaces was the main instrument: the clusters of buildings were organized around a series of parks, while linear and punctuating elements continuously connected the whole. Also important was the choice of a spatial differentiation of functional accents (for example, services dominating next to the station, residential space in outer areas), which nevertheless also entailed some functional mixture in every parcel (for example, minimum percentages of housing and public uses in the service areas, and a share of services in the residential areas).

Unexpectedly, after the urban design competition, SBB chose to cease active involvement in the process, and dropped its area out of the planning perimeter. Initially, on SBB's request, options for developments across and along the tracks had also been explored. Now only about 3 ha in the northern section of the site (formerly a freight yard) would still be included: a small share, and one without any direct link to the main transport node. According to SBB, this decision was based on technical and economic considerations (building above the tracks would be too complicated and too costly). But it also stemmed from the fact that railway land could be developed even without a zoning ordinance. Furthermore, Oerlikon station plays no strategic role in SBB's transport development programme. However, it should be noted that Zentrum Zürich Nord is the largest urban redevelopment project in Switzerland. The station could and should be the strategic link between the existing and the future centres on both sides of the tracks. It is therefore fairly obvious that a 'chance' is being missed, not only by SBB but also by the other promoters of the ZZN initiative.

Fig. 8.9 Zentrum Zürich Nord: the urban redevelopment concept, based on the winning competition entry of Ruoss and Siress Architektur. (Source: Amt für Siedlungsplanung und Städtebau der Stadt Zürich)

The prize-winning project was adopted as the basis for the elaboration of the legal planning framework (land-use plan and urban design guidelines, *sonderbauvorschriften*) and of the contracts between the partners (*rahmenvertrag* and bilateral contracts). After two years of discussions, agreement on an urban redevelopment concept (*Entwicklungsleitbild*) was finally reached in 1994 (Figure 8.9). The proposal was presented jointly by the City of Zürich, the property owners, and SBB in September of that year. For the partners, its publication marked the point where their agreement achieved a sufficient level of clarity and substance to be submitted to the outside world.

Phase 3: from the plan to the contracts, 1995–1996
At the beginning of 1995, public consultations got under way. Individuals and associations were invited to comment on the proposal and make suggestions. Until then, the decision process had been essentially restricted to the three partners, or rather to the two most active ones: the landowners and the city. Local groups had been denied information and the right to participate. Among these local groups, one had been particularly active: the association called zürifüfzg! First they demanded access to the planning process for the local population. Then they came up with their own development vision, which was defined through open workshops. Afterwards they offered comments on the official proposal. And finally they came forward with concrete suggestions as their contribution to the transformation process. Surprisingly, when the official development concept was presented in 1994, it contained many points of overlap with the proposals made by the group. Furthermore, there was a readiness to cooperate on both sides. Both zürifüfzg! and the public–private partners had the same main objective: to develop a diverse, lively urban district on the former industrial sites. The local groups were motivated by the desire to attract activities from the city centre (above all in the cultural sphere) to a peripheral neighbourhood where 'nothing much was going on'. The landowners perceived the development of a lively urban

district as a precondition for attracting investment into the area. The partners seemed to be conscious that the input of the local group 'was a sort of planning we could not do' and that their contribution was therefore welcome.

There was also a political element in the change, of course. In Zürich's fragmented and coalition-based political scene, it would have been too risky – at least from the perspective of the public authority – to open up the debate on a plan that did not yet enjoy widespread support. In particular, Ursula Koch feared that allowing the local population to take part at an early stage would have led to polarization. It would have pitted the left against the right, driven a wedge between economic and social interests, and paralysed the planning process. This political strategy seems to have paid off. The project, unlike many others in Zürich, can count on wide support in the council. And given its open-ended and process-oriented character, there is still room for external contributions. The local community seems also to have accepted the point, as it sees more opportunities for direct involvement. One remarkable turn of events in this respect is that a direct line of communication and cooperation is developing between the landowners and zürifüfzg! This readiness to collaborate – particularly unusual on the landowner side – appears to be grounded in their shared awareness of the complexity of the task. An industrial area has to be transformed into a diverse part of the city. To accomplish that goal, a plurality of initiatives and initiators is indispensable.

The planning framework derived from the winning plans of Ruoss, Schrader and Siress seems perfectly suited to this philosophy. The *sonderbauvorschriften* are taken as flexible guidelines. Guiding concepts (functional, building, open space, and traffic principles) have been clearly articulated. Nevertheless, the development aims have not been defined in detail. Their specification awaits the results of feasibility studies. The concrete form of the development could be diverse in nature (temporary or permanent) and might be initiated by different actors (market or community).

In the spring of 1996, public reactions to the urban redevelopment concept were evaluated. Both the *sonderbauvorschriften* and the contracts were elaborated so that they would be ready for submission to the relevant bodies in the course of the year. The progress towards a detailed plan was commended in December 1996 by the city executive and in the spring of 1997 by a city council commission. However, some problems (mostly connected with land reclamation issues) still had to be sorted out with the landowners. As soon as these are solved – according to expectations, in the autumn of 1997 – the plan can be submitted to the city council for final approval. At that point, it would be possible to call for a referendum and to lodge objections. If, as is presumed, no major resistance emerges, the plan could be then formalized.

Meanwhile, marketing has already started. In March 1996 the project was presented at MIPIM, the annual international real estate fair in Cannes. In principle, each property owner should market their property independently. But joint meetings are held regularly, and the main landowner, ABB, has a virtual leadership. In the summer of 1997, feasibility prospects for the plan were presented. The prospects looked good: a first series of new industrial facilities had already been built, and a concrete proposal for a shopping and housing complex had been submitted. Design competitions for parks and housing projects, among other things, had either taken place, or would soon be held.

Table 8.3 Zentrum Zürich Nord: summary of the main phases

Phase 1: from the initiative to the programme, 1988–1991

	Initiative of the property owners (ABB, OB); establishment of the partnership with the City of Zürich and the Swiss Railways; negotiations
1990	Agreement reached on the *Struktuurkonzept*

Phase 2: from the programme to the plans, 1992–1994

1992	Urban design competition (in two rounds); elaboration, discussions
September 1994	Presentation of urban development concept

Phase 3: from the plans to the contracts, 1995–1996

Beginning of 1995	Public consultation
1995/1996	Elaboration of the land-use plan and urban design guidelines (*sonderbauvorschriften*); elaboration of the contracts (*rahmenvertrag*, bilateral contracts)
March 1996	ZZN participates in the MIPIM in Cannes; international marketing starts
1996/1997	Progress noted by the city council and executive; the public and private partners work towards finalization of the contracts
Autumn 1997	(Expected) vote on land-use plan; contracts to be signed

Table 8.4 Communication plan for Zentrum Zürich Nord (up to 1995)

16 June 1989	Orientation of personalities of city districts 11 and 12
7 July 1989	Press conference of the landowners
12 June 1990	Joint press conference of the city and the landowners
16 May 1991	Joint press conference on the urban design competition
28 April 1992	Joint neighbourhood information on the urban design competition results
29 April 1992	Joint press conference on the urban design competition results
11 November 1992	Joint neighbourhood information on the result of the second round of the urban design competition
12 November 1992	Joint press conference on the result of the second round of the urban design competition
26 September 1994	Press conference and neighbourhood information on the urban development concept Zentrum Zürich Nord
5 December 1994	Information event for the local population
10 January 1995	Opening of the public consultations, with a press conference and information for the local population
January–March 1995	Public consultations

Once the approval has been given for the planning framework, the municipal government will consider its mission accomplished. However, informal involvement in the project will remain high. Thus a continuing role of the municipality as facilitator of informal contacts is to be expected. More concretely, individual development would require a building permit. It is the intention of the public and the private partners to prepare each application in close cooperation with the interested investors/users. All the actors consider the level of private, public and community interaction not only exceptional but also extremely positive, and they intend to keep profiting from it. In this respect, it is revealing to see how the evolution of the planning process and the communication plan of Zentrum Zürich Nord have run parallel and have been consistent with each other (Tables 8.3 and 8.4). To preserve this capacity for concerted effort since February 1997, and following a proposal of zürifüfzg!, an accompanying team has been installed. Their task is to foster communication between the public, private and community partners, thereby ensuring that the implementation process will run smoothly.

8.7 Property development at Zentrum Zürich Nord

8.7.1 The functional concept

The objective of the development is to transform an industrial zone into an area with an urban mix of functions in the spheres of work, living, culture, and leisure time. Five thousand residents and 12 000 workers are expected. The area has been subdivided in sub areas with a dominant accent (residential, industrial, service). Overall, about 240 000 m^2 of housing, 315 000 m^2 of services, and 270 000 m^2 of industry are to be developed (1996 data). A degree of functional mixture will be pursued in every parcel, with the exception of those reserved for industrial production and public functions. For instance, in the predominantly service-oriented area around the station, at least a minimum amount of housing will be kept. The diffuse presence of housing will help to create a socially secure environment, one that is lively at all hours of the day and night. On the other side, the presence of services in the residential sections will allow experimentation with new combinations of living and working (for example, home working, or artists' studios). The establishment of shops and restaurants, of activities that attract large numbers of visitors, and of neighbourhood-level services in all the ground-floor premises will be also promoted. Existing buildings could provide space for temporary uses such as exhibitions, ateliers, workshops, theatre, and education. Public services will eventually include a professional school (funded by the canton of Zürich), an elementary and middle school (funded by the city of Zürich), and a public engineering facility (also funded by the city of Zürich). A planning bonus of 2% will be awarded in exchange for an equivalent amount of space for decentralized public services such as daycare and community centres. Part of the site will continue to be used for industrial production (by the same landowners), but their activities will be re-oriented towards research and development, and should be able to evolve competitively.

The group zürifüfzg!, the landowners, and the city government all want to develop a true urban centre in Oerlikon. All perceive an urban centre as an attractive experience: a place where people live and work; where different forms of economic, commercial, and cultural activities take place and a social mixture is present; where a synergy exists in the supply of culture, sport, exhibitions, and food; and which has a local, regional and extra-regional significance. The proposals made by zürifüfzg! revolve around the process dimension of urbanization. That means that urbanization takes place through a gradual change in which different competing actors, trends and objectives are involved. Present and future workers, residents and city users should be seen – from the point of view of this local group – as the indispensable human resources on which to build the identity of the district. The new centre should get a distinct character and differentiate itself from other centres. This is also a basic condition for the attraction of investors. Activities connected with production and consumption of leisure time and culture are seen as particularly crucial. Some examples are sports, education, entertainment, comedies and musicals, tourist facilities, exhibitions, fashion, food, techno/disco, and open-air activities. In practice, the group proposes to start with low-investment initiatives that could make good use of the empty industrial halls. Examples of such possible initiatives are:

- A theatre, concert and event complex for 800–2000 visitors. This facility should also offer the possibility for groups to produce their own shows. It would require only a small investment to make minimal adaptations of the existing industrial buildings. The possibility is being explored with the city and interested performing groups.
- A Japanese hall: a central facility for foreign tourists to Switzerland, where the country could be presented and the visit organized. Attached facilities could be a crafts centre, a folk music school, and a transport and travel centre. Initial contacts have been already made with transport and travel organizations.
- An urban laboratory: a facility for discussions, events, meetings, and associations around the theme of urban development. A sort of meeting point, or theme-leisure centre, with a restaurant, cafe, conference rooms, library, and exhibition spaces.
- Other possibilities include artists' studios, a 24-hour computer centre, an 'action square', a 'discovery trail', and public services.

8.7.2 *The urban design and traffic concepts*

See Figures 8.9 and 8.10. The existing street grid and blocks of buildings will be maintained. New buildings can be inserted gradually without rupturing the structure. The area will be divided into five sub-areas, each with its original character. The areas will be characterized by elements peculiar to their historical development, such as old industrial structures, by building types, and by open space. In special situations, architectural competitions will be held. There will be an extensive, hierarchical system of green spaces. Each sub-area will be centred on a park, and each park will have an individual speciality (such as sports, woods, city life, or industrial heritage). Orientation will be provided by linear elements (tree lines), while punctuating elements ('pocket parks') will provide for rest areas in the working complexes.

Ecological considerations such as emission levels and energy saving have been guiding criteria in developing the traffic concept. Another concern has been that

Teilgebiet E

Teilgebiet A

Teilgebiet B

Teilgebiet C

Teilgebiet D

Fig. 8.10 Zentrum Zürich Nord: the building concept. Hatched areas are retained buildings, dark grey areas are new buildings, light grey areas are new one-level buildings. Teilgebiet means 'sub-area.' (Source: Amt für Siedlungsplanung und Städtebau der Stadt Zürich)

transport and traffic solutions should not require large investments up front. From the outset, the area is well served by public transport. The fulcrum of the development is the existing railway station of Oerlikon. Services (and thus higher levels of traffic) will be concentrated there. Another S-Bahn station serves the north side of the site. In addition, two radial and one tangential bus line on dedicated lanes will be brought into the perimeter, so that no location will be more than 300 m away from a public transport stop. In the design and the localization of public transport stops, passenger security will be a priority. For instance, easy eye and ear contact will be assured. Furthermore, the area will have an extensive network of bicycle and pedestrian paths. The volume of motorized traffic that the streets will accommodate will be kept to a minimum, and parking facilities, while concentrated in specific structures, will not surpass the current area-wide capacity of 4000. The objective is to keep car traffic at the present levels. As in Basel, an underground road link to the peripheral motorway is planned, but the plan will not be operative for another 30 years. Novel and environmentally friendly concepts have also been developed in the area of public utilities, including water and soil management, energy provision, and waste disposal.

8.7.3 *The development concept*

The development process has been the object of specific attention and measures to ensure that it stays within the planning guidelines. For instance, an element of public space will have to be attached to any private development (through direct transfer of private land and/or development fees, for example). A mix of functions will be guaranteed at all times by providing a minimum percentage of other functions at the parcel level. There are linkage mechanisms between private developments, the extension of the public transport network, and the construction of schools. In a first phase (already under way), the industrial firms will reorganize their production activities, freeing space for other uses. Then interested individual investors and users will have the opportunity to develop properties within the conditions set by the planning guidelines. It is expected that development could be completed in 20–30 years. The urban design framework is thus intended as an abstract (conceptual) system of rules. It forms a scaffolding for the actual (not entirely foreseeable) implementation options. The feasibility study is seen as the necessary instrument to further refine the plan, case by case. It is not a 'final state' that is thus envisaged, but rather a 'transformation process'.

Particularly interesting – and possibly revealing of the future development of Zentrum Zürich Nord – is the role that the local group zürifüfzg! is playing in the implementation phase. The group sees itself as a producer of ideas and proposals for the transformation of Zentrum Zürich Nord, a promoter of community involvement (as in the definition of the public uses of the area), an initiator of consortia in the fields of culture, education and leisure time, and a contributor to the urban development process by organizing discussions and documentation on culture, education, and projects. The local group has successfully proposed the formation of a project group to accompany the development process. Contacts with the private partners are intensifying, to the point where it seems that some of the group members might be employed as consultants by the landowners.

Table 8.5 Zentrum Zürich Nord: main structural data

Surface area	63 ha (station area, outside project perimeter, is 10 ha)
Area ownership	Mainly private (Asea Brown Boveri, Oerlikon Bürle)
Public open space for park and squares, transferred to the city without compensation	10%
Public traffic areas, transferred to the city without compensation	10%
Total surfaces	840 000 m² (160 000 m² of buildings preserved long term)
Residential	240 000 m² (average density 200%)
Service	315 000 m² (average density 200%)
Industrial	270 000 m² (average density 180%)
Public	15 000 m² (average density 70%)

8.8 Zentrum Zürich Nord: evaluation

From a planning perspective, the redevelopment of the railway station area of Zentrum Zürich Nord is a very interesting case. With respect to the conclusions, we note some remarkable similarities with and differences from Basel EuroVille. The first observation, concerning the initiators of the redevelopment process, highlights both.

The initiators were the private owners of the property in industrial areas north of the station. However, they soon contacted the city and the railways to form a partnership. The whole planning process has been steered by this partnership, of which the main actors are the municipality and the private landowners. The local authority had not only the vision but also the political acumen and influence to implement it. Continuity in political leadership was provided by Ursula Koch, the city alderwoman for urban development. That continuity has proved to be a decisive factor. On the other side, there were enlightened landowners with the material and cultural resources to play an active part in the process. The vision of and relationship between these two main actors are the keys to interpreting the result. An essential element was the early achievement of a cooperative atmosphere and reciprocal trust. Furthermore, the timing of the open and closed phases in the process has been of the essence. After an initial closed stage, when the agreement between the partners had to be consolidated in order to protect the politically vulnerable project, a more open stage followed. By then, within an established framework, local groups were encouraged to suggest and promote innovative uses of the site. The role of the railway company has always been ambivalent. The railways were initially active in the partnership, bringing in their own redevelopment proposals. But they have subsequently withdrawn their land from the plan. In so doing, they have arguably limited their risk, but it is also possible that they (and the initiative) are missing an opportunity. The development is the biggest of its kind in Switzerland, and, because of the attitude of the railways, the station and its immediate surroundings might be less integrated in the project than is possible and desirable.

Our second observation also refers to elements of similarity and difference. In Zürich, as elsewhere, the duration of the process has forced the actors to adopt a process approach. It is hard to identify clear stages in the development, but the process approach to development is explicit. In the former industrial areas, some buildings will be maintained in their present use, whereas others will be given new uses. Yet other buildings will be demolished and new ones built in their place. Some of the new uses could be temporary, while other ones could be or could become permanent. Built-in implementation mechanisms ensure that coherence (the urban multifunctional quality of each section, and the network of open spaces) is guaranteed in each phase. Of course, we cannot know everything that will happen within this frame. The idea is that the interplay of supply and demand (in both market and social terms) will determine much of it. The plan provides the conditions and a vision to start with, acting as a guarantee of quality and certainty for investors. A gradual transition of the area from industrial to fully urban is envisaged. The development plan (quantification of uses, urban design guidelines, public–private contracts) is the 'hard' component, while its interpretation in terms of specific functions, users, and investors is the 'soft' component.

As for the node–place concept, both aspects come to the fore in the development process. This leads us to our third and fourth observations. One of the main objectives is to achieve a broad mixture of users and uses (industrial, residential, and service) at both the area and the parcel level. That objective has been both firmly stated and imaginatively provided for in the planning framework. The guiding principle of the development is to create a multifunctional and dynamic urban district. The service sector will have a prominent function, but abundant space for modern industry, quality housing, and public amenities is also ensured. Imaginative regulations and financing mechanisms have been devised to guarantee that a true urban mixture (including less profitable elements) is obtained. Particularly innovative is the idea that the area could serve as an incubator for different uses. For example, next to permanent high-return/high-investment functions with a lower urban value (such as offices in new buildings) temporary low-return/low-investment functions with a higher urban value could also be developed (such as cultural production and consumption in refurbished buildings). A possibly vexing problem in Zürich is closely connected with other priorities of the Swiss railways: there is no clear idea of how the railway station should be integrated into the new development. Related to this is the problem of how the new and the old neighbourhoods, lying on opposite sides of the tracks, could become a functional unity.

As far as the node is concerned, the heart of Zürich Nord, Oerlikon, is the second station of the Zürich metropolitan area. It is essentially a regional station that has greatly benefited from the recently completed S-Bahn system. This provides fast and frequent connections to the city centre, the airport, and many other destinations in the metropolitan area. However, access to the national and international train network is indirect, as most national and international trains passing through the station do not stop there. It is in principle possible to increase the direct national and international links and to develop railway station capacity and services accordingly. But in reality, none of this is part of the Zentrum Zürich Nord project. For example, unlike the situation in Basel, there are no plans to put in a new station entrance on the north (project) side of the tracks or high-quality pedestrian connections from there to the existing station. This choice is related to the company policy of the Swiss railways. It may well hamper the full realization of the development potential of the site. A final point is the clear priority given to public transport: a direct (underground) connection to the motorway ring has been envisaged, but it will not be implemented for at least the next 30 years. The choice is virtually identical to that in Basel. Quite interestingly, it distances Zentrum Zürich Nord from the cases of Euralille, Utrecht, Amsterdam and Stockholm, where excellent, direct accessibility by car is seen as a precondition to property development at the railway station. Swiss cases appear alone in this. (The role of accessibility by car is marginal also in the next case, the King's Cross railway lands, but this is situated in a very different metropolitan context.)

9

King's Cross railway lands

9.1 Preamble: the national planning system

It is not surprising that Newman and Thornley (1996, pp. 27–76) labelled the planning system in the UK the *British family*. The first comprehensive law regarding physical planning was passed in 1947. It has subsequently been adjusted, but the main principles have remained unchanged. Three functions were distinguished: development control, development plans, and central government supervision. The first two functions are mainly a local responsibility. In contrast to many other countries, the development plan is not legally binding. Other material considerations can override the plan (or parts of it) in some situations. Earlier, these plans had to be approved by the central government, but this has since been changed. The central government is now responsible only for legislation regarding physical planning, and for issuing general policy guidelines. However, citizens, companies etc. have the right to lodge an appeal directed towards the central government. This is an important aspect of the system, as the central government may have a different view on the development plan in question from that held by the local authority. In formulating development plans or preparing development decisions, planners always consider the implications of any appeal to the central government. In general, as metropolitan administrative bodies have become weaker or have been eliminated altogether, the planning system in the UK has become more flexible. Local authorities and especially the central government now have a strong position (ISOCARP, 1992, pp. 240–255). With this relative shift in power towards the central government, the fiscal basis for infrastructure development at the local and regional level has also been decreased.

The influence of central government runs through the Planning Policy Guidance Notes. Basically, there are two kinds of guidance: one topic based and one area based. Examples of the first kind are topics such as housing, national parks, green belts, and archaeology. The second kind is regional and strategic guidance on specific areas, which sets out the guiding principles to which the local physical plans must conform.

Development plans are prepared at two levels: structure plans are prepared by counties, and local plans by district authorities. In metropolitan areas, these two tiers are combined into a unitary development plan. Since 1991 (with the Planning and Compensation Act) these plans have taken on more status and importance. An important turn of events is the increase in the practice of negotiation between local authorities and developers over planning permission (planning gain or planning obligations). These negotiations are conducted in secret; third parties have no right to challenge the outcome.

Although the local government would seem to be in a strong position, the planning system rather shows a centralized character. Both through the Planning Policy Guidance Notes and the decisions passed on appeals, the central government can exercise a great deal of influence. It has influence over matters of substance, and thus has a degree of power that goes beyond its administrative procedures. Another aspect is the amount of discretion shown when appeals are made. Decisions on appeals have to take many factors into account. These include central government guidelines, development plan policy, and local issues such as traffic generation, access, or effects on neighbours. The balance between the factors can easily shift, and so can priorities in central government planning policies. Another interesting point (Newman and Thornley, 1996, p. 44) is that, compared with other countries, the UK has a noticeable lack of physical plans, at both the national and the regional level. This situation enhances flexibility at the higher levels of government. All these often contradictory forces can be particularly clearly seen at work in the case of station area redevelopment. In this regard it is also important to take note of parliamentary involvement in the passage of railway bills, further adding to the complexity.

9.2 Context: railway station area redevelopment in the UK

Until recently, railway station area redevelopment has been largely restricted to London. Of course, there have been some developments in railway station areas elsewhere, such as at Bristol Parkway, and new plans have been recently launched at Leeds City station. Yet almost all the projects undertaken over the last 20 years have been in London, and most of those have been in *central* London (Figure 9.1). A literature survey carried out in 1996 (Bertolini and Spit, 1996) identified 16 station projects in the UK, 15 of which were in the London region and 13 in central London. This is no coincidence. As opposed to the other European countries studied here, apparently Britain has had no clear overarching framework at the national level to integrate, at least conceptually, individual initiatives. There was no plan for expansion of a national HST network, as in France. There were no national or regional policies promoting development at public transport interchanges, as in the Netherlands and Switzerland. And there was no national integrated transport and property strategy of the railway company, as in Sweden. Furthermore, the role of local authorities seems much more limited than elsewhere. They have been either abolished (as with metropolitan bodies) or seriously weakened (as with boroughs and towns) by the Conservative government.

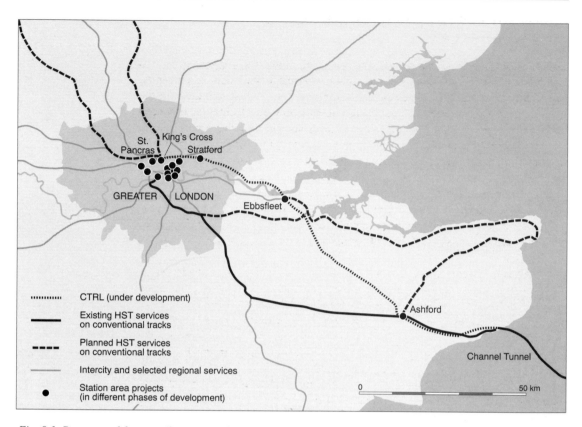

Fig. 9.1 Present and future railway network in the South-East of England and main station area projects.

In this context, two distinct rationales have been fuelling most of the railway station redevelopment plans that have been carried out in Britain thus far. One rationale is expressed in the evolution of British Rail (BR). BR started searching much more explicitly and much earlier than its European counterparts for complementary revenues – most notably property – to finance operational investments or just to improve the balance sheet. This is a trend that was already set in 1978 by the imposition of external financing limits on BR. Those limits were set by the then Labour government, and further reinforced in the Thatcher years (Olsberg, 1990). A second rationale is expressed in the initiatives of 'venture' developers. These innovative entrepreneurs were looking for opportunities that would arise as soon as railway lands and station air rights were released and put on the property market. A typical example of this last group is Rosehaugh Stanhope Developments plc. This is the company that developed several of central London's stations (including Broadgate/Liverpool Street and Ludgate), and was for some time involved in King's Cross.

The interaction between the strategies of these two actors has largely determined *where*, *when* and *how* railway stations have been developed in Britain. And this has essentially meant:

• on railway lands or station air rights in or adjoining the City of London;

- during the financial and property markets booms of the 1980s;
- as office-only complexes.

The list of implemented schemes that fit this profile includes locations at several London stations: Blackfriars, Cannon Street, Charing Cross, Fenchurch Street, Liverpool Street, Ludgate, and Victoria. In many cases (most strikingly in the Broadgate/Liverpool Street station development), the transformation has been massive and spectacular. BR has taken a generous share of the profits. In the period 1970–1989, for instance, its property division, the British Rail Property Board (BRPB), contributed £1.6 billion to BR finances. This injection accounts for £323 million, or 11% of BR turnover (which was more than its total profit), in its record financial year 1989/90 (Edwards, 1991). In all the examples cited above, BR and the developers were the ones taking the initiative. Apparently, the only contribution the local authority could make was to obtain, in exchange for planning permission, as much benefit for the local community – or planning gain – as possible.

In the past few years, this philosophy has been wearing thin. In particular, since the property market crash the wisdom of pursuing this approach has been questioned (see, for instance, London Planning Advisory Committee, 1993). Change might be afoot, as recent proposals for King's Cross-St Pancras, Stratford and Ebbsfleet suggest. These three sites can be seen as crucial test cases. Unlike many central London railway station location redevelopments in the 1980s, the development of these three areas cannot be reduced to a mere real estate operation. The plan to put in Channel Tunnel Rail Link (CTRL) interchanges at these locations (Figure 9.1) means that a much wider approach is needed, one dealing with both urban and transport complex, tangled development issues.

9.3 King's Cross railway lands as node and place

9.3.1 The node

King's Cross-St Pancras is one of the most intensely used transport interchanges in London (Figures 9.1 and 9.2). Every morning, 30 000 travellers come into King's Cross-St Pancras, more than anywhere else in the UK, except for Oxford Circus tube station. The node includes several above-ground and underground levels and stations. Two bundles of national railway lines converge here (the Midland main line at St Pancras, and the East Coast main line at King's Cross). Furthermore, the node includes the West Anglia, Great Northern and Thameslink regional railways. The latter is the only through-London rail line. Six Underground (metro) lines and numerous bus lines – urban, regional, national, and international – all stop at King's Cross-St Pancras station. Euston Road, tangential to the two main railway station buildings, is part of a London inner ringway.

Plans to strengthen the node centre hinge on the decision to locate here the second and main London terminal of the high-speed Channel Tunnel Rail Link (CTRL). Since the approval in 1996 of the CTRL Act, those plans are finally entering the implementation phase. The total cost of the CTRL is estimated at £3 billion (February 1995). About half of that amount will be contributed by central government. The other half is to be provided by London & Continental Railways (LCR), the private consortium that in 1996 won the competition to build and

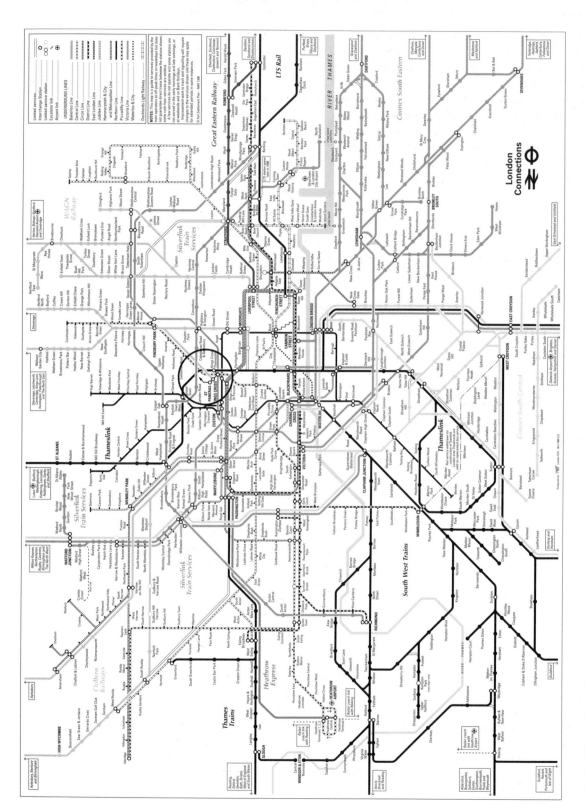

Fig. 9.2 King's Cross–St Pancras in the metropolitan public transportation networks. (Source: London Transport and Network South East)

operate the link. At King's Cross-St Pancras, even more is envisaged than the work on international and domestic CTRL tracks and platforms, which are due to open in 2003. The plans for the upgrading of the interchange include a new underground Thameslink station, improvements on the existing Underground facilities, and better connections between all modes. A fast airport rail link to Heathrow Airport is also under discussion.

The CTRL will bring increased speed and more capacity to the London–Channel Tunnel corridor. Travel time will be cut from 70 to 35 minutes, bringing the trip to Paris down to 2 hours 20 minutes, and the trip to Brussels down to 2 hours. With the greater capacity, the corridor will be able to handle up to eight trains per hour each way, or twice as many Eurostars as are now possible. It will have four stations: a main London terminal at St Pancras; two intermediate stations, one at Stratford in East London, and one at Ebbsfleet in North Kent; and the existing Channel Tunnel station at Ashford. St Pancras will be the interchange between Eurostar and the existing Intercity, regional rail and Underground services. The node is designed to allow, at peak times per hour, in each direction, five international Eurostar trains, eight express domestic trains serving north Kent, ten Midlands main line trains, and 24 Thameslink trains. Some trains will stop at Stratford, bypassing St Pancras on a new link with the West Coast main line, and continue onwards to the North-West of England (Manchester, Birmingham). Additionally, Waterloo station will be connected to the CTRL south of Ebbsfleet, and will be maintained as a second international London terminal. At peak times there will be five international trains per hour from St Pancras, three from Waterloo, and two through Stratford. Express commuter trains between Kent and London will also use the CTRL on part of their journey, significantly cutting the travel time of about 25 000 daily commuters.

9.3.2 The place

The King's Cross railway lands are adjacent to the King's Cross-St Pancras transport node (Figure 9.3). These lands form one of the largest development sites in Europe. At present, the property is occupied by partly disused freight and industrial yards (including some notable examples of the Victorian industrial heritage), and a nature reserve. The Regent's Canal cuts across the site. The area lies just outside central London, and its features reflect this anomalous location. Various public institutions –including Camden City Hall and recently the new British Library – are located there. Some offices line Euston Road. There are hotels near the terminals, and retail establishments along the major thoroughfares. More to the north of the area, and on the railway lands, there are a number of light industrial sites. On the whole, public open space is scarce and fragmented. With the exception of the south side, the area 'is set alongside a poor general environment, dysfunctional streets and roads, a deprived population and a dreadful reputation' (King's Cross Partnership, 1997). The 3 square mile (780 ha) area identified by the Single Regeneration Budget bid (Figure 9.4) as 'the stations and their surroundings' is where 16 000 people live. A third of the residents are minorities, and three-quarters live in social housing. Unemployment is well above the national average. Commercial rents are significantly lower and vacancy rates higher than in other central London areas.

Fig. 9.3 The King's Cross railway lands, viewed from the south. St Pancras and King's Cross stations are in the foreground. The development site, in the background, is now mainly occupied by partly disused freight and industrial yards, and includes some notable Victorian industrial heritage and a nature reserve. (Source: Union Railways (London & Continental))

9.3.3 The process

For the last 10 years, the redevelopment process of the King's Cross railway lands has been the subject of complex negotiations involving local and central governments, the local community, transport operators, and property developers. Negotiations have concerned both land and transport development issues, but have often been held at separate tables.

186

The Partnership Area

Fig. 9.4 The area covered by the Single Regeneration Budget bid. (Source: King's Cross Partnership)

A series of planning documents have provided a rather weak framework for the negotiations. The Greater London Development Plan (GLDP) of 1976 first identified King's Cross as a potential office location linked to an improved public transport node. A GLDP revision in 1984 attempted to impose limits on future tertiary developments in the area. The proposal called for more space for affordable housing and light industry, but it was never approved.

The 1987 borough plan of Camden, the local authority under whose jurisdiction most of the area falls, also incorporated social aims but remained vague on the quantities, leaving them open to negotiation with future developers. The Borough of Camden (BC) further specified its standpoint on the King's Cross railway lands in a community planning brief (CPB), which it adopted in June 1988. As in the borough plan, conditions and wishes were stated, but the initiative was left to the developers.

Camden acknowledged that the CPB

is deliberately much more specific on the community requirements than on the quantity of commercial activities the Council would be prepared to accept. A strong incentive is thereby provided for the developer to come forward with a scheme which respects the industrial heritage of the site, which encourages diversity and which strikes a proper balance between the interests of strategic and local, community and commerce. (Borough of Camden, 1988, p. 1)

A similar integration of interests and perspectives was also advocated by the strategic planning advice published in October 1988 by the metropolitan consultative body called the London Planning Advisory Committee (LPAC), and – albeit in a rather vague way – also by the strategic guidance for London, which was published by the central government in July 1989. The main thrust of the central government document was towards reinforcement of the position of London as an international financial centre.

The actual redevelopment process of the railway lands, or what later came to be known as the *King's Cross saga*, took off in 1987. At that time, British Rail (BR), the main transport operator and landowner in the area, invited four developers to submit bids for the area. The location at King's Cross of an international high-speed train terminal was – officially – not an issue at this point. Only later, and after leaks to the press, did BR admit that it intended to seek authorization to build an international station at King's Cross, overturning its own conclusions drawn three years earlier. Two developers were selected in a first round, and projects were shown publicly in January 1988, but the financial aspects and quantities were not disclosed. In June (1988) it was announced that the plan of the London Regeneration Consortium (LRC, a partnership of the property developers Rosehaugh Stanhope and the National Freight Corporation, a key minority landowner in the area), designed by Norman Foster, was the winner. The deal, as was to emerge later, entailed a lump-sum payment of £400 million to BR immediately, plus 70% of future profits.

In November 1988 BR sent a King's Cross Railways Bill to parliament requesting the necessary authorization, or 'powers', to undertake the infrastructure works, which included an underground high-speed international terminal at King's Cross. In April 1989, BR submitted an outline planning application (OPA) to the Borough of Camden, requesting planning permission for the redevelopment of land. With these two submissions, the stage was set for negotiations that were expected to take place within a relatively short period. In reality, only now (after almost 10 years) has a solution come within reach. Two periods characterized by radically different approaches can be distinguished in the process: a first round, from 1987 to 1992; and a second round, starting in 1994. In between, 1993 was a year when everything, and nothing, seemed possible.

The first round

In the first phase of negotiations (1987–1992), the roles of the most important actors were quite diverse. The Borough of Camden and the LRC had been negotiating successive modifications of the planning application. The two actors held quite different visions, as the different philosophy of the community planning brief and the LRC plan show. But both needed resources, either legal or financial, that the other actor had. Furthermore, both seemed willing to give up something. The Borough was willing to concede on some points in order to avoid a public inquiry and risk losing its say. The developers were willing to give in to speed up the process and possibly build a positive image. On the other side were the local groups. As time went by, they were progressively identified with an umbrella organization called the King's Cross Railway Lands Group (KXRLG). They made a concerted effort (negated by the LRC and not obstructed by Camden) to rally support for alternative plans. In the end, everything depended on the outcome of the debate in parliament (where every actor involved had its own lobby) on British Rail's King's Cross Bill.

The OPA presented by the LRC in April 1989 was the biggest one ever submitted in the UK (44 boxes and 616 kg of documents!). A decision from Camden was expected at the beginning of 1990, as soon as the Bill had passed through parliament. However, the cycle of examinations, amendments, and resubmissions proved endless. The substance of the negotiations did not vary much. Each time, Camden made amendments to the plan to scale up the social and environmental aspects. And each time the LRC formally agreed, but only just. To each new application, the municipality responded by making new requirements. A solution soon proved difficult. Because of its contract with BR, LRC could not give up too much, if any, of its profit-generating uses. This applied most to the offices, which constituted more than 70% of the functional programme. Camden, for its part, could afford to bide its time until the fate of BR's parliamentary Bill became known.

At the same time, the KXRLG formulated its own proposals, with the participation of the local population. Basically, they entailed taking on and perfecting the social and environmental programme of the Community Planning Brief but also explicitly arguing for a lower office content. The local groups allied themselves initially with a local 'enlightened' developer supported by a King's Cross Team (KXT) of professionals. But later the group decided to pursue the cause on its own. The result was two distinct alternative proposals: a more 'radical' one (the KXRLG's) and a more 'realistic' one (the KXT's). The former was formalized in an OPA in December 1991. The main problem for the local groups was how to break the basic assumption on which the LRC's proposals were built. The LRC contended that high-profit-generating uses were needed to compensate for the high costs of putting in the infrastructure, which the government was not prepared to finance. To break this logic, the local group advocated either a less expensive above-ground terminal at St Pancras or – better yet – an alternative terminal at Stratford in East London, and possibly (and more provocatively) a different political context in which to consider public investment in infrastructure.

The complicated, multilateral dispute was protracted, and showed few significant shifts. That changed in July 1992, when the Borough declared its intention to grant, under certain conditions, planning permission to the LRC proposal. The conclusion drawn by Camden's officials who were evaluating the development options epitomizes the dilemma created by the institutional context. Given the cost of the transformation – as Camden's officials argued – any substantial reduction in the amount of office space would jeopardize its feasibility, with the result of putting at risk the entire regeneration policy for the area (Borough of Camden, 1992). Property and transport development have been interdependent at King's Cross. These two interests were locked into a spiral of ever greater costs and profits that left very little room for programme alternatives. The basic assumption was so compelling that all other considerations were dwarfed. The perceived need for office space overshadowed the possibility that the complications created by the office bias could cause the entire operation to collapse. Ironically, this extreme scenario was precisely the one that came to pass.

The second round

The year 1993 was packed with events on different fronts. Completely new transformation prospects emerged. Let us review what happened from the point where we left off in the overview of the first round: the conditional intention to grant planning permission by Camden's officials. The most important condition set by the Borough was the approval of BR's Bill, which was still under discussion in parliament. This was a crucial point. The localization at King's Cross of an underground high-speed international terminal was the pivot of the whole LRC initiative. However, the choice of King's Cross became increasingly controversial. In February 1993, Union Railways (UR, the independent company set up in 1992 by BR to develop the high-speed link to the continent) published a study in which the underground terminal hypothesis was abandoned. Instead, UR proposed using the existing terminal at St Pancras. The conclusion drawn in this study was that the St Pancras option would be less complex and less costly to build, while being more attractive in environmental, operational, business and safety terms. The study also pointed out the opportunity to realize a second station in Stratford. (Ironically, both conclusions came close to what had been long contended by the local community groups!) In January 1994, following further evaluations, the government also declared its preference for St Pancras. In addition, the government announced its intention to launch a competition to attract private capital for the whole high-speed link, including the terminal. A definitive solution was not yet in sight (when, if ever, would private capital be available?). But the option of an underground terminal was abandoned, implying that the entire LRC plan had to go back to the drawing board. A worse signal, however, came from the property market, as the boom had turned to bust. The crisis also struck Rosehaugh Stanhope, the property developers associated in the LRC, shaking the financial credibility of the operation to its very roots.

Fig. 9.5 The Interim Uses Initiative. (Source: M. Parkes and D. Mouawad with the King's Cross Railway Lands Group)

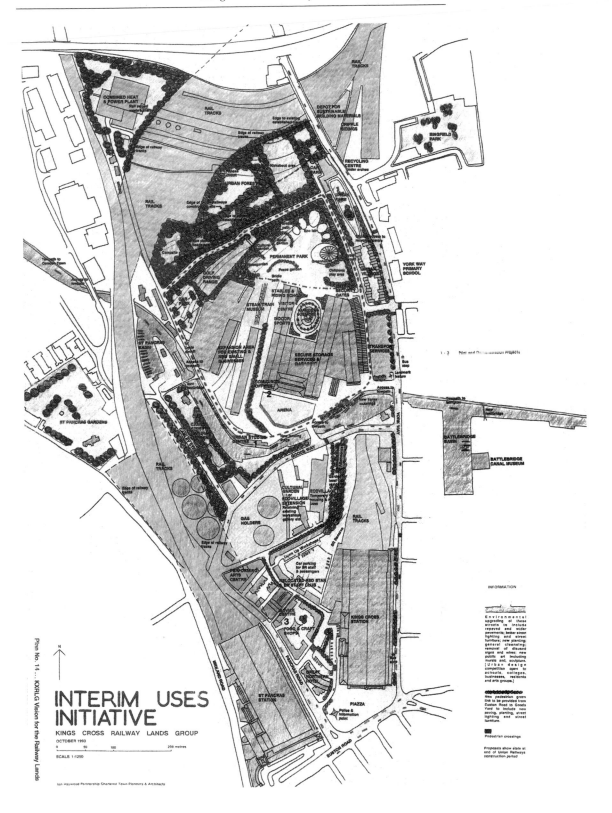

Plan No. 14 ... KXRLG Vision for the Railway Lands

**INTERIM USES
INITIATIVE**

KINGS CROSS RAILWAY LANDS GROUP

OCTOBER 1993

SCALE 1:1250

Ian Haywood Partnership Chartered Town Planners & Architects

The dramatic changes in context were underscored by the Draft Advice on Strategic Planning Guidance for London, published in June 1993 by LPAC. In this document, LPAC contended that development in King's Cross above 140 000–185 000 m^2 (a third of what was being proposed by LRC!) would not accord with strategic planning objectives, while even that amount would depend on all the planned infrastructure being in place and in any case would not be feasible until after the year 2000. Furthermore, LPAC believed that the current situation opened up opportunities for temporary uses and for a permanent mixed use development (LPAC, 1993, pp. 30–31). The Borough of Camden must have reached similar conclusions; by spring, it had commissioned the KXRLG to produce an 'Interim Uses Initiative' (see the resulting plan in Figure 9.5).

In the course of 1994 events followed each other quickly, partly confirming and partly complicating the emerging picture:

- In April, the LRC withdrew its planning application and sued BR for breaking the contract.
- In August, a shortlist of four private consortia were invited by the government to submit offers for the construction and operation of the Channel Tunnel Rail Link (CTRL), including railway station areas. The condition of self-financing was confirmed, but to partially bypass this limitation the idea emerged to use the line for express commuter trains from Kent too, as this would entitle it to subsidies.
- In November UR presented a CTRL Bill to parliament; at that point, the underground option for the terminal was abandoned, and the proposal to use St Pancras was submitted.
- Also in November the Borough of Camden approved and published a new community planning brief (November 1994) registering the changes in context. In the same month, the Borough launched CrossMillennia, a bid for a share of the national lottery funds that the government will make available for special projects to celebrate the new millennium. It envisaged at King's Cross, next to the international terminal, the development of an events hall in a telecommunication and media complex, to be built in partnership with British Telecom and the London film industry (Figure 9.6). The bid proved unsuccessful.
- In the course of the same year, the KXRLG reviewed its planning application, contested the disruptive idea of allowing Kent commuters into St Pancras, and tried with limited success to get landowners interested in the Interim Uses Initiative.

To many, the situation at this time would have appeared hopeless. However, in the ensuing months a new framework for the development of the area had been gradually taking shape, as distinct processes have been recomposed with each other. Two chains of events are important here. A first one was triggered by an initiative of the Borough of Camden. In September 1995, after a first unsuccessful attempt, neighbouring Camden and Islington Boroughs – together with the local community, the voluntary sector, and private sector participation (P&O

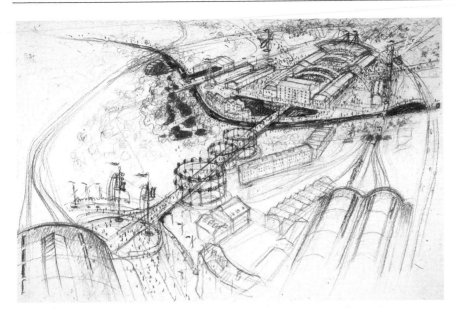

Fig. 9.6 The CrossMillennia proposals. (Source: London Borough of Camden. Design: Building Design Partnership)

developments, National Freight Corporation, Railtrack*, and Union Railways) – made a second bid to the Single Regeneration Budget (SRB), the new central government programme substituting all previous urban initiatives. The bid asked for £37.5 million from the government, to be more than matched by investment from the private sector and the local public sector. The bid covered the railway lands and their surroundings, with a surface of approximately 3 square miles (780 ha) (Figure 9.4). This time it was successful: £37.5 million was to be granted in seven years, matched by £43.6 million in local public funds (mostly local authority and housing association) and £171.4 million in private investment, complementing the impact of an expected £2 billion CTRL investment in St Pancras.

In March 1996 the King's Cross Partnership (KCP) was launched to coordinate and provide the strategic framework for the seven-year regeneration initiative. At the same time it was supposed to counter the potential marginalization of the local population. The initial focus of its work has been on education, training, and advice, and on studies that will eventually feed into a strategic framework for the regeneration of the area, to be ready by mid-1998. The hope is that by the end of 2003, a 'new quarter' could be completed. However, coordination with the railway works – also scheduled for the same period (see below) – remains a major problem, as up to 2003 the area will essentially be a gigantic construction site. It remains to be seen whether the KCP will develop into a genuine partnership. All the relevant actors participate in it, but the power is very unevenly distributed among them. Its main appeal, besides a budget that is only relatively significant, may well be its ability to build consensus through persuasion.

---

* Railtrack was the new company that in 1994, as BR was privatized, took over the ownership and management of all track, signalling, infrastructure, buildings, and operationl land. However, in the light of the special situation created at King's Cross by the CTRL, Railtrack's competences were in this case limited to the King's Cross station building.

Table 9.1 King's Cross railway lands: summary of the main phases

Phase 1: rise and fall of a property-led approach, 1987–1992

1987	BR invites four property developers to submit bids for the area
June 1988	The London Regeneration Consortium wins the contest; the Borough of Camden adopts the Community Planning Brief
November 1988	British Rail sends the King's Cross Railways Bill to parliament, including an application for an underground HST terminal
April 1989	The London Regeneration Consortium submits an Outline Planning Application to the Borough of Camden
	Negotiations and debate; property slump begins
December 1991	The King's Cross Railway Lands Group submits an alternative planning application
	Negotiations and debate continue; property slump worsens

Phase 2: withdrawals and attempts at redefining the issue, 1993–1995

February 1993	Union Railways suggests the alternative use of existing St Pancras for the HST terminal
December 1993	The Interim Uses Initiative is published; the reception of the landowners is cold
January 1994	The central government also declares its preference for St Pancras
April 1994	The London Regeneration Consortium withdraws its planning application
August 1994	A shortlist of four private consortia are invited by central government to submit offers for the construction and operation of the Channel Tunnel Rail Link (CTRL)
November 1994	Union Railways sends the CTRL Bill to parliament; the Borough of Camden publishes a new Community Planning Brief and launches the (unsuccessful) CrossMillennia bid for national lottery funds
September 1995	Camden and Islington Boroughs, together with private and community interests, make a bid to the Single Regeneration Budget (SRB)
	Debate in Camden and in parliament

Phase 3: towards parallel transport- and regeneration-led approaches, 1996–1997

February 1996	London and Continental wins the competition to build and operate the CTRL
March 1996	Following success of the SRB bid, the King's Cross Partnership is launched
December 1996	Royal assent is granted to the CTRL Bill
In the course of 1997	Planning applications for the CTRL works are processed; studies commissioned by the King's Cross Partnership are undertaken

Table 9.1 continued

Phase 4: implementation, 1998–2003?	
1998–2003	London and Continental expects to begin construction of the CTRL in 1998 and terminate in 2003
mid-1998 to end of 2003	The King's Cross Partnership hopes to publish a strategic framework for the regeneration of the area by mid-1998, and that a 'new quarter' will be completed by the end of 2003

In King's Cross, most agree that the critical factor in the decision of government in favour of the King's Cross regeneration bid was in all likelihood the impending decision on the CTRL. In fact – and this is the second important chain of events – throughout 1995 and 1996 the CTRL Bill had been passing through parliament. King's Cross boroughs and local groups obtained only minor amendments, but in the process a second station at Stratford was secured, in connection with a link with the West Coast main line bypassing St Pancras. Royal assent was finally awarded to the Bill, and it became an Act in December 1996. Eight years (!) after the first King's Cross Bill was presented by BR to parliament, there was finally legal certainty on the development of the transport infrastructure. The CTRL Act authorized the construction and operation of the new railway, including powers of compulsory purchase and outline planning permission for the railway and its structures. Local council approvals were needed only on details. However, the Act made no provisions for the development of the King's Cross railway lands other than those required for the construction of the CTRL and associated works. Approval for any future land development proposals would be sought from the London boroughs of Camden and neighbouring Islington under normal planning procedures. The unitary development plan (UDP) of Camden was here to provide the statutory framework, alongside the UDP of Islington, the strategic guidance for London, and other central government documents. Camden's UDP was then under discussion. However, it already appeared that the King's Cross railway lands were to be allowed particular flexibility. Also, on the Islington side there was readiness to cooperate beyond the letter of the plan.

During examination of the CTRL Bill in February 1996 it was announced that London and Continental (L&C, a consortium supported by Richard Branson of Virgin, among others) had won the competition to undertake the works and operate the line. Costs were estimated at £3 billion. Partially countering a previous declaration, the government stated that it would finance half the amount, while the rest would have to be raised on the market. Construction was expected to begin in 1998, and the line and stations should be opened in 2003. L&C Stations & Property, a subsidiary of L&C,

> will manage the acquisition of the land required for the CTRL and the disposal of surplus land, and manage all the group's property assets including stations. Working in close cooperation with the local authorities, other landowners and development agencies it will unlock the regeneration benefits of the CTRL and its new stations, particularly around Stratford, the Thames Gateway and St Pancras. (Cited from London & Continental brochure)

9.4 Property development at King's Cross railway lands

The intention to create the second international high-speed train terminal of the British capital at King's Cross (the first, already in use, is at Waterloo) has prompted a variety of redevelopment proposals for the area. Two distinct waves of plans can be identified, corresponding to the first and second rounds of negotiations discussed above.

9.4.1 The first wave

In the first wave, on the table was the review of the outline planning applications (OPAs). These were submitted by the developers and minority landowners, who jointly formed the London Regeneration Consortium (LRC) and were contractually linked to British Railways (BR, the main landowner), and by the coalition of local groups gathered in the King's Cross Railway Lands Group (KXRLG). A third proposal had been put together by the King's Cross Team (KXT) for the local 'enlightened' developer Clarke, but it was not formalized in an OPA. The plans for King's Cross sponsored by the LRC and designed by Norman Foster (Figure 9.7) have long been featured on the pages of specialized

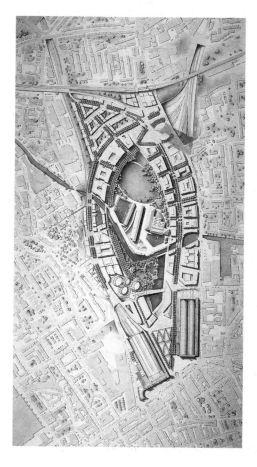

Fig. 9.7 The LRC plan designed by Norman Foster, July 1990 version. (Architects: Foster Associates)

Table 9.2 Property development proposals for King's Cross (floor space in m²)

	LRC	KXRLG1	KXRLG2	KXT
Social housing (units)	50 321	130 000	153 750	149 186
	(+575, −77)	(1440)	(1710)	(1444)
Housing for the market	100 641	65 000	51 250	74 593
(units)	(1.111)	(820)	(660)	
Offices	544 858	180 000	22 000	373 665
Industry	18 850	39 000	39 000	35 855
Retail	27 870	30 000	30 000	20 758
Leisure	16 752	22 255	22 255	21 337
Community	16 772	22 255	22 255	21 334
Hotel	9 290	10 000	10 000	15 000
Total	785 054	498 510	350 510	711 728

Source: Parkes and Mouawad (1991)

and less specialized magazines. Those plans have been the object of numerous conferences, workshops, and field trips. In contrast, little attention has been given to the alternative hypotheses that have been advanced since the beginning of the process. In trying to sketch a balanced picture of the transformation prospects, these should be analysed too. Their relevance has been underscored by recent insights and orientations emerging on several points.

The first-wave proposals, as they were formulated in 1991, are summarized in Table 9.2. The LRC proposal, designed by Norman Foster, envisaged a circle of buildings between eight and ten storeys high and two 44-storey towers around a central park. Access to the international terminal underground was located between the two existing railway stations, and the plan reserved (limited) surfaces for housing and light industry at the northern end of the site. The LRC pursued 'a mixed development, combining a living with a working environment and with shops, social and leisure facilities to match' (*King's Cross Extra*, 1989). Such a declaration does not, however, appear totally coherent with the actual functional programme and area layout. The share taken by the office component, following a recurring philosophy in the redevelopment of railway stations in central London in the 1980s, is overwhelming. Furthermore, most other uses, and most notably housing and light industry, are pushed to or concentrated on the margins of the site, making the achievement of a 'mixed' district problematic. Also, the projected number of users is somewhat deceptive: 25 000 office workers and only 5000 inhabitants.

The balance of uses put forward by the KXRLG is radically different, mainly because the share of offices is much lower. The KXRLG presented two proposals (KXRLG1 and KXRLG2 in Table 9.1). The second proposal assumes a political and economic context where urban regeneration is not dependent on real estate profits (and thus *not* London of the 1980s and early 1990s). The result is that offices become a secondary element, to the advantage of housing, space for small businesses and social facilities. These are the priorities that emerged from consultation with the local community.

In the first round, the visions for the future of the area appear to be irreconcilable. For a concrete example of what the LRC might have had in mind, one can, as the LRC itself invites the public to do, visit Broadgate. This is an office complex that the same developers, in partnership with BR, have built above and around Liverpool Street station. Broadgate contains about 300 000 m² of offices, plus a few shops and restaurants and other facilities catering for about 25 000 employees. All of these functions have been inserted in a carefully designed network of pedestrian streets and squares. From a strictly real estate point of view, the success of Broadgate is difficult to contest. Bordering on the City, being highly accessible, offering up-to-date office space, realized in record time, and employing advanced construction and financial techniques imported from the USA, it did not have any trouble finding tenants in a market that was (at that time) in full expansion. Part of the profits has permitted the reconstruction of Liverpool Street railway station, providing a model of cooperation that the developers and the railways would in all probability have wanted to apply to King's Cross. The balance sheet is more uncertain, however, from the perspective of another actor: the local population. The overwhelming majority of the people working in Broadgate come from faraway suburbs, while the restaurants and shops are totally out of the range of local people. Of course, the station has been renewed, and each traveller can find convenient shopping opportunities. But the barrier separating the railway station from the derelict neighbourhoods nearby could not be more striking. Not even the pavement tiling runs across the property line! The overcrowded Bangladeshi ghetto of Brick Lane is just a few blocks away. That area, plagued with the highest unemployment and deprivation indexes, could not offer a more striking contrast with its up-market neighbour.

The Interim Uses Initiative elaborated by the KXRLG (Parkes and Mouawad, 1993), while formalized at a later stage to fill a vacuum in the development process, is possibly the best representation of the different sort of environment envisaged by the local groups. The proposals (Figure 9.5) include a City Garden Festival, anticipating the creation of permanent park and other 'green' initiatives; areas and facilities for sport and recreation; a documentation centre on the environment and on local history, with connected commercial and tourism facilities; space for events in the arts and entertainment spheres; and temporary housing. Other proposals call for a market, craft workshops, the rationalization of existing storage and distribution activities, the expansion of production (both existing and to be promoted, such as a recycling centre), and a job training and employment promotion centre. Most of these are temporary uses, in the spirit of the Interim Uses Initiative commissioned by Camden. Nevertheless, the KXRLG believes that the proposed activities could be a first step towards more permanent uses. Eventually,

> The traveller arriving on the TGV from Paris or Milan in 2003 should thus expect to emerge from St Pancras into a many-faceted, thriving district, combining a wide variety of both temporary and permanent activities. Such offices as there may be are likely to be spin-offs from the University, the British Library, contemporary dance or the dozens of charities and trades unions in the area – rather than corporate headquarters. The resident population may have increased, making a contribution to reverse commuting and to benign pedestrian and cycle trips, helping to support all-day and year-round activity and sustaining a strong multiethnic culture. (Parkes and Mouawad, 1993, p. 7)

The Borough of Camden appears to be torn between these two contrasting visions, lacking the means to force through its own middle way, as envisaged by the community planning brief. However, the dramatic changes in context, which distinguish the first round from the second round in the negotiations, seem to make more space for such a third option and a second wave of initiatives.

9.4.2 The second wave

The shift in emphasis that accompanied the transition from the first to the second round of negotiations is well documented in the differences between the original 1988 community planning brief (CPB) of the Borough of Camden and its revised version of 1994. The first brief (Borough of Camden, 1988) basically sets a loose framework for the negotiations of community benefits in exchange for planning permission to develop the commercial parts (following the planning gain approach). While the 1988 CPB contained a rather detailed list of the desiderata of the community, the definition of the commercial elements was left up to the developers. The second brief (Borough of Camden, 1994) stressed and specified the need for housing (930–1000 units, of which 25–50% would have to be affordable), the conservation of present economic activities as long as possible, space for light industry and workshops (15 000–20 000 m²), diversified small-scale shopping, social and community facilities, and leisure facilities exploiting the architectural and natural features of the area. Most importantly, it also explicitly indicated a maximum of 150 000–185 000 m² of offices, going along with LPAC's advice (LPAC, 1993). Furthermore, while a concentration of commercial activities around the station node was suggested, integration of uses across the whole site was also advocated. Temporary uses were also promoted, in order to counteract the mounting dereliction that persisting uncertainty had been bringing to the area, but also in order to initiate a more incremental development strategy. One more point is the orientation towards broader partnerships. Alignment was promoted not only with the private sector, but also with other public bodies (the bordering Borough of Islington, for instance) and with the local community.

The CrossMillennia and SRB bids of 1994–1995 are the direct results of a more proactive approach by the local authority, a stance implicitly encouraged by the new CPB. The borough has been able to get the support of all the relevant public, private and community actors to these initiatives. The second – and successful – SRB bid was the most important one as it outlined the path that is currently being pursued. The September 1995 bid envisaged the railway lands as a lively and successful urban quarter, capitalizing on its unique access to Europe but also on its local heritage. The station complex is to become a 'spectacular new gateway to Britain', profiting also from the adjacent new British Library. To ensure that local people will benefit from the project there will be accompanying programmes in the domains of education, training and employment, business support, housing, public health, and crime reduction. Most projects (41.5% of SRB funding) are geared towards creating a framework within which the new quarter and gateway could develop, opening key sites for development, and attracting private investment by establishing a clear and positive identity. The bid is seen as adding value to government plans 'by accelerating and coordinating redevelopment, and providing opportunities for local businesses and residents'. The focus of the economic development strategy will be on the cultural, entertainment and tourism sectors. In itself, this will represent a clear shift away from the office city. The creation of local jobs and the tackling of social problems in the area is seen as a condition of development, also in view of the security implications.

The estimates show a potential for developing 200 000 m^2 of commercial floorspace in the area, and the prospects for collaboration with the landowners (L&C, Railtrack, and the National Freight Corporation) appear good. The list of projects already committed in the bid includes:

- 46 000 m^2 of shops and offices that P&O will develop on a 3.2 ha site next to the railway lands;
- a 14 000 m^2 hotel partly in St Pancras, to be developed by L&C;
- a new concourse in front of King's Cross station, to be built by Railtrack;
- environmental improvements to be made by the Borough of Camden;
- 200 new homes;
- refurbishment of around 1500 council or housing association homes;
- improved pedestrian access.

Furthermore, at present 94 up-market apartments are already being developed at Battlebridge Basin overlooking the Regent's Canal, just outside the perimeter of the railway lands.

The vision has been further elaborated by the board of King's Cross Partnership (KCP), the board installed in April 1996 to administer the SRB funds. The KCP seeks to create at King's Cross 'an important and successful part of a world city, an interchange for travel, information and culture and a destination'. The area 'must be of high quality and safe and pleasant to live in, work in, visit and travel through' (KCP: brief précis). 'King's Cross is now an interchange . . . we aim to make it into a destination' (our interview with KCP). One of the initial activities of the effort to turn this vision into reality has been to carry out a series of studies: for example, on mobility issues and activity development thresholds. The purpose of the studies is to provide a foundation for the incremental definition of a 'strategic framework' for development – not to formulate a master plan, as all actors emphasize. Development is expected to be evolutionary rather than cataclysmic. In any event, the development will be carried out step by step until the CTRL works are completed. The idea is to progress towards such a framework by identifying thresholds, or the critical mass, for each activity, and by under-standing the role of each activity in building the new urban quarter. The current direction also deviates from previous approaches in the role given to feasibility studies. These are seen as an *ex ante* tool to help shape a programme rather than an *ex post* tool to test an existing one.

A particularly important tool is the site implementation study (SIS), which got started in September–December 1996 and was expected to be ready in May 1997. The SIS was an initiative of the Borough of Camden, which saw it as a means to test the new community planning brief. Once under way, the SIS fell within the framework of the SRB, under the supervision of the Borough of Camden, the Borough of Islington, L&CR, English Partnerships, the Government Office for

London, the KCP, and the KXRLG. Its objective is to 'clarify, analyse and assess the development constraints and potential of the King's Cross railway lands and provide advice on the practical steps that should be taken to secure the earliest possible comprehensive regeneration'. It is supposed to set out 'the tasks and stages which should be followed to allow the Council and the KCP to best achieve their regeneration and urban planning objectives for the railway lands'. From the legal point of view it will become a 'material consideration', alongside the planning brief, the UDP, strategic planning guidance, etc. when considering planning applications. Its most important function could be that of allowing the actors to take their first steps in concert towards a more specific shared vision for the area. At that point, conflicts may emerge again, however, especially when specific quantities have to be indicated. For instance, the local community gives priority to affordable housing and workplaces. L&C, in contrast, appears to be more interested in luxury housing and commercial accommodation, to complement a conference and hotel centre. Conceivably, there might be physical space for both, but will there be enough room in the budget?

The most important question of all concerns the interaction with the CTRL works and its related developments, which L&C will be initiating. L&C maintains that its first priority is now the construction of the line and stations. It sought control of the land around stations essentially in order to support the firm's transport activities. Of course, the land has a potential value, but profits from property development would provide only a fraction of the revenues needed from CTRL ownership and operation to make the whole viable. Ownership of land is seen as necessary for reasons other than extracting profits from it. With an eye to CTRL development, property ownership ensures that infrastructure construction can proceed smoothly: the projects would not be obstructed by fragmented ownership of the land. With an eye to CTRL operation, ownership ensures that stations would not become 'islands in the middle of nowhere'. A stake in projects for station areas would help to ensure that stations evolve into attractive places, well integrated in their surroundings. The latter is seen as particularly important because the 'travel experience' is a whole set of activities that include getting to and leaving a station. L&C will not develop the land by itself. Instead, the firm will look for property development partners when the time comes (that is, 'infrastructure is in place, policies are in place'). L&C has also declared its intention to work closely with local authorities, private interests and communities along the line 'in order to identify early projects' and 'develop strategic frameworks'. Indeed, L&C is involved in partnerships at railway stations, including the KCP. On the other hand, as no major land development is likely until the bulk of CTRL works are completed (in the year 2003, if all goes well), a 'wait and see' attitude is the most advantageous for L&C, allowing the firm to ensure that 'options are left as open as possible'. But how does this relate to the aim of the KCP to have the 'new urban quarter' in place *by* 2003, when the partnership's mandate expires?

The future of the King's Cross railway lands is still uncertain. However, accountable land and transport development frameworks seem finally to have emerged. The main instances are in the first case the KCP and in the second LCR. Both frameworks are summarized below.

9.4.3 Land development

The KCP is increasingly becoming the forum where a common vision for the King's Cross railway lands could emerge. It is becoming the point from which the actions of the different actors could be coordinated, in order to solve conflicts and achieve synergistic effects. The board of the SRB includes four representatives of local government, three representatives of a public agency (police, health, education), six from the private sector (including Railtrack, L&C, and other landowners), and four community representatives. The chairperson is a seventh private party, selected 'to ensure that the implementation and management of the project is essentially private-sector led'. The KCP must:

- gain and maintain support from all sectors for the regeneration plan for King's Cross;
- secure the successful implementation of the regeneration plan;
- act as agent to the local authorities for the development of Challenge Fund grants in King's Cross.

In essence, the task of the KCP is seen as finding ways of 'influencing', through the SRB budget, that can add value to CTRL and other investments in the area by multiplying their regeneration content: for example, a temporary construction bridge could be of better quality and become permanent, or tourist information could enhance the impact of a new hotel. Perhaps more importantly, the KCP can foster communication and consensus, thereby helping to ensure coordination and coherence. A crucial but delicate task is to keep the resident community from becoming marginalized.

9.4.4 Transport development

The financing for the design and planning work that precedes the CTRL has been provided by shareholders of the winning private consortium L&C and a group of banks. The private share of the financing for the construction will consist of a stock market flotation and cashflow from Eurostar (UK), the subsidiary operating HST services between London and the Continent. London & Continental Railways (LCR) and its subsidiaries will be fully responsible for the construction and the commercial risks. Some well-defined exceptions are specified; in these instances, the government will be exclusively or partially responsible. Furthermore, the government's financial contribution will 'be reduced in the event of LCR achieving a high level of profit from the development of lands, principally at King's Cross and Stratford, which are to be transferred to them.'

LCR has a number of subsidiaries:

- Eurostar (UK), operator of cross-Channel HST services in conjunction with the Belgian and French railways (a seemingly booming business, also thanks to a massive marketing campaign: the number of passengers went up to 6.4 million per year, from 3.9 million per year in the 12 months prior to August 1996);
- Union Railways, developing the CTRL;

- L&C Engineering, designing and planning the CTRL (actual construction contracts will be competitively tendered);
- L&CR Pathways, the firm that will manage the line when ready;
- L&C Stations & Property, which 'will manage the acquisition of the land required for the CTRL and the disposal of surplus land, and manage all the group's property assets including stations. Working in close cooperation with the local authorities, other landowners and development agencies it will unlock the regeneration benefits of the CTRL and its new stations, particularly around Stratford, the Thames Gateway and St Pancras.' (From London & Continental brochure).

Finally, an overview of the main structural data is given in Table 9.3.

9.5 King's Cross railway lands: evaluation

The redevelopment of the King's Cross railway lands has been characterized by particularly high instability. This has been true for the planning stages, and will in all likelihood remain true for the implementation stages. What can we learn from this case?

First, we see the importance of the change in approach between the first and second rounds and between the first and second waves. Together, the new framework that is emerging appears much better suited to the complex inter-relationships between node and place dynamics in the King's Cross situation. Shifts in context (in the property market, for example, or in decisions concerning the main infrastructure) had here a decisive role, but not an exclusive one. Local agents were also important. The changes manifested themselves as follows:

- from essentially property led (BR looking for profits to balance its budget) to essentially transport led (LCR commercially developing a high-speed railway link and accessory facilities);
- from a contract between BR (a transport company) and LRC (a property developer), with LRC taking the initiative, to an ad hoc transport company

Table 9.3 King's Cross railway lands: main structural data

Surface area	Railway lands: 58.7 ha
	SRB area: around 3 square miles (780 ha)
Area ownership	Railway lands: mostly London & Continental and National Freight Corporation, then Railtrack and Borough of Camden
	SRB area: various additional, P&O a main one
Offices, houses, shops, hotel and congress, etc.	Functional mix and quantities being defined/negotiated (a 'potential for 200 000 m² of commercial development' exists in the SRB area)
Costs	£3 billion (total CTRL, around 50% public)
	£249 million (expected seven-year investment in the SRB area, 32% public, 68% private)

integrating property interests for the CTRL (LCR), next to more conventional land and infrastructure owners and users;

• from land-use negotiations in a local arena and a parallel debate on the transport component in a national arena, to a parliamentary Act providing a firm foundation and simplified procedures for the infrastructure works and a weak partnership structure (KCP) for the property development and urban regeneration components.

A second observation concerns the line-up of actors. As the process proceeded – and it moved ahead slowly – the interests of the actors shifted. Accordingly, new proposals – enticing though they might be – delayed the development process further. This may be interpreted as a negative aspect of the development process, as delays accumulated. Yet at the same time the actors were engaged in a learning process. In that way the basic issues in the project could be better understood and eventually dealt with. It can be concluded that all of the actors have learnt a great deal, and a common vision might be finally emerging, though at a very high price (for example, in terms of dereliction in the area due to uncertainties, and in terms of waste of resources on all sides). But given the institutional context, perhaps there was no other way to proceed.

There are still some crucial unanswered questions: how to balance in time infrastructure works (which have not wholly secured funding yet) and property development/urban regeneration? how to balance in space more profitable and less profitable uses? how to achieve a consensus on the 'right' mix of functions, and – most importantly – fund it?

The absence of a basis for a strong plan opened up the possibility of a rolling agenda. Proposals could easily be amended, new proposals introduced, and redundant proposals withdrawn. This mechanism brought increased flexibility into the development programme, but at the same time it led to greater uncertainty among the participants – a situation that is not entirely overcome. The comparatively unique way in which the process unfolded has to do with the specific character of the UK planning system in combination with specific developments in King's Cross. Looking at the future, it could point at possible weaknesses in the now established project–institutional framework. The KCP may be said to be too informal. Its organizational structure is weak (because of factors such as its time limits, and the accountability to multiple constituencies). Its partners are unequal in strength, giving private actors a dominant position. All this leads to the crucial issue: will the KCP be capable of steering through answers to the 'still unanswered questions' mentioned above?

A third observation deals with the node–place concept. Extensive infrastructure works at King's Cross-St Pancras include: refurbishing and extending the St Pancras train shed; making new track connections from St Pancras to the East Coast main line, the Midlands main line, and the West Coast main line; enabling works for a new underground Thameslink station and a track connection to the Great Northern Line; realigning roads; and making utility diversions. London Underground will upgrade its facilities and connections to the terminus. The Channel Tunnel rail terminal will serve as a focal point for urban regeneration, including projects funded from the government's Single Regeneration Budget. In the past, the degree of entanglement between developments in the node and the place impeded progress of the initiative. Now, paradoxically, coordination in the place and autonomy of the node are sought at the same time. The KCP is a promising but rather weak instrument for achieving a higher level of coordination. On the other side, the CTRL Act strongly guarantees the autonomy of the transport developer. For instance, and typically, while the contractor will endeavour to adopt solutions that would reduce the adverse environmental impacts, the local authorities shall 'have regard to construction costs and programme implications and shall not seek to impose unreasonably stringent standards in respect of land use, planning, design or environmental matters'. True, all participants have a stake in ensuring that the project will be a success. Ultimately, both their collective and individual image depends on this. But will such a 'soft' binding factor be enough?

Part Three
Conclusions

10
Conclusions

10.1 The redevelopment of railway station areas: its urgency and complexity

As shown in Part One, an adequate analysis of complex planning problems such as the redevelopment of railway station areas would have to take all three aspects of the planning triangle (sections 1.1 and 4.1) into account. In this view, *context* variables (institutional arrangements and developments) ought to be combined with *process* variables (actors and organizations) and *object* variables (the node and place dimensions).

In principle, the starting point of analysis should be the railway station area itself, the object of redevelopment. However, as the pressure for transformation is fuelled by developments in the wider context, that wider field becomes so predominant that it should be considered first. Analysis of the redevelopment process becomes important at a later stage. Context variables show their relevance, as much of the variety in outcomes can be explained by referring to these variables, either in the direct context (the national planning system, or changes in transport policy, for example) or in the wider context (technological developments, economic developments, etc.).

Each railway station area redevelopment initiative can be seen as part of wider processes. These processes determine the urgency of the initiative. Throughout the discussion of the cases, we have seen those driving forces in action, each time in a different combination. This combination of forces makes the task a complex one. The complexity is enhanced when factors become obscure in the course of the process, as both realities and their perceptions change. As a result, decisions have to be made under conditions of limited knowledge and high uncertainty. A basic objective of this study is to shed some light on this complexity, and at least to make the observer aware of it, so that decisions can be taken in a more informed manner. With this goal in mind, a selected number of factors fuelling railway station area redevelopment will be highlighted. These factors, as they are encountered in the case studies, will be the subject of our discussion here.

- Environmental (that is, promoting public transport use) and local economic development policies are the driving forces behind many plans discussed here. Increasingly, these appear to be the two policy discourses shaping the debate on station area redevelopment. However, the two are not equal in strength. While there are differences, the economic argument tends to dominate. There is also a third policy discourse, which could be labelled *civic design* or *urban upgrading*: for example, healing the urban fabric, removing physical barriers, integrating railway station and neighbourhood, providing more liveable public spaces, or making the area a part of the city. However, it appears to be subordinate to the first two, of which it is merely an instrument. This construction (economic argument as dominant, environmental argument as supportive, civic design/urban upgrading as tool) can be most clearly observed in the two Dutch cases and in Basel. In the other cases, the policy balance was rather different. In Euralille, for instance, the economic argument appears to be far more important. Stockholm – after a more opportunistic start – seems to be going in a similar direction. Intriguingly, in Zürich Nord, civic design and urban upgrading, or 'city-building', issues carry more weight than elsewhere, and economic and environmental arguments seem more instrumental. Furthermore, economic, environmental or even civic design arguments appear to be rather abstract policy attributes, as they can be given significantly different accents. The King's Cross story, for instance, shows particularly well how there might be quite different views of what local economic development is, and of what actions it requires.
- Positive and negative technological changes shape the opportunities but also increase the number of constraints on railway station area redevelopment. A location at the crossroads of the north European HST network in Lille triggered the whole urban development operation there. Massive national and regional investment programmes in rail infrastructure are the essential conditions that make ambitious projects thinkable, as demonstrated by the Utrecht Centrum Project and the Zuidas in the Netherlands, and EuroVille in Switzerland. Centrality in the new S-Bahn network is a basic condition of the Zentrum Zürich Nord plan. Besides opportunities, the largely autonomous dynamics of infrastructure development also shape the basic constraints to property development. For instance, no development was possible in King's Cross until there was clarity on the Channel Tunnel Rail Link. The physical and organizational coordination of transport and property transformations may be seen as a crucial condition, as shown by the examples of Lille, Stockholm, Amsterdam, and possibly Utrecht. An alternative strategy is to keep the two orders of development separate from each other, as in Basel, Zürich, and now seemingly in King's Cross.
- Reorganization of the national railway companies has an impact on all the examples analysed here. The indefinite status of the privatization process means that a vital actor may radically, often destructively, change its role and perspective in the course of the process. Some stability in the institutional status of the railways appears to be an absolute precondition for station area redevelopment processes, perhaps even more crucial than the sort of organizational structure arrived at. This was particularly evident in the King's Cross case, but also in Utrecht. On the other hand, in Stockholm the horizontally

integrated development strategy of a privatized railway company is a fundamental force driving the project. The same situation could be emerging in both the Dutch cases and in King's Cross. In this respect, the role of the SNCF in France appears to be much less significant. Switzerland offers a contrasting picture, with an integrated railway company logic possibly emerging in Basel but as yet absent in Zürich.

- Property market cycles are an essential explanation in the vicissitudes of the King's Cross and Stockholm development processes. In the first phase of King's Cross they were an outright driving factor. In all other cases, the property market is seen as a condition of implementation rather than as a compelling factor. This may reflect an emerging trend, as a property-led perspective is also being abandoned in London. This does not mean, however, a decrease in the weight of property markets. Fiscal austerity implies that private resources are needed. This need influences the definition of the functional programme. Accordingly, financial feasibility studies are becoming an increasingly crucial tool (possibly the most crucial one) when putting together a functional programme. This is a very clear message, emerging from all seven cases.

- Internationalization and metropolitanization form the context of several of the arguments supporting the initiatives discussed in this book. In particular, where local economic development discourses dominate, these are typically set in the context of the competition of locations within a globalizing economy. Interestingly, governments continue pursuing a policy of big urban projects even though evidence of the benefits is lacking, while the costs are increasingly evident. Also, the content of the project tends to show little imagination, as international business centres are being conjugated in all possible ways. City marketing considerations of this kind are an essential factor of the station area initiatives in Lille, Utrecht, Amsterdam, Stockholm, and Basel. A more original approach might be emerging in Zentrum Zürich Nord, where the holistic quality of the station area as an attractive place for different sorts of people, firms and activities is seen as the essential competitive asset. In King's Cross, public policy has been less proactive and more subordinate to other forces than in other cases. More recently, however, a division of tasks between a private railway company essentially pursuing transport development objectives and a public–private–community partnership pursuing local regeneration objectives might have shaped the conditions for more innovative programmes.

Together, these factors fuel railway station redevelopment. However, their influence may differ in time and per location. Within each case study, elements of these factors can be observed, either contributing to a successful redevelopment process or increasing its complexity and impeding it. With reference to the inherent complex structure of the redevelopment of railway station areas, the latter is the most likely scenario. Chapter 4 showed that contextual factors emphasize both the differences between railway station areas in Europe (divergence) and the similarities (convergence). As the external pressures grow from a wider context – as might be expected in an 'open' Europe, where internationalization becomes more and more important – the latter gains in importance as well. Study of the redevelopment processes of railway station areas in Europe teaches us that converging processes culminate in similar dilemmas. It is precisely at this point that we can learn from each other. The next section deals with the main dilemmas as analysed in the case studies.

10.2 The characteristic dilemmas of station area redevelopment

In the preceding section, we have shown how different factors combine to form the unique challenge of each station area redevelopment initiative. But beyond the particularities of each case, what are the common dilemmas that characterize railway station area redevelopment? In answering this question, we must go back to Chapter 2, where the fundamental ambivalence of railway station areas, both nodes and places, was considered. In Chapter 4, we highlighted the way in which similar developments can occur (convergence). But we also showed how existing differences between railway station areas can be emphasized in the development process (divergence). Elements of divergence and convergence mix. Thereby, each railway station area develops according to the interplay of various diverging and converging developments in its context. The seven distinctive features, as discussed in section 4.4, can be traced in a systematic search for convergence of railway station area development in Europe.

10.2.1 Node and place, and the distinctive features of railway station area redevelopment

In Chapter 3, the node and place dimensions were placed in the context of current trends. This has made it possible to better define the specificity of the task of station area redevelopment. From a transport development point of view, we highlighted the flexible accommodation of growing infrastructure capacity and the furthering of both physical and organizational integration of different transport modes. From a property development point of view, we stressed the need for an understanding of the specific urban context (in which city and at what particular location in that city?), of the peculiar combination of strengths and weaknesses of the location, and of the implications of the accessibility issue. In the last section of Chapter 3, we pointed out the need for an integrated node–place perspective on station area redevelopment. However, it has also been said that a satisfactory analytical framework could be introduced only after a close examination of the case studies.

Railway stations are very peculiar locations. They are, ambivalently, both nodes and places (Bertolini, 1996a, 1996b). On the one hand they are (or may become) important nodes in emerging, heterogeneous transport and communication networks. On the other hand they identify a 'place', a temporarily and permanently inhabited portion of the city, an often dense and diverse assemblage of uses and forms accumulated through time, which may or may not share in the life of the node. As redevelopment objects, most railway stations areas are thus – and fundamentally – neither essentially nodes, as are airports for instance, nor predominantly places, as for example obsolete urban industrial lands or waterfronts. *Both* node *and* place dynamics tend to be equally strong at railway stations, resulting in a set of characteristic redevelopment dilemmas. These are described below.

A physical dilemma

In the compressed space of station areas, growing amounts of node-related and place-related structures must be accommodated, catering both to passengers passing through and residents, employees and visitors living in the location. The property development ideal of maximum land exploitation and the transport development ideal of maximum infrastructure flexibility must find an improbable synthesis. In order to realize synergies and manage conflicts very creative planning, architectural and engineering solutions are required, while exceptionally high costs seem inevitable. Some individual examples, such as Euralille in France, or national programmes, as the Swedish national railways' Travel Centres programme, have been more successful than others in coping with this unique challenge. In Lille, development of a critical mass of urban activities has been physically combined with construction of the HST station and improvement of the urban–regional connections. In Sweden, property developments at stations are programmatically seen as a complement of a specific transportation potential.

Four sorts of possible strategy can be identified in this respect. A first one is the physical integration of transport and property developments, as has been most notably done in Lille. Also, in Amsterdam the whole Zuidas plan hinges on the choice of an appropriate model for integration of infrastructure and property development. This is an attractive strategy, but a difficult one to implement. As we have seen, Euralille was in many ways an exceptional case, and in Amsterdam several questions are still to be answered. In most other situations a second, more flexible strategy could be more apt. Partly in the Utrecht Centrum Project and entirely in Basel EuroVille, the answer to the physical dilemma has been to keep the two orders of development as separate as possible, breaking up the plan into several autonomous subprojects. Nevertheless, the existence of an accountable, long-term framework of infrastructure works, as can be seen in Basel but not yet in Utrecht, appears to be a necessary condition for successful application of this strategy. In King's Cross in London, property–transport coordination strategies have long proved inadequate, but more recently a way out is being sought by giving priority to transport development concerns. In this, King's Cross typifies a third, essentially transport-led possible strategy. The opposite is being done in Zentrum Zürich Nord, where an urban development perspective (which is *not* property-led) dominates, representing a fourth possible option. The limit of both these latter approaches is however that synergies might get lost as opportunities on the other side of the equation are missed (that is, urban regeneration in King's Cross, public transport growth in Zürich).

This dilemma coincides with the distinctive feature *scale and complexity*.

A functional dilemma

Ideally, development of station areas will always be a matter of conceiving and implementing short-circuits between modifications in the accessibility and modifications in the activity profiles of the location, in both the material and the perception spheres. As a result, rich, 'urban' mixtures of uses are being advocated in most situations. Multifunctionality is desired because it is an essential element of the liveability, attractiveness and security of the station area, and because it improves both public transport and long-term property exploitation prospects. Many believe that without a high, 'urban' degree of functional mix, station areas will never regain the centrality that they have lost.

However, there are two main problems. First, a less vague, more situation-specific commitment to multifunctionality than now often is the case is needed. Among the cases analysed, this has been – or is being – achieved in Lille Euralille and in Zentrum Zürich Nord, while it could be emerging in King's Cross. In Lille, it has been done through an early and firm commitment to a diversified package of activities. In Zürich, it is being done through the indication of minimum percentages of 'other' functions for each parcel. In King's Cross, it could be done through an incremental identification of diverse programme elements by a public–private–community partnership. Less convincing, because they are too vague, appear as yet the strategies adopted to promote multifunctionality in Amsterdam, Utrecht, Stockholm, or Basel. A second point is that achievement of multifunctionality in practice tends to remain highly problematic. Realizing multifunctionality requires a difficult combination of 'providing orientation' and 'letting it happen', imaginatively catering for both profitable *and* less profitable elements. Only the most innovative approaches seem capable of achieving this synthesis. Among those researched, Euralille and Zentrum Zürich Nord certainly deserve – again – citation, together with emerging views of the King's Cross development.

The functional dilemma can be seen as a result of both *partiality* as a distinctive feature and *colliding functional interests*. Functional differences lead almost automatically to a subdivision of such projects. It seems obvious that functionality plays a leading role as a criterion for subdivision. That interests may collide in the interplay between players in the process is a more or less self-evident outcome, which is visible throughout all of the case studies.

A financial dilemma

The technical difficulties and conflicting requirements of railway station area development tend to be translated into high additional costs. Constraints on public expenditure imply that compensation is increasingly sought in the property market, especially when investments beyond those in the main transportation infrastructure are concerned. This may ignite a circular logic (Edwards, 1992, unpublished; Bertolini, 1996b): it demands more intensive exploitation of land and consequently yet more complications and higher costs, with the possible paradoxical result of paralysing the entire initiative, as in King's Cross at the beginning of the 1990s. A second problem is that, whatever the initial commitment to diversified functional programmes, the reciprocal attraction between high costs and high profits implies that offices tend to chase away all other uses, as most strikingly in Central London during the 1980s. Also, in the Amsterdam case and (above all) the Utrecht case great amounts of offices tend to be seen more as a necessary condition of feasibility than as a valuable element in their own right. Seemingly only in those examples where the public actor has had a strong and imaginative role in the definition of the programme, and has also been capable of assembling enough resources to sustain it, has a different course been followed. Both in Euralille and Zentrum Zürich Nord this has been the case. In both examples, a diversified programme was put together on its own merits, while financial feasibility studies and the early and direct involvement of private partners helped in building support for it.

The financial dilemma is directly related to the actors' opinion of *risk and risk management* as a feature. The case studies focus on financial risk, which is the most visible. But upon closer examination the case studies also reveal other kinds of risk (management), such as public safety or security.

A *temporal dilemma*

This is perhaps the most important dilemma. The place-development and node-development processes of railway station areas each tend to follow an autonomous track. This is translated into different kinds of uncertainty.

On the property side, conditions change constantly and unpredictably, sometimes dramatically. For instance, many station initiatives were conceived during the property boom of the 1980s but reached the implementation stage in the midst of the property slump of the early 1990s. In several cases (King's Cross and Stockholm City West, for example) this brought the development process to a total halt. The sponsors were forced to reconsider both their goals and the means to attain them. Elsewhere, only a few examples were flexible or solid enough to withstand the property crisis without drastic amendments (as at Euralille).

On the transport side, public transport investments and policies appear also to a great extent exogenous to single station area development initiatives and thereby difficult to foresee. The general implication is that a plan that is too dependent on a particular property market or transport policy context could thus easily and rapidly become outdated. This has been most clearly the case for the London Regeneration Consortium plan for King's Cross, but it is also true of the early approaches in the Amsterdam and Zürich areas. In London, changed property market conditions and a different terminal solution forced withdrawal of the plan. In Amsterdam and Zürich, efforts were initially directed towards central station locations. Inherent complications and market preference for peripheral locations were first ignored, but had later to be acknowledged and capitalized upon. On the other hand, the need to activate and/or manage in time largely autonomous property and transport dynamics is central in the current approach to the Amsterdam Zuidas. Also, in London a more flexible approach is on the rise. Swiss projects such as Basel EuroVille and Zentrum Zürich Nord go particularly far in trying to combine flexibility of the parts and coherence of the whole. Both combine a 'hard' framework (for example, the network of public spaces, a package of infrastructure investments, the conditions of implementation) and a 'soft' filling, allowing for variations in social and market demand. While profiting from an exceptional combination of circumstances, Euralille also is much more adaptable and articulated than a superficial consideration would suggest, as it accounts for – but is not dependent upon – future expansion of its office content.

The temporal dilemma is closely connected to both *scale and complexity* as a distinctive feature, and to *partiality* and *interdependence of design*. The argument is that, because of their scale and complexity, such processes tend to get divided: thus a separate plan has to be developed for each (functional) part. Again, because of the complexity of all plans involved, the development and implementation generally take a long time, thereby generating a temporal dilemma.

A management dilemma

The ambivalence of railway station areas does not stop when their redevelopment is completed. Most cases analysed here are still in a planning or early implementation stage, but the management challenges that will be posed by the renovated station area – both as transport interchange and as urban activity complex – are already apparent. The uncertain status of the future node–place conglomerate – neither public nor private, but both public and private – adds to this problem. Innovative future management structures are already being discussed in Utrecht and Amsterdam. In Euralille, after completion of the development phase, the responsibility for its management will fall on the municipality. The local authority says that it will treat it just like any other district, but not everybody is convinced that this could really happen. Elsewhere, the issue has not yet been explicitly raised. But it is likely to emerge, especially where extensive interaction between the railway station and the city is desired. Some (e.g. Euricur, 1997) have proposed adopting the (air)port model of an autonomous (air)port authority. However, as discussed in Chapter 2, railway station areas are nodes and places of a very different nature. In brief, the public place, or 'urban' component, has a much greater influence than in most (air)ports, implying a much more dense and diverse array of functions present and of actors involved.

All of the distinctive features mentioned earlier come together in the management dilemma. In addition, all other dilemmas culminate in management, too. Therefore it is no coincidence that the management of such a development process appears to be one of the most important emerging factors for success.

The dilemmas, as outlined above, are always present in railway station area redevelopment processes. They often represent the source from which problems or difficulties start, although most of these are felt only when brought forward by one of the parties involved, thus drifting away from its real source. A profound understanding of these dilemmas and the difficulties they create during the process improves the understanding between the parties. Compromises and cooperation can be reached more easily in a redevelopment process when a far-reaching understanding of the respective positions can be established. In this way, respect can grow between the parties, and the shared objective to redevelop the railway station area is strengthened.

The above sketch of the dilemmas, however, also raises a practical question: how can they be addressed and surmounted? The case studies show a wide range of approaches and varying results. Success, however, does not depend on any one factor, but always on a number of factors in combination. This will be dealt with in the next section.

10.3 Making it happen: building a capacity to act

At the end of Chapter 3, we pointed out the benefits of an integrated node–place perspective, in which process and context variables were adequately accounted for. Further on, in Chapter 4, we emphasized the importance of an analysis in which the object variables formed the point of departure. An integrated perspective on the interaction between node and place variables offers a good starting point. Such a perspective puts the participating actors and their relationships in a prominent analytical position. In this way, the building blocks of the earlier sections (factors fuelling development as well as the dilemmas connected to it) can be elaborated in an effort to gain deeper insight into the factors for success.

Railway station redevelopment processes are the work of a multifarious array of both node- and place-based actors. The local government and the national railway company are two principal ones, as most explicitly seen in Stockholm, Basel, and King's Cross. These actors might form an alliance, as they did in the first two cases, or may be antagonists instead as in the third. Depending on the local context, other actors will play a decisive role too. These include different levels of public administration, different transport companies, and – most significantly – market actors such as developers, investors, and users. In Euralille, a coalition was formed across local, regional and national government levels and with investors. In Zentrum Zürich Nord, a municipality–landowner partnership has been the driving force. In Utrecht, the relationship between the municipality, the railways, the building owners and the users has been crucial, and a similar construction is emerging in Amsterdam. Furthermore, local residents and businesses may also be crucial, particularly at station locations set in dense, historically stratified urban districts. Among the cases analysed, this occurred in Utrecht, Basel, King's Cross, and Zürich, with less (Utrecht, Basel, King's Cross until recently) or more (Zürich, possibly King's Cross now) constructive outcomes.

The objectives of this heterogeneous array of actors are often conflicting and at best uncoordinated. This was the case in Euralille initially and in Utrecht, Amsterdam, and King's Cross for a long while. Contrasts may even exist within the strategy of one and the same actor. This is typical for railway companies torn between transport and property goals, and for local governments uneasily trying to balance social, environmental, and economic objectives. The first phase of King's Cross epitomizes the former problem, while the Utrecht Centrum Project is a good example of the latter.

The fragmentation of both goals and means at stations epitomizes a key feature of the present urban system. The urban system is characterized by 'diverse and extensive patterns of interdependence', where 'the paradigmatic form of power is that which enables certain interests to blend their capacities to achieve common purposes' (Stoker, 1995, pp. 270–272). Following the lead of regime theorists, we could call it the ability to build a *capacity to act*. This is the capacity, from whatever side it comes, to mobilize and involve in the process a plurality of public, private and community actors, spanning both the transport and the land-use domains. Whatever the external and internal divisions, a high degree of active consensus appears indispensable for the implementation of station area projects. A catalyst role has possibly been the most important function of, for instance, the local government in Lille, or of the coalition between railway and municipality in Stockholm. The absence or insufficiency of such a catalyst has been the cause of great difficulties in King's Cross and Utrecht.

National institutional contexts and local political traditions play a leading role in facilitating or obstructing the effort to build up this capacity to act. However, the role must not be understood so much in a formal way – that is, through the national planning system – but through the actors and interests involved. Most important in this respect is that, through the persons of the actors involved, links are often made between positions in the national planning system. This can be done either through a person's formal role (such as a mayor, for example) or informally through contacts established in a present or earlier position. The case studies present ample evidence of the variety of possibilities on this point. The most prominent is visible in the case of Lille, where Pierre Mauroy (mayor for more than 20 years, former prime minister, senator, president of the Communauté Urbaine and president of the Société d'Economie Mixte Euralille) played a mobilizing and binding role.

The institutional context shapes the conditions within which redevelopment processes take place. Consequently, the institutional context functions both as a factor, fuelling redevelopment processes (section 10.1), and as a condition, influencing development during the process. For instance, in the redevelopment process in King's Cross, changes in the process can be traced down towards changes in the contextual conditions. From a property-led development it changed towards a more transport-led development, not only because of changes in insight, but also under the pressure of a shift in the property market context. This is an important observation. As railway station area redevelopment takes a long period of time (by definition), it is (also by definition) vulnerable to changes in its context. In order to narrow down the broad concept of context, the case studies show that changes in the economic context dominate. Property development and transport – together representing the central building blocks for redevelopment – are highly influenced by economic developments. Other context developments are government policies, such as retrenchment measures and transport investment. Awareness of the risks can be translated into the redevelopment process. For instance, in trying to speed up the process the risks can be reduced. But also, introducing explicit stages in the redevelopment process contributes to the reduction of risks from context developments.

In both the transport function and the real estate function, developments in the institutional context can generate converging and diverging processes between the potential of railway station areas, anywhere in Europe.

10.4 Towards an agenda for research and practice: putting railway station locations in their urban–regional context

The points discussed in the previous sections can be seen as sources of reflection for practice and sources of inspiration for a research agenda. Some of the themes to be explored have already been treated in this book but need further refinement and empirical verification. A first point concerns fostering the circulation of knowledge among researchers and practitioners on specific aspects of each of the node–place dilemmas discussed above, and of problems and solutions in practice. A second contribution of research should be to improve the understanding of the role of context and process variables in specific railway station area re-development situations, giving attention to the scope of generalizations. This appears to be a condition for learning lessons.

There are some areas of enquiry that this book has touched upon only marginally. Perhaps the most intriguing ones are the implications of the wider spatial–functional context of a railway station location. Because of its ambivalent nature, this context is shaped both by the accessibility of the transport network and by the features of the railway station surroundings. Multiple geographical scales are represented in the compressed space of railway station areas. Railway stations are the interface of transport and information flows that span the immediate surroundings, the urban region, and selected national and international spaces. Their capacity to link physically and symbolically distant domains is the source of both their potentials, their constraints, and their contradictions. Metropolitan space is increasingly organizing itself around specialized activity poles, distributed over vast *urban regions*. Within emerging multicentred systems, traditional and emerging subcentres are connected with each other and with centres outside the region through material and immaterial networks. The generalized trend towards clustered redistribution of activities in this urban–regional space is further accelerated and may possibly be structured by innovation in rail transport. Here we refer to the expansion of regional railway systems (such as S-Bahn in Germany and Switzerland, and RER in France) on the one hand and the HST network on the other. The possibility is particularly interesting if set within the framework of a sustainable approach to urban development.

The most dynamic railway station areas are invariably those that seem to be caught up in these urban–regional dynamics. Some examples, though not fully capitalized upon, can already be cited. In Germany, the initially opposed location of Kassel's HST station on the periphery of the city has induced the emergence there of tertiary concentration, while the central station area is searching a new role as *Kultur-Bahnhof* (culture station). In Zürich, controversy and uncertainty still permeate the redevelopment of central HauptBahnhof Süd West and its surroundings, while Zentrum Zürich Nord promises to be one of the most intriguing large-scale urban projects in Switzerland. In the Paris region, the opening of TGV stations on the metropolitan periphery, as at Massy or Marne-La Vallée-Chessy, offers both unconventional challenges and opportunities for urban and transport development. In Amsterdam, the realization of an office centre around the central station, while strongly supported by the municipality, has come to a standstill. In contrast, 'spontaneous' property dynamics around peripheral railway stations have been intense. The local government is now trying to catch up, by giving some direction and meaning to the reality of 'eccentric clustering'. In the UK, an overarching development strategy for station areas along the Channel Tunnel Rail Link is being sought, even though it is still unclear which organization could promote it. This has required looking beyond the King's Cross-St Pancras terminal to the Stratford railway lands and to locations further down the east Thames corridor.

A negative but nonetheless equally interesting theme is the non-materialization of urban development effects at new exurban HST stations. This is the problem at the infamous TGV 'desert stations' in France, but also at peripheral X 2000 stations in the Stockholm area. Finally, among the cases surveyed, Lille Euralille and Stockholm City West are the most intriguing examples of how a station complex could be developed into a link between an urban region and an (inter)national space.

Awareness of these multicentred dynamics is still limited, and so is the elaboration of its implications, for the economy, the environment, and the general quality of life of an urban region. In order to provide a firmer foundation to railway station area redevelopment programmes, more fundamental research is needed on the potential roles of railway station locations in the emerging multicentred urban regions of Europe. Station areas could be seen as potential 'centres of centres' within the region and as links between the region and the (inter)national space: that is, between the local and the global. The focus should be on relationships of competition and complementarity between locations in the context of evolving transport and land-use patterns. The conditions required to realize this vision need to be explored in depth, but so do the limits to the potentials of railway station locations (for instance, owing to the dominance of private transport). In the process, the combinations of factors behind current station area redevelopment initiatives discussed in this book could be further disentangled, making choices and their implications clearer to those involved.

References

Acosta, R. and Renard, V. (1993) *Urban Land and Property Markets in France*. London: UCL Press.

Agence de développement et d'urbanisme de la métropole lilloise (1996) *Lille aprés Euralille. La métropole en mutation*. Lille: Agence de développement et d'urbanisme de la métropole lilloise.

Alexander, C. (1965) A city is not a tree. Reprinted in Legates, R. and Stout, F. (eds) (1996) *The City Reader*, pp. 118–1131. London: Routledge.

Amar, G. (1996) Complexes d'échanges urbains, du concept au project. *Les Annales de la Recherche Urbaine*, **71**, pp. 93–100.

ARCAM (1988) *Boom Town Amsterdam*. Amsterdam: ARCAM.

Arenas, M., Basiana, X., Guasa, M. and Ruano, M. (eds) (1995) *Barcelona Transfer*. Barcelona: ACTAR.

Bach, B. and De Jong, M.I. (1997) *Ontwerp-aanbevelingen Stationsomgeving, Topologische- topografische- en programmatische aspecten in relatie tot de stadsplattegrond*. Delft: TU Delft.

Bakker, H.M.J. (1994) *Stationslocaties: geschikt voor winkels?* Amsterdam: MBO.

Banister, D. (ed.) (1995) *Transport and Urban Development*. London: E & F N Spon. 711·7 , 711·75

Banister, D. and Hall, P. (1993) The second railway age. *Built Environment*, **19** (3/4), pp. 157–162.

Batisse, F. (1994) World trends in railway traffic. *Rail International*, January, pp. 13–20.

Bayliss, D. (1991), Transport in London: entering the 1990s. *Built Environment*, **17** (2), pp. 107–121.

Bell, P. and Cloke, P. (1990) *Deregulation and Transport: Market Forces in the Modern World*. London: David Fulton Publishers.

Bertolini, L. (1996a) Des gares en transformation, noeuds de réseaux et lieux dans la ville. *Les Annales de la Recherche Urbaine*, **71**, pp. 86–91.

Bertolini, L. (1996b) Nodes and places: complexities of railway station redevelopment. *European Planning Studies*, **4** (3), pp. 331–345.

Bertolini, L. (1996c) Knots in the net: on the redevelopment of railway stations and their surroundings. *City*, **1** (1/2), pp. 129–137.

Bertolini, L. and Spit, T. (1996) *Realizing the Potential: European Lessons for the Utrecht Centrum Plan and Amsterdam Zuid-WTC*. Utrecht: Stepro.

Bestuurlijk Overleg Zuidas (1996a) *Ontwerp Master plan Zuidas. Toelichting.* Amsterdam: Bestuurlijk Overleg Zuidas.

Bestuurlijk Overleg Zuidas (1996b) *Ontwerp Master plan Zuidas. Ontwikkelingsstrategie.* Amsterdam: Bestuurlijk Overleg Zuidas.

Bestuurlijk Platform UCP (1996) *UCP: analyse, diagnose en oplossingsrichting.* Utrecht: Bestuurlijk Platform UCP.

Bewoners Overleg City Projekt (BOCP) (1992) *UCP, wij denken mee: standpuntennota BOCP.* Utrecht: Bewoners Overleg City Projekt.

Bogaard, H.P. (1981) *Utrecht centrum in beweging.* Real estate agent professional thesis, Ijsselstein.

Bongenaar, A. (1994) A-locaties hebben broeinestfunctie. *Stedebouw en Volkshuisvesting,* **75** (3), pp. 29–31.

Bongenaar, A. (1996) Spoorzoeken in Japan. *Bouw,* July (7/8), pp. 34–37.

Bonneville, M., Buisson, M. and Rousier, N. (1994) *L'internationalisation des villes: De nouveaux rapports ville-region.* Paper presented at the international conference 'Cities, Enterprises and Society at the eve of the XXIst century', Lille, 16–18 March.

Borja, J. and Castells, M. (1997) *Local & Global. Management of Cities in the Information Age.* London: Earthscan.

Borough of Camden (1988) *The King's Cross Railway Lands. A Community Brief.* London: Borough of Camden.

Borough of Camden (1992) *Outline planning applications for the redevelopment of the King's Cross Railway Lands.* Report of the director of the Environment Department, London, 29 July. London: Borough of Camden.

Borough of Camden (1994) *King's Cross Railway Lands. Community planning brief.* London: Borough of Camden.

Boursier-Mougenot, I. and Ollivier-Trigalo, M. (1993) La territorialité du réseau SNCF. *Flux,* n.12, April–June, pp. 19–28.

Bovy, P., Orfeuil, J. and Zumkeller, D. (1993) Europe: a heterogenous 'single market'. In: Salomon, I., Bovy, P. and Orefeuil, J.P. (eds), *A Billion Trips a Day: Tradition and Transition in European Travel Patterns,* pp. 21–32. London: Kluwer Academic Publishers.

Bowers, P. (1995) Commercialisation, local and international access on the rails. *Public Transport International,* No. 1, pp. 25–29.

Brooks, M. and Button, K. (1995) Separating transport track from operations: a typology of international experiences. *International Journal of Transport Economics,* **22** (3), pp. 235–260.

Brotchie, J., Batty, M., Hall, P. and Newton, P. (eds) (1991) *Cities of the 21th century. New Technologies and Spatial Systems.* Harlow: Longman Cheshire.

Bruijn, J., Jong, P. de, Korsten, A. and Zanten, W. van (1996) *Grote projecten: besluitvorming & management.* Alphen a/d Rijn: Samsom H.D. Tjeenk Willink.

Bruinsma, F. and Rietveld, P. (1995) De structurerende werking van infrastructuur. In: Brouwer, J. and Voogd, H. *Investeren in Ruimte,* pp. 98–110. Alphen a/d Rijn: Samsom H.D. Tjeenk Willink.

Bureau voor Stedebouw ir. F.J. Zandvoort BV (1986), *Verdichting rond stations.* Utrecht: Bureau voor Stedebouw ir. F.J. Zandvoort BV.

Camagni, R.P and Salone, C. (1993) Network urban structures in northern Italy: elements for a theoretical framework. *Urban Studies,* **30** (6), pp. 1053–1064.

Castells, M. (1989) *The Informational City. Information Technology, Economic Restructuring and the Urban–Regional Process.* Oxford: Blackwell.

CEAT (1993) *La mise en valeur des terrains de gare: Conditions de réalisation et de mise en oeuvre.* Lausanne: CEAT.

Clark, T.N. and Ferguson, L. (1983) *City Money: Political Processes, Fiscal Strain and Retrenchment.* Chicago: University of Chicago Press.

Clarke, S.E. (ed.) (1989) *Urban Innovation and Autonomy, Political Implications of Policy Change, Urban Innovation.* Volume 1. Newbury Park, CA: Sage.

Cornet, J. (1993) From a government institution to a publicly or privately run transport enterprise: the challenges facing the railways. *Rail International,* Aug/Sept, pp. 41–44.

Cullingworth, B. (1997) *Planning in the USA: Policies, Issues and Processes.* London: Routledge.

Custers, J. (1994) Hoge ambities niet gehaald; verslag discussiebijeenkomst NIROV. *Stedebouw en Volkshuisvesting,* **75** (3), pp. 10–11.

De Volkskrant (1994) Kruispunt van Europa. 22 January, p. 3 of the supplement 'Vervolg'.

De Volkskrant (1995) Automobiel levert samenleving twee miljard gulden op. 27 July, p. 2.

De Volkskrant (1996) Sweden heeft een nieuw model: het spoor. 12 October, p. 45.

Dematteis, G. (1988) The weak metropolis. In: Mazza, L. (ed.), *World Cities and the Future of the Metropolis,* pp. 121–133. Milano: Electa-XVII Triennale.

ECMT (1988) *Investment in Transport Infrastructure in ECMT Countries.* Paris: European Conference of Ministers of Transport.

ECMT (1992) *Statistical Trends in Transport 1965–1988.* Paris: European Conference of Ministers of Transport.

ECMT (1996) *Trends in the Transport Sector (1970–1994).* Paris: European Conference of Ministers of Transport.

Economist, The (1996) Transport and infrastructure, Europe's new model railways. 28 September, pp. 81–87.

Edgington, D.W. (1990) Managing industrial restructuring in the Kansai region of Japan. *Geoforum,* **21** (1), pp. 1–22.

Edwards, M. (1991) How should we manage the land resources of the state railways? Some lessons from London Paper presented at the seminar 'Stazioni e ferrovie urbane in Europa: Prospettive per il mercato immobiliare e per le pubbliche amministrazioni', Torino, 25 October.

Edwards, M. (1992) Potentialities and contradictions in resistance to 'development' in Mrs Thatcher's London. Unpublished paper.

Ellwanger, G. (1990) The railways' role in environmental conservation. *Rail International,* July, pp. 7–12.

Euricur (1997) *The High-Speed Rail: Servicing the Planning and Development of Europe's Metropolitan Cities.* Brussels: Eurocities.

Fancello, M. (1993) High-speed rail and real estate in Europe. Part I: Belgium & France. Master thesis, International Business School, Marseille.

Fischhoff, B. (1981) *Acceptable Risk.* Cambridge: Cambridge University Press.

Fitzroy, F. and Smith, I. (1995) The demand for rail transport in European countries. *Transport Policy,* **2** (3), pp. 153–158.

Friedmann, J. and Miller, J. (1965) The urban field. *Journal of the American Institute of Planners,* **31** (4), pp. 312–320.

Gemeente Amsterdam (1996) *De Zuidas Amsterdam.* Amsterdam: Gemeente Amsterdam.

Gemeente Utrecht, N.V. Nederlandse Spoorwegen, Algemeen Burgerlijk Pensioenfonds e Koninklijke Nederlandse Jaarbeurs (1993) *Utrecht City Projekt. Master plan.* Utrecht: Gemeente Utrecht, N.V. Nederlands Spoorwegen, Algemeen Burgerlijk Pensioenfonds e Koninklijke Nederlandse Jaarbeurs.

Gemeentevervoerbedrijf Amsterdam, NS, and Midnet (1997). *Knoop Zuid.* Amsterdam: Gemeentevervoerbedrijf Amsterdam, NS, and Midnet.

Grübler, A. (1990) *The Rise and Fall of Infrastructures: Dynamics of Evolution and Technological Change in Transport.* Heidelberg: Physica Verlag.

Grübler, A. and Nackicenovic, N. (1991) *Evolution of Transport Systems: Past and Future.* Laxenburg, Austria: International Institute for Applied Systems Analysis.

Guardian, The (1993) Dirty from the cradle to the grave. 30 July, p. 17.

GVU, Midnet and NS (1996) *Mainport Utrecht*. Utrecht: GVU, Midnet, NS.

Hall, P. (1991) Moving information: a tale of four technologies. In: Brotchie, J., Batty, M., Hall, P. and Newton, P. (eds) *Cities of the 21st Century: New Technologies and Spatial Systems*, pp. 1–21. Melbourne: Longman Cheshire.

Harvey, D. (1989) *The Condition of Postmodernity*. Oxford: Blackwell.

Hayer, M.A. (1996) Heterotopia Nederland of wat Bunnik mist. *Stedebouw & Ruimtelijke Ordening*, **77** (6), pp. 4–10.

Healey, P. and Williams, R.H. (1993) European urban planning systems: diversity and convergence. *Urban Studies* 1993 (4/5), pp. 701–720.

Hoogerwerf, A. (1995) *Politiek als evenwichtskunst: Dilemma's rond overheid en markt*. Alphen a/d Rijn: Samson H.D. Tjeenk Willink.

ISOCARP (1992) *International Manual of Planning Pracice*. The Hague: ISOCARP.

Jansen, G.R.M. (1993) Commuting: home sprawl, traffic jams. In: Salomon, I., Bovy, P. and Orfeuil, J.P. (eds), *A Billion Trips a Day: Tradition and Transition in European Travel Patterns*, pp. 101–127. London: Kluwer Academic Publishers.

Jonker, T. (1996) Private integrale ontwikkeling van edge cities in Japan. *Rooilijn*, **10**, pp. 489–494.

Kargadoor, Milieu-sektie van de (1979) *Hoog Catharijne een aanwinst voor Utrecht?* Utrecht: Milieu-sektie van de Kargadoor.

King's Cross Extra (1989) A new district for London. May, p. 2.

King's Cross Partnership (1997) *King's Cross Partnership News*, no. 1. London: King's Cross Partnership.

Kloosterman, H. and Venema, P. (1997) Kantoorgebruiker wil steeds meer ruimte innemen. *Vastgoedmarkt*, January, pp. 15–19.

Korver, W., Jansen, G.R.M. and Bovy, P. (1993) The Netherlands: ground transport below sea-level. In: Salomon, I., Bovy, P. and Orefeuil, J.P. (eds), *A Billion Trips a Day: Tradition and Transition in European Travel Patterns*, pp. 329–348. London: Kluwer Academic Publishers.

Kreukels, A.M.J. and Spit, T.J.M (1990) Public–private partnership in the Netherlands. *Tijdschrift voor Economische en Sociale Geografie*, **81** (5), pp. 388–392.

Kunzmann, K.R. (1996) Euro-megapolis or themepark Europe? Scenarios for European spatial development. *International Planning Studies*, **1** (2), pp. 143–163.

Kurata, N. (1994) Lo spazio in concorrenza. Ferrovie private e sviluppo urbano. *Casabella*, January/February (608–609), pp. 100–107.

Lambooy, J.G. (1994) *Stationslokaties op weg naar morgen*. Paper presented at the congress Stationslocaties, Amersfoort, 15 February.

l'Architecture d'Ajourd'hui (1992) Euralille (dossier), n.280.

Lemstra, W. (1987) Public–private partnerships. *Economische en Statistische Berichten*, **71** (3607), pp. 514–517.

Louter, P. (1996) Economische ontwikkeling in multi-nodale stedelijke gebieden. In: Dieleman, F.M. and Priemus, H. (eds), *De inrichting van stedelijke regio's*, pp. 141–156. Assen: Van Gorcum.

LPAC (1993) *1993 Advice on Strategic Planning Guidance for London/Draft*. London: London Planning Advisory Committee.

Lutter, H. (1994) Accessibility and regional development of European regions and the role of transport systems. Paper presented at the Research Colloquium on Spatial Development in Europe, Copenhagen, 17–18 March.

MBO (1993) *Jaarverslag*. Amsterdam: MBO.

Menerault, P. and Stissi-Epée, P. (1996) Euralille: territoire des réseaux? *Transports Urbains*, No. 93, October–December, pp. 31–36.

Ministerie van Volkshuisvesting, Ruimtelijke Ordening en Milieubeheer, Ministerie van

Verkeer en Waterstaat e Nederlandse Spoorwegen (1992) *Ontwikkeling Stations-lokaties in de stedelijke knooppunten.* Den Haag: Ministry VROM.

Ministry of Housing, Physical Planning and Environment (1991a) *Fourth report (EXTRA) on physical planning in the Netherlands.* Den Haag: Ministry VROM.

Ministry of Housing, Physical Planning and Environment (1991b) *The Right Business In the Right Place: Towards a Location Policy for Businesses and Services in the Interests of Accessibility and the Environment.* Den Haag: Ministry VROM.

Munck Mortier, E. de (1996) Hollen en stilstaan bij het station; onderzoek naar de beleving van de omgeving van Rotterdam CS door reizigers en passanten. Thesis, University Utrecht.

Nagengast, E. (1997) Over de Zuidas. *Rooilijn,* No. 2, pp. 73–78.

Needham, B., Koenders, P. and Kruijt, B. (1993) *Urban Land and Property Markets in the Netherlands.* London: UCL Press.

Newman, P. and Thornley, A. (1995) Euralille: 'boosterism' at the centre of Europe. *European Urban and Regional Studies,* **2** (3), pp. 237–246.

Newman, P. and Thornley, A. (1996) *Urban Planning in Europe: International Competition, National Systems and Planning Projects.* London: Routledge.

NIROV/Sectie SEIROV (1995) Stationslocaties op de rails. Unpublished proceedings of the congress of the same name, Arnhem, 23 February.

NSC (1994) Stationslocaties. Unpublished proceedings of the congress of the same name, Amersfoort, 18 February.

Nspirit (1996) December, pp. 19–20.

Observatoire des bureaux de la métropole lilloise (1996) *Lille Métropole. Marche des bureaux et grands aménagements.* Lille: Observatoire des bureaux de la métropole lilloise.

Olsberg, S. (1990) Gains for trains. Masters thesis, University of London.

Ontwikkelingsmaatschappij UCP (1995) *Het ruimtelijk funktioneel concept UCP.* Utrecht: Ontwikkelingsmaatschappij UCP.

Orfeuil, J. (1993) France: a centralized country in between regional and European development. In: Salomon, I., Bovy, P. and Orfeuil, J. (eds), *A Billion Trips a Day: Tradition and Transition in European Travel Patterns,* pp. 241–256. London: Kluwer Academic Publishers.

Orfeuil, J.P. (1994) Traffic restraints in the context of urban regions. Paper presented at the Congress Car-free Cities, Amsterdam, 24–25 March.

Orfeuil, J.P. and Bovy, P. (1993) European mobility is different: a global perspective. In: Salomon, I., Bovy, P. and Orfeuil, J.P. (eds), *A Billion Trips a Day: Tradition and Transition in European Travel Patterns.* London: Kluwer Academic Publishers.

Ottens, H.F.L. and Ter Welle-Heethuis, J.G.P. (1983) Recent urban research at Utrecht. *Tijdschrift voor Economische en Sociale Geografie,* **74** (5), pp. 387–396.

Oum, T.H. and Yu, C. (1994) Economic efficiency of railways and implications for public policy: a comparative study of the OECD countries' railways. *Journal of Transport Economics and Policy,* **28**, pp. 121–138.

Page, E.C. and Goldsmith, M.J. (1987) *Central and Local Government Relations: A Comparative Analysis of West European Unitary States.* Newbury Park, CA: Sage.

Parkes, M. and Mouawad, D.C. (1991) *Towards a People's Plan. Full Report.* London: King's Cross Railway Lands Group.

Parkes, M. and Mouawad, D.C. (1993) *Interim Uses Initiative. Full Report.* London: King's Cross Railway Lands Group.

Parkinson, M., Bianchini, F., Dawson, J., Evans, R. and Harding, A. (1991) *Urbanisation and the Functions of Cities in the European Community.* Commission of the European Community: DGXVI.

Perrow, C. (1984) *Normal Accidents. Living With High-Risk Technologies.* New York: Basic Books.

Porter, M.E. (1990) *The Competitive Advantage of Nations.* London: Macmillan.

Portheine, H.E. (1994) NS Vastgoed groot-grondbezitter op A-locaties. Paper presented at the congress Stationslocaties, Amersfoort, 18 February.

Pressman, J.L. and Wildavsky, A (1973) *Implementation.* Berkeley CA: University of California Press.

Provincie Zuid Holland (1991) *Lokaties op Sporen.* Den Haag: Provincie Zuid-Holland.

Pucci, P. (1996) *I nodi infrastrutturali: luoghi e non luoghi metropolitani.* Milano: FrancoAngeli.

Pucher, J. (1988) Urban travel behaviour as the outcome of public policy: the example of modal split in Western Europe and North America. *Journal of the Amercian Planning Association,* **54** (4), pp. 509–520.

Pucher, J. (1990) A comparative analysis of policies and travel behavior in the Soviet Union, eastern and western Europe, and North America. *Transportation Quarterly,* **44** (3), pp. 441–465.

Pucher, J. and Lefèvre, C. (1996) *The Urban Transport Crisis in Europe and North America.* London: Macmillan Press.

Rail Business Report (1994) Europe's railways to spend ECU 120 bn, pp. 31–36.

Railway Gazette International (1992) Train and plane can be partners. May, pp. 351–352.

Railway Gazette International (1994) Performance survey. July, pp. 465–468.

Railway Gazette International (1996) Kinnock charts path to rail's comeback. February, pp. 74–76.

Renner, M. (1988) *Rethinking the Role of the Automobile.* Washington, DC: Worldwatch Institute.

Rienstra, S.A., Rietveld, P., Bruisma, F.R. and Gorter, C. (1996) Zuidas: Werk Scheppen of werk verschuiven? *Stedebouw & Ruimtelijke Ordening,* **77** (6), pp. 24–28.

Roty, T. (1996) Eki (le relais): la gare au Japon. *Les Annales de la Recherche Urbaine,* No. 71, pp. 75–85.

Rutten, J. and Cüsters, J. (1994) Overheid laat kansen liggen. *Stedebouw & Volkshuisvesting,* **75** (3), pp. 26–28.

Salomon, I., Bovy, P. and Orfeuil, J.P. (1993) Introduction: Can a billion trips be reduced to a few patterns?' In: Salomon, I., Bovy, P. and Orfeuil, J.P. (eds), *A Billion Trips a Day: Tradition and Transition in European Travel Patterns,* pp. 3–12. London: Kluwer Academic Publishers.

Sands, B. (1993) The development effects of high-speed rail stations and implications for California. *Built Environment,* **19** (3/4), pp. 257–285.

Simon, M. (1993), *Un jour, un train. La saga d'Euralille.* Lille: La Voix du Nord.

Simonis, J.B.D. (1983) *Uitvoering van beleid als probleem.* Amsterdam: Uitgeverij Kobra.

SJ and Stockholms Stad (1997) *Stockholm City West. Programme for feasibility studies.* Stockholm: SJ and Stockholms Stad.

SJ Real Estate Division (n.d.) *SJ Real Estate Division* (presentation brochure). Stockholm: SJ.

Smallenbroek, A. and Spit, T. (1992) Regions and regionalization in the Netherlands. *Tijdschrift voor Economische en Sociale Geografie,* **83** (5), pp. 234–240.

Spit, T. (1993) *Strangled in Structures: An Institutional Analysis of Innovative Policy by Dutch Municipalities.* Netherlands Geographical Studies 160. Utrecht: University Utrecht.

Spit, T. (1995) Regionalization and regional land policy in the Netherlands. Paper presented at the 9th AESOP Congress, Glasgow, 16–19 August.

Spit, T. and Jansen, L. (1997) *De ruimtelijke effecten van investeren in infrastructuur; een internationale verkenning.* Utrecht: URU.

Stein, J. (1993) *Growth management: The Planning Challenge of the 1990s*. Newbury Park: Sage.

Stoker, G. (1995) Regime theory and urban politics. In: LeGates, R. and Stout, F (eds), *The City Reader*, pp. 268–281. London: Routledge.

Sudjic, D. (1992) *The Hundred Mile City*. London: Andre Deutsch.

Suzuki, T. (1996) Une métropole étendue: le cas de Tôkyô. *Les Annales de la Recherche Urbaine*, No. 71, pp. 156–158.

Sweden Today (1994) Sweden's best property under development. February, one-page reprint.

Teisman, G.R. (1992) *Complexe besluitvorming, een pluricentrisch perspektief op besluitvorming over ruimtelijke investeringen*. Den Haag: VUGA Uitgeverij B.V.

Townroe, P. (1995) The coming of Supertram: the impact of urban rail development in Sheffield. In: Banister, D. (ed.), *Transport and Urban Development*, pp. 162–181. London: Spon.

Treiber, D. (1995) OMA a Euralille: una angosciata modernità. *Casabella*, No. 623.

Troin, J. (1995) *Rail et aménagement du territoire*. Aix-en-Provence: Edisud.

Urbanisme (1993) Dossier: métropole lilloise: l'Europe à trés grande vitesse. No. 263.

Utrecht Centrum Project (1997) *Voorlopig Stedebouwkundig Ontwerp*. Utrecht: UCP.

Van der Berg, M. (1996) De Randstad, de symbiose tussen stad en land. In: Dieleman, F. and Priemus, H. (eds), *De inrichting van stedelijke regio's. Randstad, Brabantse stedenrij, Ruhrgebied*, pp. 12–34. Assen: Van Gorcum.

Van Nierop, I. (1993) Verdichting rond stations. Thesis, Universiteit van Amsterdam.

Varlet, J. (1992) Réseaux de transports rapides et interconnexions en Europe occidentale. *L'Information Géographique*, No. 56, pp. 115–120.

Webber, M.M. (1986) Automobility for everyone. *Urban Resources*, **4** (1), pp. 47–50.

Websters's Ninth New Collegiate Dictionary (1986).

Wolting, A. (1995) Financiering, vastgoed- en investeringsstrategie. Paper presented at the congress Stationslocaties op de rails, Arnhem, 23 February.

World Resources Institute (1992) *The Going Rate: What Really Is the Cost to Drive?* Washington, DC: The World Resources Institute.

Zembri, P. (1995) Il TGV, le reti e il territorio: un'interconnessione imperfetta. *Archivio di studi urbani e regionali*, **26** (53), pp. 145–154.

Zembri, P. (1997) Les fondements de la remise en cause du Schéma Directeur des liaisons ferroviaires à grande vitesse: des faiblesses avant tout structurelles. *Annales de Géographie*, n. 593–594, pp. 183–194.

Zoete, P.R. (1997) *Stedelijke knooppunten: virtueel beleid voor een virtuele werkelijkheid?* Amsterdam: Thesis Publishers.

Index